T0319681

The Economics of Sports Betting

NEW HORIZONS IN THE ECONOMICS OF SPORT

Series Editors: Wladimir Andreff, *Department of Economics, University of Paris 1 Panthéon Sorbonne, France* and Marc Lavoie, *Department of Economics, University of Ottawa, Canada*

For decades, the economics of sport was regarded as a hobby for a handful of professional economists who were primarily involved in other areas of research. In recent years, however, the significance of the sports economy as a percentage of GDP has expanded dramatically. This has coincided with an equivalent rise in the volume of economic literature devoted to the study of sport.

This series provides a vehicle for deeper analyses of the demand for sport, cost–benefit analysis of sport, sporting governance, the economics of professional sports and leagues, individual sports, trade in the sporting goods industry, media coverage, sponsoring and numerous related issues. It contributes to the further development of sports economics by welcoming new approaches and highlighting original research in both established and newly emerging sporting activities. The series publishes the best theoretical and empirical work from well-established researchers and academics, as well as from talented newcomers in the field.

Titles in the series include:

Contemporary Issues in Sports Economics
Participation and Professional Team Sports
Edited by Wladimir Andreff

The Economics of Sport, Health and Happiness
The Promotion of Well-being through Sporting Activities
Edited by Plácido Rodríguez, Stefan Késenne and Brad R. Humphreys

The Econometrics of Sport
Edited by Plácido Rodríguez, Stefan Késenne and Jaume García

Public Policy and Professional Sports
International and Australian Experiences
John K. Wilson and Richard Pomfret

The Economics of Competitive Sports
Edited by Plácido Rodríguez, Stefan Késenne and Ruud Koning

Disequilibrium Sports Economics
Competitive Imbalance and Budget Constraints
Edited by Wladimir Andreff

Sport Through the Lens of Economic History
Edited by John K. Wilson and Richard Pomfret

The Economics of Sports Betting
Edited by Plácido Rodríguez, Brad R. Humphreys and Robert Simmons

The Economics of Sports Betting

Edited by

Plácido Rodríguez

University of Oviedo, Spain

Brad R. Humphreys

Department of Economics, West Virginia University, USA

Robert Simmons

Lancaster University Management School, UK

NEW HORIZONS IN THE ECONOMICS OF SPORT

 Edward **Elgar** PUBLISHING

Cheltenham, UK • Northampton, MA, USA

Published by
Edward Elgar Publishing Limited
The Lypiatts
15 Lansdown Road
Cheltenham
Glos GL50 2JA
UK

Edward Elgar Publishing, Inc.
William Pratt House
9 Dewey Court
Northampton
Massachusetts 01060
USA

A catalogue record for this book
is available from the British Library

Library of Congress Control Number: 2017931761

This book is available electronically in the **Elgar**online
Economics subject collection
DOI 10.4337/9781785364556

ISBN 978 1 78536 454 9 (cased)
ISBN 978 1 78536 455 6 (eBook)

Typeset by Servis Filmsetting Ltd, Stockport, Cheshire
Printed and bound in Great Britain by TJ International Ltd, Padstow

Contents

List of contributors   vii
List of abbreviations   xii

Introduction   1
Plácido Rodríguez, Brad R. Humphreys and Robert Simmons

1   Consumer spending on spectator sports, physical activity, and
    gambling: evidence from Canada   5
    Brad R. Humphreys, Jane E. Ruseski and Jie Yang

2   Should gambling markets be privatized? An examination of
    state lotteries in the United States   21
    Kent R. Grote and Victor A. Matheson

3   Price setting and competition in fixed odds betting markets   38
    Xiaogang Che, Arne Feddersen and Brad R. Humphreys

4   Evaluating probabilities for a football in-play betting market   52
    Stephen Dobson and John Goddard

5   Forecasting football match results: are the many smarter than
    the few?   71
    Jaume García, Levi Pérez and Plácido Rodríguez

6   New empirical evidence on the Tote–SP anomaly and its
    implications for models of risky choice in gambling markets   92
    Babatunde Buraimo, David Peel and Robert Simmons

7   Market efficiency and the favorite–longshot bias: evidence
    from handball betting markets   105
    Arne Feddersen

8   "Hot arms" and the "hot hand": bettor and sportsbook
    reaction to team and pitcher streaks in Major League Baseball   118
    Rodney Paul and Andrew Weinbach

9   Investigating the "hot hand" hypothesis: an application to
    European football   139
    Robert Simmons and Rhys Wheeler

10   Sports corruption and developments in betting markets   162
     David Forrest

Index   183

Contributors

 Babatunde Buraimo is Senior Lecturer in the Management School at the University of Liverpool, United Kingdom. He has a PhD in Economics from Lancaster University. Babatunde's main research interests are economic and statistical analyses of sports and he has published numerous papers in peer-reviewed journals as well as a number of edited contributions in major volumes on the subject. Babatunde is currently working on a number of themes that involve the application of econometric analysis. These include racial discrimination in sport, managerial contribution to organizational success, the economics of broadcast rights and television audience ratings, and labour market issues in professional team sports.

 Xiaogang Che is a Lecturer (Assistant Professor) at Durham University Business School, United Kingdom. His research interests are applied microeconomic theory, applied game theory, auctions and contest. He has published in several scientific journals such as *American Economic Journal: Microeconomics*, *Mathematical Social Sciences*, *Economics Letters* and *Review of Industrial Organizations*.

 Stephen Dobson is Professor of Economics at Hull University Business School, United Kingdom. He is an expert in sports economics and his other research interests include industrial organization and the economics of developing countries. He has recent publications in *Theoretical Economics Letters*, *World Development*, *Economics Letters*, and *European Journal of Operational Research*. He is coauthor of the monograph *The Economics of Football* (Cambridge University Press, 1st edition 2001; 2nd edition 2011).

 Arne Feddersen is Professor MSO of Industrial vEconomics in the Department of Sociology, Environmental and Business Economics at University of Southern Denmark, Campus Esbjerg. His research is primarily focused on sports economics, media economics and the economics of betting markets. He is the editor-in-chief of the *International Journal of Sport Finance* and has published in journals such as *Economic Inquiry*, *Labour Economics*, *Journal of Sports Economics* and *International Journal of Sport Finance*.

David Forrest is Professor of Economics at the University of Liverpool, United Kingdom and Honorary Professor, Macau Polytechnic Institute. He specializes in analysis of the sports and gambling industries. He is a member of the Responsible Gambling Strategy Board, which advises the UK authorities on problem gambling issues. He contributes substantially to literature on sport and gambling markets. Outlets include journals such as *Economic Inquiry*, *Labour Economics*, *Journal of the Royal Statistical Society*, *International Journal of Forecasting* and *European Journal of Operational Research*.

Jaume García is Professor in the Department of Economics and Business at the Pompeu Fabra University, Barcelona, Spain. He is Academic Advisor of the School of International Trade (ESCI), Universitat Pompeu Fabra, Barcelona, Spain. He is one of the authors of the *Handbook on the Economics of Sport*, edited by Edward Elgar. He has published articles in journals such as *Journal of Sports Economics*, *European Sport Management Quarterly*, *Health Economics* and *Oxford Bulletin of Economics and Statistics*. He is former President of the Spanish Institute of Statistics.

John Goddard is Professor of Financial Economics at Bangor Business School, United Kingdom. He is an expert in sports betting and his other research interests are in industrial organization, the economics of financial institutions and the economics of professional sports. He has recent publications in *Journal of Money Credit and Banking*, *Journal of Banking and Finance*, *Journal of Forecasting*, *European Journal of Operational Research* and *International Journal of Industrial Organization*. He is coauthor of the monograph *The Economics of Football* (Cambridge University Press, 1st edition 2001; 2nd edition 2011).

Kent R. Grote is Assistant Professor of Economics at Lake Forest College in Lake Forest, Illinois, USA. His research focuses on US lottery and gambling markets and he has published articles in such journals as *Public Finance Review*, *Eastern Economic Journal* and *Journal of Gambling Business and Economics*.

Brad R. Humphreys is Professor in the Department of Economics at West Virginia University, USA. He belongs to several editorial boards and has published articles in *Southern Economic Journal*, *Applied Economics*, *Journal of Sport Management*, *Journal of Sports Economics* and *Contemporary Economic Policy*.

 Victor A. Matheson is Professor in the Department of Economics at the College of the Holy Cross, Worcester, Massachusetts, USA. He is an expert in sports economics, especially in the analysis of great sports events' impact, public finance and gaming economics. He has collaborated as an expert in magazines such as *Forbes*, *ESPN The Magazine* and *The New York Times*.

 Rodney Paul is Professor in the Department of Sport Management at Syracuse University, USA. His research focuses on sports economics and gambling economics. His research has appeared on Buffalo Sabres Gamenight and Forbes.com, in *CFO Magazine*, and in various newspaper and radio outlets, including recent interviews on National Public Radio. He has also published in specialized journals such as *Journal of Sports Economics*, *Journal of Economics and Finance* and *Atlantic Journal*.

 David Peel is a Professor in Economics at Lancaster University, United Kingdom. He was educated at the University of Warwick. He has held previous posts at the University of Liverpool, Aberystwyth and University of Cardiff. Professor Peel has published widely on empirical and theoretical issues in macroeconomics and the economics of gambling markets. He has published pioneering papers in the application of nonlinear ESTAR models to purchasing power parity deviations, the political theory of the business cycle, uncertainty and football attendance, central banks with asymmetric preferences and political popularity series modelled as fractional processes.

 Levi Pérez is Associate Professor in the Department of Economics at the University of Oviedo, Spain. He is an expert in lottery markets and gambling economics, and has published several articles in scientific journals such as *The Journal of the Royal Statistical Society: Series C – Applied Statistics*, *Papers in Regional Science*, *Journal of Economic Surveys* and the

Journal of Gambling Studies. He is also co-author of a chapter published in the book *Recent Developments in the Economics of Sport*, edited by Wladimir Andreff.

 Plácido Rodríguez is Professor EU of Economics in the Department of Economics at the University of Oviedo, Spain. He is the co-editor of the books *Sports Economics after Fifty Years: Essays in Honour of Simon Rottenberg*, *Governance and Competition in Professional Sports Leagues*, *Threats to Sports and Sports Participation* and *Social Responsibility and Sustainability in Sports*. He was formerly President of Real Sporting de Gijon Football Club and currently is the Director of the Fundación Observatorio Económico del Deporte and the Honorary President of the IASE (International Association of Sports Economists).

 Jane E. Ruseski is Associate Professor of Economics at West Virginia University, USA. She is an applied microeconomist with specializations in health, sports and gambling economics. She has published in several journals including *Contemporary Economic Policy*, *Health Economics*, *Southern Economic Journal*, *Journal of Sports Economics* and *International Journal of Sport Finance*. She is a co-editor of *Contemporary Economic Policy* and *International Journal of Sport Finance*.

 Robert Simmons is Senior Lecturer of Economics at Lancaster University Management School, United Kingdom. He is an expert in labour economics and sports economics. He has been consultant to the International Labour Organization. He is also a member of the editorial board of the *Journal of Sports Economics*. He has published in numerous journals such as *Economic Enquiry*, *Applied Economics*, *Economica*, *Journal of Sports Economics* and *Southern Economic Journal*.

 Andrew Weinbach is Professor of Economics in the Department of Economics and Finance, Wall College of Business at Coastal Carolina University, USA. He is the author of more than fifty publications on sports betting and consumer demand for sports. His current research areas encompass sports betting markets, human behaviour in financial markets and the demand for sports on television. His research has been published in a number of journals, including *Journal of Sports Economics*, *Journal of Prediction Markets*, *Journal of Economics and Finance* and *Journal of Economics and Business*.

Rhys Wheeler is a PhD student and Associate Lecturer at Lancaster University, United Kingdom. His research areas are applied microeconomics and behavioural economics, focusing on the economics of gambling. He is also interested in health economics, in particular the economics of addiction. His current projects involve modelling demand and evaluating the taxation of gambling product, and also researching the welfare impact of gambling.

 Jie Yang was a Research Associate at the University of Alberta, Canada until April 2016. His main skills are data analyses, econometrics, qualitative and quantitative research and statistical modelling.

Abbreviations

AIDS	Almost Ideal Demand System
B365	Bet365
BW	Bet & Win
CPI	Consumer Price Index
CPT	Cumulative Prospect Theory
EMH	efficient markets hypothesis
EPL	English Premier League
GB	Gamebookers
GGY	Gross Gambling Yield
IV	Instrumental Variables
IW	Interwetten
LB	Ladbrokes
LFS	Labour Force Survey
NBA	National Basketball Association
NCAA	National Collegiate Athletic Association
NFL	National Football League
NHL	National Hockey League
OLS	Ordinary Least Squares
OLSDV	Ordinary Least Squares Dummy Variable
PASPA	Professional and Amateur Sports Protection Act of 1992
RPI	Retail Price Index
SB	Sportingbet
SELAE	The Spanish National Lottery Agency
SHS	Survey of Household Spending
SJ	Stan James
SP	starting price
VC	VC Bet
WH	William Hill

Introduction

**Plácido Rodríguez, Brad R. Humphreys and
Robert Simmons**

Sports betting has become increasingly popular in recent years, with a greater diversity of betting products now on offer. The growth of sports betting is facilitated by the increased availability of online betting opportunities. It seems reasonable to conclude that sports betting and spectator viewing are complementary goods. Sports fans can now watch sporting contests on television in the comfort of their own home and simultaneously place bets on the outcome through online bookmakers. At many UK football stadia, bookmakers have facilities within the premises for fans to place bets. Many European football teams now have shirt sponsorship provided by betting companies. The growth of sports betting gives rise to several important issues for scholars to analyse and the present volume exhibits state of the art research on a variety of key questions including how betting markets function. Specifically, can bettors usefully exploit imperfections in betting markets so as to generate profits for themselves?

The first five chapters in this book concern strategic issues in sports betting including recent trends and current policy concerns. The question of the extent of complementarity between sports betting and spending on spectator sports viewing is addressed in Chapter 1 by Brad Humphreys, Jane Ruseski and Jie Yang using Canadian household spending data. They find that spending on betting and spending on spectator sports are indeed complementary. Intriguingly, they also find that betting and spending on sports participation are substitutes. This suggests that further deregulation of sports gambling in Canada could well lead to less physical activity and more sedentary life styles for Canadians.

In North America and Europe, many sports betting operations are state-owned and could be argued to suffer from inefficiency and failure to innovate. Privatization of state betting operations could raise efficiency and lead to more product innovation. In Chapter 2 Kent Grote and Victor Matheson use the case of the Illinois State Lottery to analyse whether privatization could lead to increased lottery revenues and hence greater transfers to public projects. The privatization case they consider did not yield extra revenues and the authors examine why this might be so.

Chapter 3 by Xiaogang Che, Arne Feddersen and Brad Humphreys shows how bookmaker commissions, termed 'over-round', have fallen over time through greater competition, hence offering improved value for bettors. They take the English Premier League as their test case and focus on the two largest UK bookmakers. The findings are most interesting. First, over-rounds have fallen over time. Second, this reduction is attributable to the emergence of a betting exchange, Betfair, which has become increasingly popular in the UK. Third, perhaps surprisingly, the reduced commissions are not related to the growth of online bookmakers in the UK. Thus, it is increased competition from the betting exchange and not from online bookmakers that has exerted downward pressure on bookmaker over-rounds.

A recent popular development in sports betting markets is the emergence of in-play betting where gamblers can post bets online during a sporting contest. Betting products available for 'live' or in-play betting include the match result, the exact score and the identity of the next scorer. This market has shown spectacular growth for European football. In a novel contribution in Chapter 4, Stephen Dobson and John Goddard investigate the efficiency of the in-play football betting market as applied to exact scores in the English Premier League over two seasons. They compare betting exchange implied probabilities with probabilities generated from a statistical model and find some discrepancies after key events, especially just after a goal is scored or a player is dismissed from the field of play.

Chapter 5 by Jaume García, Levi Pérez and Plácido Rodríguez poses the fundamental question of whether bookmaker probabilities offer superior predictions of match outcomes to bettors themselves. Their test case is Spanish football and the comparison gamblers are football pools bettors who play a game where they forecast match outcomes. The authors find, first, that there is a favourite–longshot bias in Spanish fixed-odds football results betting and, second, bookmakers' predictions outperform those of football pools bettors.

The next four chapters question the existence of betting market efficiency and focus on possible market anomalies, biases or failures. The key question uniting most of these chapters is whether sports betting markets are efficient so that outcome probabilities associated with betting odds are exactly correlated with match outcomes with any deviation being due to 'luck'. The last chapter analyses manipulation of individual sporting contests.

In North America and Europe, the dominant mode of horse race betting is pari-mutuel where the operator takes a fixed commission and winners share a pool of betting money. In the United Kingdom, this betting format is known as the 'Tote'. But unlike Europe and North America, United Kingdom bettors can choose to bet on the pari-mutuel form or at fixed-odds offered by on-course and off-course bookmakers. This raises the question, addressed in Chapter 6 by Babatunde Buraimo, David Peel and Robert Simmons, of whether returns for winning bets are similar across both types of market. The authors investigate UK horse racing and find that returns for winning bets are superior in the pari-mutuel market, compared to fixed-odds bets, for long shots but not at short odds. The authors rationalize this finding in terms of how odds are set by bookmakers together with gamblers' attitudes to risk, bearing in mind that the pari-mutuel sector is a more risky proposition for a gambler given that odds are unknown ex ante.

Considerable attention has been devoted to the presence of favourite–longshot bias in sports betting markets where favourites are 'under-bet' with odds that are superior to those predicted under fully efficient markets. Underdogs are 'under-bet' with odds that are even more unfair than those that would be predicted under market efficiency. The favourite–longshot bias has been well-documented in horse racing. In Chapter 7, Arne Feddersen extends the analysis of favourite–longshot bias to European handball leagues covering six countries. The chapter uses regression-based analysis to demonstrate the presence of favourite–longshot bias in handball with market inefficiency observed as a consequence.

A significant strand of literature on sports betting investigates how bettors and betting markets respond to winning streaks by players or teams. This literature began with basketball and refers to the 'hot hand' effect of in-form players and teams which suggests that bettors and/or bookmakers believe this streak will continue. Do gamblers benefit from backing a player or team that is on a winning streak or would they gain superior returns by assuming that the streak will end in the next game? Chapter 8 by Rodney Paul and Andrew Weinbach tests the 'hot hand' hypothesis in betting on Major League Baseball games. Interestingly, they find different results for bets based on the momentum of the team and on individual pitchers. Their results show that the baseball betting market believes in the 'hot hand' and there is potential for positive returns for gamblers when betting that a team's hitting streak will end i.e. bettors would benefit from pursuing a 'contrarian' strategy. In contrast, wagering on pitchers with successful streaks delivers superior returns to bets against the streak.

In Chapter 9, Robert Simmons and Rhys Wheeler test the 'hot hand' hypothesis in European football and analyze returns to simple betting rules relating to team momentum effects. They detect some evidence that the market believes in the notion of winning streaks but such beliefs are fully incorporated into bookmaker fixed-odds. In European football, it appears there is no scope for gamblers to exploit team winning streaks so as to generate profits for themselves.

In Chapter 10, David Forrest takes a broad look at malfeasance in betting markets through match-fixing. He confronts the critical issue of how and why match-fixing might occur in some sporting competitions. This chapter sets out economic motives for players to engage in match-fixing and also establishes the structural features of betting markets that lead to fixes. The solution, however, is not to make betting markets illegal as this would be counter-productive and would harm consumer welfare. Instead, Forrest argues for the need for sports governing bodies and national and supranational governments to cooperate in detecting and punishing match-fixing.

We hope that this book demonstrates the richness and depth of contemporary research into sports betting markets. We believe that opportunities for fruitful research into sports betting markets will continue to open up as these markets grow and develop.

We thank the sponsors and stakeholders who made this book possible: Ayuntamiento de Gijón (Sociedad Mixta de Turismo), CajAstur, Consejo Superior de Deportes, Fundación del Fútbol Profesional, University of Oviedo, PCTI Asturias, Fundación Observatorio Económico del Deporte (FOED), Facultad de Comercio, Turismo y Ciencias Sociales Jovellanos and Departamento de Economía de la Universidad de Oviedo. Plácido Rodríguez acknowledges financial support from grant GRUPIN14-064 of the Regional Government of Principado de Asturias (Consejería de Economía y Empleo).

1. Consumer spending on spectator sports, physical activity, and gambling: evidence from Canada

Brad R. Humphreys, Jane E. Ruseski and Jie Yang*

1.1 INTRODUCTION

Recent developments in North America underscore the importance of understanding the economic relationship between consumer spending on leisure activities, gambling, and exercise or participation in physical activity. Both labor force participation and participation rates in physical activity continue to decline worldwide, suggesting that consumers spend more time pursuing other leisure activities. Legal opportunities for gambling have expanded, and sports betting opportunities also appear to be expanding. In Canada, the federal government has considered amending the Criminal Code to legalize betting on individual sporting events. In the US, states have pushed for legalized sports betting. The outcome in both countries is still undecided. This chapter analyzes the relationship between spending on sports betting and other leisure-related consumer spending to understand how increasing access to sports betting opportunities might affect other types of spending.

We use detailed household-level data from the Survey of Household Spending (SHS), a large-scale annual Canadian survey of consumer economic activity to estimate an Almost Ideal Demand System (AIDS) for these three consumer goods and services. AIDS models have been used extensively in recent research to analyze consumer spending, including spending on gasoline and consumer transportation (Chang and Serletis, 2013), consumer travel (Mangion et al., 2012), consumer non-durables (Blow et al., 2012), food (Koohi-Kamali, 2013), and residential energy (Guta, 2012; Gebreegziabher et al., 2012).

Flexible functional form demand models like AIDS allow for the estimation of own and cross price elasticities for consumer goods and services that can be interpreted as approximations to general consumer choice models. These models generate estimates consistent with aggregation across households, which make them ideal for use with consumer expenditure survey data like the SHS data analyzed here.

We find that household spending on sports betting and attendance at spectator sports are complements, but household spending on sports betting and spending on leisure time exercise are substitutes, based on estimates from an Almost Ideal Demand System using spending data from 145,560 Canadian households over the period 1997–2009. Since household spending on sports betting and spending on attendance at sporting events are complements, professional sports leagues in North America have little reason to worry that the expansion of legal sports betting opportunities will reduce attendance-based revenues; instead, our evidence suggests that expanding legal sports betting may increase attendance at live sporting events, generating larger revenues for sports teams and leagues.

However, the evidence that consumer spending on sports betting and spending on exercise and physical activity are substitutes suggests that increasing access to legal sports betting may have unintended consequences, if the reduced household spending on physical activity and exercise reflects reduced participation in physical activity, since reduced participation in physical activity has been linked to adverse health outcomes (Humphreys et al., 2014).

1.2 GAMBLING, EXERCISE, AND ATTENDANCE

Gambling, including sports betting, is a highly regulated economic activity in Canada. The other two categories of consumer spending analyzed here, spending on live attendance at sporting events and spending on leisure time physical activity, are not regulated. Professional sports, and Division I intercollegiate athletics in North America are produced by monopoly sports leagues. Access to sports betting depends on both government regulations and the willingness of certain individuals to violate these regulations. Simmons (2007) analyzed factors influencing gambling regulations. He identified a tension between consumers, who view gambling as entertainment or a financial transaction, and governments, who view state sponsored monopoly gambling as a source of revenues. Significant illegal sports betting operations exist in many countries, particularly the US. Strumpf (2003) documented the number and nature of the extensive US illegal sports betting operations.

Sauer (2001) analyzed the regulation and availability of legal gambling using a public choice model in which governments set regulations in response to lobbying by interest groups, including pro-gambling consumers whose welfare rises with gambling access and falls with gambling regulation, and an anti-gambling lobbying group who wants to restrict gambling access. The anti-gambling lobbying group includes individuals and organizations like churches that disapprove of gambling for different reasons. In the case of sports betting, the anti-gambling group may also contain professional and amateur sports organizations like the NFL, NBA, NHL and NCAA. The gambling regulations predicted by this model depend on the relative lobbying efforts made by the two groups.

Forrest and Simmons (2003) reviewed the economic and public policy context for sports betting. They highlighted the recent and rapid growth in sports betting worldwide and discussed the implications for revenue generation for government and sports organizations. They identified a number of negative aspects of sports betting, including incentives for corruption. They also emphasized the symbiotic nature of the relationship between sport and sports betting, and pointed out the importance of complementarities between watching sport and sports betting as well as the tensions generated by this relationship. The importance of complementarities in consumption drives demand for sports betting and puts pressure on governments to expand sports betting opportunities, while the corruptive factors fuel the desires of anti-sports gambling groups and leads to increased pressure to restrict sports betting opportunities.

Even though gambling, and sports betting, is highly regulated in both Canada and the United States, government regulators are currently debating policy changes that would significantly increase access to legal sports betting in both countries. In Canada, the Criminal Code currently prohibits single-event sports betting but allows parlay-style betting on two or more sporting events. However, Bill C-290 ("an Act to amend the Criminal Code") that would legalize single-event sports betting was passed unanimously by the Canadian House of Commons in December 2012 and is currently being debated by the Senate. The governments of eight Canadian provinces have formally supported passage of the bill. The National Hockey League (NHL) has vocally opposed the bill, claiming that legal single-event sports betting will lead to reduced revenues and increase the likelihood that gamblers will try to fix game outcomes. During legislative hearings on the bill, experts testified that Canadians currently spend between $10 and $40 billion annually betting on single sporting events with illegal bookmakers and about $4 billion annually betting on single sporting events with on-line offshore bookmakers that are not regulated by Canadian provinces.

In the US, the State of New Jersey passed a law legalizing single-event sports betting in 2012 following a successful 2011 referendum on the issue. Single-event sports betting is currently legal at casinos in Las Vegas, and, under the federal Professional and Amateur Sports Protection Act (PASPA) of 1993, sports betting can be legalized in four states (Nevada, Oregon, Delaware and Montana). The four major professional sports leagues operating in the US, the National Football League (NFL), Major League Baseball (MLB), the National Basketball Association (NBA) and the National Hockey League (NHL) along with the National Collegiate Athletic Association (NCAA) challenged New Jersey's legalization of sports betting immediately after the law was passed and obtained an injunction against the implementation of the law. The sports leagues claimed that increased access to sports betting would damage the public perception of professional sports, leading to long-term and irreparable economic damage in the form of lost revenues.

Little evidence about the relationship between legal sports betting and professional sports leagues currently exists. Forrest and Pérez (2011) show that the presence of high-profile football matches on the betting coupon increases the volume of bets placed in La Quiniela, a football pool betting game operated by the Spanish National Lottery. García and Rodríguez (2007) and García et al. (2008) reported evidence of important complementarities between watching or following sporting events and sports betting in La Quiniela in Spain. No formal evidence of such complementarities exists in other countries.

Canadians have access to legal sports betting as part of a group of government-sanctioned lottery games. These games have different names in different parts of Canada. In Quebec, the lottery-based sports betting game is called Pari Sportif; in Ontario and Atlantic Canada this game is called Pro-Line; in Manitoba, Saskatchewan and Alberta it is called Sports Select; in British Columbia it is called Sports Action. In western Canada, consumers also have access to a lottery-based game based on point spreads. All of these lottery-based sports betting games are available at lottery outlets. In some provinces, sports betting and other lottery tickets can be purchased on the internet. In 2011, total sales of government sponsored lottery products in Canada were $4.76 billion dollars. Canadians have easy access to lottery outlets. About $237 million of these sales came from sports betting games, just over 5 per cent of total sales. In 2011 there were 30,090 lottery outlets in Canada, roughly one lottery outlet for every 900 persons age 18 and older.

These Canadian lottery-based sports betting games, except Point Spread, are based on fixed odds bets on game outcomes and total points scored in professional and amateur sports leagues, including games in the major North American sports leagues and US college football and basketball games. These games feature parlay-style betting where gamblers must pick the outcome of between two and 12 games.

Winnings in Canadian sports betting games are not pari-mutuel; lottery corporations make profits based on over-round, the amount by which the win probabilities implied by the fixed betting odds offered on specific outcomes exceed 100. The over-round on Canadian sports betting games varies with the number of events selected in the lottery ticket. The minimum over-round is 160 per cent and it can exceed 300 per cent depending on the bets placed. Winnings are capped at $2,000,000 per card no matter how large the odds on the selected events or the number of games included in the parlay wager.

Given that Canadians currently have access to a form of sports betting offered at lottery outlets throughout the country, data on household spending on government operated lotteries and other related consumer goods can provide new insights into the relationship between sports betting and other sectors of the economy like professional sports. In the following sections, we describe the data source, empirical methods, and results of this analysis.

1.3   DATA DESCRIPTION

The data come from the SHS conducted by Statistics Canada. We used the SHS confidential micro data from 1997 to 2009, which includes detailed information about household expenditure. In particular, the SHS contains information about household expenditure on attendance at live sporting events, physical activity/physical fitness and the government-run lottery as well as detailed household demographic characteristics.

The SHS has been conducted in the ten Canadian provinces annually since 1997 and in the three Canadian territories biannually since 1999. The coverage of the population is about 98 per cent in the provinces and 90 per cent in the territories. However, there was a drop in coverage in Nunavut in 2005 (68.3 per cent) due to changes in sampling methods. The SHS contained about 20,000 eligible households each year before 2007. However, the sample size was reduced by nearly 30 per cent after 2008 due to Statistics Canada budget cuts. The response rates for the SHS have been about 66 per cent, varying from 63.4 per cent in 2008 to 76.2 per cent in 2001.

In the SHS, detailed information about household expenditure for the reference (calendar) year is collected during the personal interview. A paper questionnaire was used before 2006 and replaced by computer assisted personal interviews, starting in 2006. Also starting in 2006, the

SHS collected information about dwelling characteristics and household equipment at the time of the interview instead of at the end of the reference year. Another important change since 2006 was that there was no distinction between "part-year" and "full-year" household members. Data were collected for every household member as of the time of the interview.

The SHS sample uses stratification and multi-stage selection from the Labour Force Survey (LFS) sampling frame. From 1997 to 2003, SHS used 1991 Census geography and population counts; from 2004, SHS used 2001 Census geography and population counts after the major sample redesign of the LFS. SHS also used Census of Population and T4 data from the Canada Revenue Agency to adjust the survey weights. For comparisons over these years, data from the 1997–2003 SHS were also re-weighted using the new weighting methodology. However, since the SHS employed a complex survey design and also considered uneven respondent selection probabilities, estimation and variance calculations using the weighted sample over these years may be problematic for certain subgroups or variables.

Extra questions were included in several survey years, but none of these relate to this topic. The final data set contains all SHS households reporting positive total expenditure on attendance at live sporting events, physical activity and exercise, and government-run lotteries (which includes sports betting) from the SHS confidential micro data files. The sample contains 145,560 observations including data from more than 40,000 Canadian households from 1997–2009. Due to the nature of confidential data, we cannot determine whether the same households participated in the surveys in multiple years. Thus, we assume that all 145,560 observations were from different households. Summary statistics are shown on Table 1.1. Note that we cannot report the maximum and minimum values in the sample due to the Statistics Canada confidentiality policy. Instead, we report the values at the 0.02 per cent percentile and 99.98 per cent, which can almost be regarded as the minimum and maximum values.

The reported Real Expenditure on Table 1.1 is the total real annual household expenditure for admissions to live sporting events, total fees (including membership and single usage fees) and dues for sports activities, sports and recreation facilities, and health clubs, and spending on government-run lotteries. It varies from about $1 to over $15,000. Table 1.1 also shows the shares of total expenditures for those three spending categories. On average, the share of spending on spectator sports event attendance is the smallest, only about 10 per cent of spending. Spending on government-run lotteries and sports betting is the largest, accounting for over one-half of this spending. For each of the three goods and services, there were always some households that spent nothing on one or two

Table 1.1   Summary statistics

Variable	Mean	Std. dev.	0.02nd percentile	99.98th percentile
Budget share, admissions to live sports events	0.101	0.237	0	1
Budget share, expenditure on physical activities	0.364	0.411	0	1
Budget share, expenditure on government-run lottery	0.535	0.435	0	1
Real Expenditure	518	847	1.02	15,734
Reference Person Age	48.3	15.5	17	94
Real Household Income (000)	62.41	79.38	0	1,163.52
Urban Household	0.786	–	0	1
Housing tenure				
Homeowner without mortgage	0.334	–	0	1
Homeowner with mortgage	0.360	–	0	1
Tenants – regular	0.266	–	0	1
Tenants – rent-free	0.009	–	0	1
Mixed tenure	0.031	–	0	1
Major income source				
No income	0.001	–	0	1
Paid employment	0.664	–	0	1
Self-employment	0.065	–	0	1
Investment income	0.014	–	0	1
Government transfer payments	0.185	–	0	1
Miscellaneous income	0.071	–	0	1
Household type				
Single female	0.110	–	0	1
Single male	0.097	–	0	1
Couple only	0.276	–	0	1
Couple with children	0.379	–	0	1
Single mother	0.060	–	0	1
Single father	0.014	–	0	1
Other	0.063	–	0	1
Household employment status				
Reference person and spouse unemployed	0.213	–	0	1
At least one has a part-time job	0.461	–	0	1
Both have full-time jobs	0.325	–	0	1

of these (share = 0) or only spent money on one of the goods and services (share = 1).

Real Household Income is the household's total annual income before taxes in the reference year. The average income in our sample is just above $62,000; the top-earning households in the sample earned over $1 million. Reference Person Age is the age of the reference person in the reference year. For one-person or single-parent households, the household income is mainly earned by the reference person. From an economic point of view the age of the reference person can be regarded as the age of the household. For couples, the age of the spouse of the reference person is highly correlated with the age of the reference person. As a matter of fact, the ages of couples are usually very close to each other. Hence we can use the reference person's age as the age of the household.

The rest of the variables on Table 1.1 are all indicator variables. Urban identifies whether the household is in an urban area. Most households (78.6 per cent) in our sample lived in urban areas. The definition of urban area follows the census definition: "minimum population concentrations of 1,000 and a population density of at least 400 per square kilometre." The other 21 variables are categorized in four groups: housing tenure, major income source, household type and household employment status.

The SHS identifies five types of housing tenure. The shares of households with and without a mortgage are both about one-third of the sample. Regular renters account for a bit more than one-quarter of the sample. Also, nearly 1 per cent are special tenants who don't pay rent. Roughly 3 per cent of households are in the mixed tenure group. They both owned and rented their dwellings in the reference year. Major household income sources are divided into six groups. Over two-thirds of the households reported income from paid employment as the major source of income. Less than 20 per cent of households depended on government transfer payments as the major source of income. A significant part of this subgroup was retired.

Since the SHS reflects household spending, accounting for household type is important when analyzing expenditure. The SHS identifies four basic household types: one-person households, couples, single-parent households, and other household types. We further broke households down into seven types: single female households, single male households, couples-only households, couples with children and/or other persons, single mothers, single fathers and other households. The rationale here was to separately identify the impacts of gender and the presence of children on expenditure patterns. In the fourth household type, couples with children and/or other person(s) living in the household, other persons refer to children whose marital status is not "single, never-married", relatives by birth or marriage, and unrelated persons. The definition is complex, but basically most households in this type are just couples with children. About 20 per cent of the sample is one-person households. Single females and single males constitute similar shares of the sample. Couples accounted for almost two-thirds of the households in the sample. Couples with children were more common than couples without children. Six per cent of the households in the sample are single mother households, about four times the share of single father households.

Household employment status consists of three variables identifying three different labor market outcomes: (1) both the reference person and the spouse have no job (if reference person had a married or common law spouse); (2) at least one of the couple has a part time job; and (3) both of the couple have full time jobs. The largest group in the sample is type (2) households. In 46.1 per cent of the sample households, at least one person was working during the reference year, but both members of the couple did not have full time jobs. Also a little more than 20 per cent of households had no jobs at all.

1.4   EMPIRICAL METHODS

Deaton and Muellbauer (1980) developed the AIDS model, which represents "an arbitrary first-order approximation to any demand system" (Deaton and Muellbauer (1980)). This model satisfies all standard axioms of choice and aggregates perfectly over consumers. Its simple functional form makes it relatively easy to estimate.

Expressed in budget shares, the AIDS demand function is:

$$w_i = \alpha_i + \sum_j \gamma_{ij} \log p_j + \beta_i \log\left(\frac{m}{a(p)}\right) \qquad (1.1)$$

where w_i is the share of the household budget spent on good or service i, p_i is the price of good or service i and the price index $a(p)$ is defined by:

$$\log a(p) = \alpha_0 + \sum_k \alpha_k \log p_k + \frac{1}{2}\sum_j \sum_k \gamma_{kj} \log p_k \log p_j \qquad (1.2)$$

We used the Consumer Price Index (CPI) component for spectator entertainment (excluding cablevision and satellite services) as the price of attending sports events, and the component for use of recreational facilities and services as the price of physical activity. Since the price of a ticket in the sports lottery was constant over time, $1 or $2 per ticket, we used the inverse of the CPI to approximate this price. There are three restrictions on the parameters of Equation (1.1), which ensure the demand function system satisfies: (1) the sum of the share functions equals 1 ($\sum w_i = 1$);

(2) each share function is homogeneous of degree zero in prices and (3) Slutsky symmetry.

$$\sum_{i=1}^{n} \alpha_i = 1, \sum_{i=1}^{n} \beta_{ij} = 0, \sum_{i=1}^{n} \gamma_{ij} = 0 \tag{1.3}$$

$$\sum_{j} \gamma_{ij} = 0 \tag{1.4}$$

$$\gamma_{ij} = \gamma_{ji} \tag{1.5}$$

The effect of changes in prices on the budget shares is reflected in the parameters γ_{ij} and changes in expenditure (m) reflected in the parameters β_j. Goods with an increasing expenditure when income increases, luxury goods, have a positive β_i and goods with a decreasing budget share as income increases, necessities, have a negative β_i.

As Deaton and Muellbauer (1980) pointed out, if individual prices are highly collinear, variation in the log price index $\ln[a(p)]$ decreases, making the identification of α_0 difficult. They suggested assigning a value to α_0 a priori. Banks et al. (1997) further argued that the lowest value of log expenditure placed an upper bound on α_0. Here, we assign the parameter α_0 to the largest integer just below the minimum level of $\ln m$. We also tested a grid of values for α_0 and our results remained robust to different values assigned to α_0. We also adopt the price scaling technique introduced by Ray (1983), who incorporated demographic characteristics into the original AIDS model in his research on the cost of children. The compensated price elasticity estimates from AIDS models are found using the standard Slutsky decomposition.

1.5   RESULTS AND DISCUSSION

The full parameter estimates, standard errors and p-values obtained from estimating the basic AIDS model and the AIDS model augmented with demographic characteristics, based on an unweighted sample from the SHS, are shown in Table 1.2. Flexible demand system models contain a large number of parameters; these results are reported primarily for completeness. Note that we do not report the parameter estimates from the year and province indicator variables since their effects are not our primary interest here. We do not report the parameter estimates on the demographic characteristics for the AIDS model augmented with household demographic characteristics shown on the right panel of Table 1.2, as there are a very large number of parameters in this model. The full results are available on request from the authors.

Table 1.2   AIDS model estimates

	AIDS model			Augmented AIDS model		
	Coef.	Std. err.	p-value	Coef.	Std. err.	p-value
$\alpha 1$	−0.281	0.023	< 0.001	−0.194	0.063	0.002
$\alpha 2$	0.519	0.036	< 0.001	1.164	0.088	< 0.001
$\alpha 3$	0.762	0.031	< 0.001	0.030	0.064	0.642
$\beta 1$	0.002	0.0004	< 0.001	0.024	0.006	< 0.001
$\beta 2$	0.104	0.001	< 0.001	0.219	0.010	< 0.001
$\beta 3$	−0.107	0.001	< 0.001	−0.243	0.010	< 0.001
$\gamma 11$	−0.202	0.025	< 0.001	−0.230	0.069	0.001
$\gamma 21$	0.280	0.028	< 0.001	0.293	0.079	< 0.001
$\gamma 31$	−0.078	0.005	< 0.001	−0.063	0.013	< 0.001
$\gamma 22$	−0.457	0.033	< 0.001	−0.543	0.093	< 0.001
$\gamma 32$	0.176	0.006	< 0.001	0.249	0.019	< 0.001
$\gamma 33$	−0.098	0.005	< 0.001	−0.187	0.014	< 0.001
Observations	145,560			145,560		

In Table 1.2 the $\alpha_i's$ are estimated intercepts, $\beta_i's$ estimated parameters on the income variable, and γ_{ij}'s reflect the effect on changes in own price and other prices on expenditure share. Like other research on demand systems, we focus on estimated price and income elasticities.

In general, the estimated parameters in both models are precisely estimated, as the p-values are quite small. The key parameters of interest in demand system models are the γ_{ij}'s which indicate the impact of changes in the price of good j on the budget share of good i. In Table 1.2 these parameter estimates are all statistically different from zero at conventional significance levels. Note that the inclusion of the demographic variables has little effect on the sign and significance of the key parameter estimates of interest; the results are robust to these different model specifications. The results are also robust to the use of sample weights from the SHS.

We focus primarily on the estimates income and price elasticities, since these have the most straightforward economic interpretation. The estimated income and price elasticities are shown in Table 1.3. The left panel contains estimates from the basic AIDS model and the right panel the AIDS model augmented with demographic characteristics.

In Table 1.3 "Attendance" refers to consumer spending on attendance at live sporting events; "Exercise" refers to consumer spending on leisure time physical activity and exercise and "Lottery" refers to consumer spending on government sponsored lotteries, which includes sports betting. In each 3 × 3 cell, the diagonal elements are the estimated own price elasticities and the off-diagonal elements are the estimated cross price elasticities.

Table 1.3   Estimated income and price elasticities

	AIDS model			Augmented AIDS model		
	Attendance	Exercise	Lottery	Attendance	Exercise	Lottery
Expenditure Elasticity	1.023	1.287	0.801	0.971	1.253	0.834
Compensated own and cross price elasticities						
Attendance	−2.902	3.159	−0.257	−3.185	3.263	−0.078
Exercise	0.875	−1.699	0.824	0.906	−2.036	1.130
Lottery	−0.048	0.560	−0.512	−0.016	0.769	−0.753
Uncompensated own and cross price elasticities						
Attendance	−3.005	2.787	−0.805	−3.283	2.909	−0.598
Exercise	0.745	−2.167	0.135	0.770	−2.492	0.459
Lottery	−0.129	0.269	−0.940	−0.100	0.466	−1.199

Estimates of the expenditure elasticity for good j are shown on the first row; the first set of estimates in row i, column j contains the uncompensated cross price elasticity of expenditure category i with respect to the changes in the price of good j. These uncompensated price elasticity estimates hold income and other prices constant, but allow utility to change with the price changes as consumers adjust their consumption bundle. The second set of estimates contains the "Hicksian" compensated price elasticity estimates that hold utility constant.

The uncompensated and compensated own price elasticities are uniformly negative, as predicted by standard consumer theory. As the price of each good or service goes up, consumer spending on that good or service falls, other things equal. Attendance at live sporting events has the highest price elasticity, and the estimated price elasticity on sports betting is relatively price inelastic.

The uncompensated and compensated estimated cross price elasticity between the price of sports betting and spending on live attendance at sporting events is negative; these goods are complements, and as the price of sports betting decreases, demand for both sports betting and live attendance at sporting events increases, other things equal. The opposite estimated cross price elasticity, between the price of attending live game sporting events and spending on lotteries and sports betting, is also negative. This provides additional support for the idea that these two types of consumer spending are complements.

This estimate has important implications. States and provinces across North America have recently been pushing for increased legal access to sports betting, especially in Canada, where the federal government has considered legalizing betting on individual sporting events. Sports leagues have generally opposed this proposed change, claiming that their revenues will be harmed by expanding access to legal betting. This estimated cross-price elasticity suggests that sports betting and spending on live attendance in Canada are complements. To the extent that increased legal opportunities to bet on sports reduces the price of betting on sports, these results predict that consumer spending on live game attendance will actually increase, contrary to the claims made by sports leagues.

The uncompensated and compensated estimated cross price elasticity between the price of sports betting and spending on participation in leisure time physical activity is positive; these goods are substitutes, and as the price of sports betting decreases, demand for participation in leisure time physical activity and exercise decreases, other things equal. The same relationship exists between the price of attending live sporting events and participating in physical activity: these are also substitutes.

These estimates also have important implications. If expanding legal access to sports betting reduces the price of sports betting, this will likely lead to a decrease in consumer demand for participation in leisure time physical activity and exercise. Increasing legal access to sports betting will tend to make Canadians more sedentary and less physically active. Since participation in physical activity and exercise has been shown to produce health benefits (Humphreys et al., 2014), expanding legal access to sports betting may have an unintended consequence of making Canadians less healthy, which may lead to increased national spending on health care.

1.6   CONCLUSIONS

This chapter develops evidence that spending on government sponsored lotteries, which encompasses sports betting in Canada, and spending on attendance at live sporting events are complements. When the price of one of these goods decreases, consumer spending on both increases. This relationship suggests that increasing access to legal sports betting, which can be interpreted as an increase in the supply of sports betting opportunities, should decrease the price of sports betting, and increase consumer spending on both sports betting and attendance at live sporting events. This evidence contradicts the claims made by professional sports leagues and the NCAA when opposing the expansion of legal sports betting in both Canada and the United States. If these results can be applied to proposed increases in access to legal sports betting in North America, professional and intercollegiate athletic teams and leagues in both countries could expect to see an increase in their revenues following the expansion of legal sports betting opportunities.

Sports teams and leagues have also raised the issue that increased access to legal sports betting will damage the public's perception of the legitimacy of the games sponsored by these leagues, by increasing the incentive for gamblers to influence the outcomes of the games by fixing games or matches. Existing evidence suggests that a significant amount of illegal sports betting already takes place in North America, and gamblers have access to on-line bookmakers. The presence of these alternatives would seem to already provide an incentive for gamblers to fix games or matches. Also Forrest and Simmons (2003) pointed out that the presence of legal sports betting opportunities actually allows law enforcement officials and sports leagues to detect match fixing more easily than would be possible in the absence of legal sports betting opportunities; after all, bookmakers stand to lose money when game or match outcomes are fixed by gamblers. These factors also argue against the claims made by sports teams and leagues when arguing against the expansion of legal sports betting opportunities.

The chapter also contains interesting evidence about a negative consequence of expanding legal opportunities to bet on sports as well as expanding opportunities to attend live sporting events. The results from the AIDS models suggest that household spending on leisure time physical activity is a substitute for spending on both government sponsored lotteries/sports betting and spending on attendance at live sporting events. As the price of sports betting and the price of attendance at live sporting events declines, demand for participation in physical activity and exercise also declines, as proxied by household spending on fees (including membership and single usage fees) and dues for sports activities, sports and recreation facilities, and health clubs. Reduced participation in physical activity and exercise can have adverse effects on both health outcomes and worker productivity, suggesting that expanding access to sports betting or live sporting events may have negative consequences on the health of individual Canadians and on the Canadian economy.

The results presented here require some caveats. The empirical results come from a sample of Canadian households that reported a positive level of spending on at least one of the three goods and services analyzed here. An expansion of access to legal sports betting could also have an effect on the spending of consumers who did not purchase any of these three goods or services. The behavior of these consumers could differ systematically from the behavior of the households that make up the sample analyzed here. We have used the price of purchasing a lottery ticket as the price of government sponsored lotteries and sports betting, which was either $1 or

$2 throughout the sample period. The effective price of lottery gambling and sports betting can also depend on the expected return from these activities, which depend on the odds of winning, the size of the prizes and, in the case of sports betting, the over-round on the posted odds on various game outcomes. Although the own price elasticity estimates are negative and significant, the simple price measure for government sponsored lotteries and sports betting used here may not fully capture the prices faced by consumers making decisions to participate in sports betting.

NOTE

*   We thank Irene Wong for her kind help in the University of Alberta Research Data Centre.

REFERENCES

Banks, J., Blundell, R., and Lewbel, A. 1997. Quadratic Engel curves and consumer demand. *Review of Economics and Statistics*, **79**(4): 527–539.

Blow, L., Lechene, V., and Levell, P. 2012. Using the CE to model household demand. In *Improving the Measurement of Consumer Expenditures*, NBER Chapters, National Bureau of Economic Research.

Chang, D. and Serletis, A. 2014. The demand for gasoline: Evidence from household survey data. *Journal of Applied Econometrics*, **29**(2): 291–313.

Deaton, A. and Muellbauer, J. 1980. An almost ideal demand system. *The American Economic Review*, **70**(3): 312–326.

Forrest, D. and Pérez, L. 2011. Football pools and lotteries: Substitute roads to riches? *Applied Economics Letters*, **18**(13): 1253–1257.

Forrest, D. and Simmons, R. 2003. Sport and gambling. *Oxford Review of Economic Policy*, **19**(4): 598–611.

García, J., Pérez, L., and Rodríguez, P. 2008. Football pool sales: How important is a football club in the top division? *International Journal of Sport Finance*, **3**(3): 167–176.

García, J. and Rodríguez, P. 2007. The demand for football pools in Spain: The role of price, prizes, and the composition of the coupon. *Journal of Sports Economics*, **8**(4): 335–354.

Gebreegziabher, Z., Mekonnen, A., Kassie, M., and Köhlin, G. 2012. Urban energy transition and technology adoption: The case of Tigrai, northern Ethiopia. *Energy Economics*, **34**(2): 410–418.

Guta, D.D. 2012. Application of an almost ideal demand system (AIDS) to Ethiopian rural residential energy use: Panel data evidence. *Energy Policy*, **50**: 528–539.

Humphreys, B.R., McLeod, L., and Ruseski, J.E. 2014. Physical activity and health outcomes: Evidence from Canada. *Health Economics*, **23**(1): 33–54.

Koohi-Kamali, F. 2013. Estimation of equivalence scales under convertible rationing. *Review of Income and Wealth*, **59**(1): 113–132.

Mangion, M.-L., Cooper, C., Cortes-Jimenez, I., and Durbarry, R. 2012. Measuring the effect of subsidization on tourism demand and destination competitiveness through the AIDS model: An evidence-based approach to tourism policymaking. *Tourism Economics*, **18**(6): 1251–1272.

Ray, R. 1983. Measuring the costs of children: An alternative approach. *Journal of Public Economics*, **22**(1): 89–102.

Sauer, R.D. 2001. The political economy of gambling regulation. *Managerial and Decision Economics*, **22**(1–3): 5–15.

Simmons, R. 2007. Prohibition of gambling. In Meadowcroft, J. (ed.), *Prohibitions (Readings in Economics)*. Institute of Economic Affairs.

Strumpf, K. 2003. Illegal sports bookmakers. University of North Carolina Chapel Hill Working Paper.

2. Should gambling markets be privatized? An examination of state lotteries in the United States

Kent R. Grote and Victor A. Matheson

2.1 INTRODUCTION TO LOTTERIES IN THE US

Since 1964, when New Hampshire became the first state to offer a state-run lottery in the twentieth century, lotteries have become commonplace around the US. As of 2013, 43 states and the District of Columbia offered lotteries and these games have become a small but important component of state revenues. In 2011, state lotteries generated more than $18 billion for state governments, representing 1.7 percent of all government revenues generated by states excluding transfers from the federal government (Humphreys and Matheson, 2013).

Early in American history, lotteries were quite common but also were generally operated by private organizations, not by state governments. For example, the construction and expansion of many early private American universities, including Harvard and Princeton, were financed in part through lottery sales. Prominent American leaders also lent their support to lotteries designed to raise funds for public works. John Hancock's signature appears on lottery tickets sold to fund the construction of Faneuil Hall while George Washington administered the unsuccessful 1768 Mountain Road Lottery in Virginia, and Ben Franklin organized a lottery during the American Revolution to finance the purchase of cannons to aid in the defense of Philadelphia (Matheson and Grote, 2008).

While the organization and operation of lotteries in early America was generally undertaken by private individuals and groups, governments still had a role in authorizing lotteries. For example, in 1612 King James I of England issued a royal decree authorizing the Virginia Company to create a lottery to provide funds for Jamestown, the first English colony in America. Between 1612 and 1621, the company raised 29,000 pounds sterling to support the colony (Jamestown-Yorktown Foundation, 2013). Indeed, the rules regarding the authorization of lotteries were an issue of contention in the run-up to the Revolutionary War when, in 1769, the British crown attempted to prevent the sale of lottery tickets by groups or individuals that had not received royal permission (Dunstan, 1997).

Lotteries began to fall out of favor in the early 1800s as governments developed alternative methods of generating revenue, moral objections to lotteries began to rise, and concern about fraud in privately run lotteries increased. New York became the first state to ban new games in 1821 when its constitution was amended to prohibit lotteries not otherwise "previously provided for by law" (Benjamin, 2013). In 1833, New York ended lotteries completely and was joined in its prohibition by Pennsylvania and Massachusetts. Within just a few years most states had stopped authorizing lotteries and by 1860 only Delaware, Kentucky, and Missouri still allowed these games of chance (Dunstan, 1997).

Lotteries returned after the American Civil War as states in the South desperately searched for new sources of revenue during Reconstruction. These lotteries were generally short-lived with one very notable exception. The last existing lottery of the nineteenth century was run by the Louisiana State Lottery Company, a private firm granted a 25-year charter in 1868 by the Louisiana state legislature in exchange for a $40,000 annual payment to the state. The legislature also banned other organized gambling at the same time, giving the Louisiana State Lottery Company a monopoly on gambling in the state. The company also actively sold tickets around the US, generating over 90 percent of its revenue outside of the state of Louisiana, but the company's ability to evade lottery prohibitions in other states came to an end in 1890 when the US Congress banned the interstate transportation of lottery tickets and advertisements, a law whose constitutionality was upheld by the Supreme Court in 1892. The company's charter was not renewed by the state of Louisiana in 1893, despite heavy lobbying by the company that included large bribes offered to members of the state legislature (Louisiana Lottery Corporation, 2013). The company then moved its operations to Honduras and continued to illegally sell lottery tickets in the US until its final closure by US law enforcement in 1907.

Lotteries began to return to the US in 1964 when New Hampshire opened the first state-sanctioned game of the twentieth century. An overwhelming majority of states followed in the subsequent decades with state lotteries spreading to 43 states and the District of Columbia by 2013. State-authorized lotteries in the twentieth and twenty-first century were distinctly different than those of the nineteenth century, however, in that in all cases the lotteries were directly operated by the state governments themselves. In the nineteenth century, a "state lottery" was more likely to mean a lottery operated by private individuals but with a state sanction, rather than the modern American meaning of the word where a "state lottery" is essentially a state-owned enterprise under the direct control of the state government and with the state government being the residual claimant of any operating profits. This operational structure has begun to change in the past two years in the US as numerous state governments have begun to privatize their lottery operations.

Private operation of public lotteries is nothing new in the rest of the world. Since its beginning in 1994, the UK Lottery has been operated on a for-profit basis by the private company Camelot in exchange for a profit allowance of 0.5 percent of gross ticket sales. The Italian Lottery is operated by the private firm Lottomatica.

In the United States, Illinois was the first state to privatize the operations of its lottery when it handed over control to the Northstar Corporation in July 2011. Northstar is a joint venture of Scientific Games, a New York-based manufacturer of lottery tickets and gaming equipment, and GTECH, a wholly owned subsidiary of Lottomatica. Northstar beat out UK rival Camelot in its bid to become the first private company to operate a state lottery in the US. Indiana handed control of its lottery over to GTECH in 2012. In 2013, New Jersey awarded operations of its lottery to Northstar NJ, another joint venture of Lottomatica, Scientific Games, and a third venture partner. Pennsylvania agreed in principle to award control of its lottery to Camelot in 2013 as well, but public pressure and internal divisions with the Pennsylvania government scuttled the deal.

2.2   INTRODUCTION TO CASINOS IN THE US

Throughout much of American history, many taverns and roadhouses permitted card and dice games, but large dedicated casinos were rare. In the early 1800s, the same moral objections that rose against lotteries led to a disapproval of this type of gaming, particularly in the East. By the 1840s, the center of casino gaming had moved to riverboats on the Mississippi River and to New Orleans (Dunstan, 1997). While recreational gambling was generally considered acceptable in the region, professional gamblers and card sharps were looked down upon with severe disfavor.

The American Civil War along with the burgeoning rail system in the country led to the decline of the great riverboats. In their place, casinos began to flourish temporarily in mining boom towns such as San Francisco (1849); Cripple Creek and Central City, Colorado (1859); Virginia City, Nevada (1859); and Deadwood, South Dakota (1874). As miners either moved away when the mines played out or were replaced by more genteel residents that gentrified former mining towns, the "Wild West" atmosphere that encouraged the development of casinos also disappeared. By the turn of the twentieth century, casino gaming was again illegal through-out the country. Nevada re-legalized casino gaming in 1931 and it held a nationwide monopoly on the activity (at least legally) until New Jersey introduced casinos to Atlantic City in 1975 (Dunstan, 1997).

Other states legalized the operation of privately operated casinos over the next three decades although these casinos were generally limited in number or stakes. Often gambling legalization harkened back to the his-torical roots of gambling in the state. For example, gambling in states along the Mississippi was frequently limited to riverboats, and states with a mining heritage opened up former mining towns such as Cripple Creek, Central City, and Deadwood to casinos. As of the end of 2012, 513 com-mercial casinos operated in 23 states generating $37.3 billion in gambling related revenue (American Gaming Association, 2013).

The Seminole Tribe in Florida opened a casino on tribal land offer-ing high stakes bingo in 1979. The state sued to close the facility, but in *Seminole Tribe v. Butterworth* (1981), the Federal Appeals Court for the region determined that, since the state allowed charitable organizations in the state to offer bingo, it did not have the jurisdiction to prohibit the sovereign government of the Seminole Tribe from offering a similar game even at higher stakes, nor did the state have the right to limit attendance at the Tribe's casino to Tribe members.

The US Supreme Court followed up this decision with its own ruling in *California v. Cabazon Band of Mission Indians* (1987), which granted Native American Tribes the right to offer gambling options largely free of state control on tribal reservations as long as the state allowed a regulated version of the game to operate elsewhere in the state. Tribal casinos were not permitted to offer games that were criminally prohibited by state law or banned by federal statute.

Given the rise of Indian casinos following these favorable court rulings, the federal government passed the Indian Gaming Regulatory Act of 1988, which provided uniform and formalized gaming rules for Native American reservations across the country. The Act divided gambling activity into three classes. Class I gaming included traditional tribal and social gaming for low stakes. Such activity was not subject to regulation from outside of tribal government. Class II gaming included activities where players exclu-sively played against one another rather than the house such as bingo and poker. Such games were permitted without state regulation if these games were permitted in any fashion elsewhere in the state. Class III gaming included gambling activities where bettors played against the house such as blackjack, slot machines, craps, and roulette. The establishment of an Indian casino with Class III gaming requires a compact with the state in which the tribal reservation is located. As of the end of fiscal year 2011,

421 tribal casinos operated in 28 states generating $27.2 billion in gaming revenue (National Indian Gaming Commission, 2012). Between Native American casinos and commercial gaming establishments, 39 states currently offer some form of casino gambling.

2.3 INTRODUCTION TO PARI-MUTUEL BETTING IN THE US

Horse racing and other forms of pari-mutuel racing are another form of gambling with a long history in the US. The first horse racing track was laid in 1665 on Long Island in New York, and tracks spread throughout the country with the expansion of the nation. In 1865, pari-mutuel betting was invented by Pierre Oller, a French perfume shopkeeper and rapidly became the standard for horse racing. By the early 1900s, the general anti-gambling ideals of the nation, which led to the decline of legal casinos and lotteries, also eliminated betting at horse tracks everywhere in the country except for Maryland and Kentucky (Nash, 2009). The advent of the Great Depression in the 1930s led to an expansion of many forms of gambling as a form of economic stimulus including horse racing and charitable bingo.

After peaking in the mid-1970s, horse racing has suffered a gradual decline in general interest, at least in part due to the expansion of other types of legalized gambling, including lotteries and casinos (Nash, 2009). The total handle wagered on US races totaled $10.9 billion in 2012 although net betting revenue is a fraction of this figure (LaMarra, 2013). As of 2012, 78 tracks in 28 states offered thoroughbred racing and 36 tracks in 16 states offered harness racing. Most tracks have a betting window that offers a variety of general pari-mutuel bets. Many tracks also offer simulcast betting on races at other tracks, and 49 tracks in 14 states also offer some type of additional gaming ranging from full service casinos to video lottery terminals or other electronic gaming devices (American Gaming Association, 2013).

2.4 INTRODUCTION TO SPORTS GAMBLING IN US

As noted previously, gambling on horse racing has a long history in the US. Betting on other sporting events grew in line with the growth of organized sports in the late nineteenth and early twentieth centuries. Indeed, the history of nearly every league in the US goes hand in hand with a story of gambling corruption. Baseball's National League, the forerunner of Major League Baseball and the oldest American professional sports league still in existence, was formed in 1876. By 1877, the Louisville Grays ended the season mired in a betting scandal and ceased operation at the end of the year. The Ohio League, a precursor of the National Football League, was formed in 1903 as a loose association of American football teams. Just three years later, the Canton Bulldogs–Massillon Tigers betting scandal led to the demise of the Canton club and a decline in the popularity of the league. Of course, the 1919 "Black Sox" scandal where members of the Chicago White Sox were accused of throwing the World Series remains American sports' most famous case of gambling corruption, while the 1948 NCAA basketball point-shaving incident highlighted corruption in the college ranks.

Following the formation of professional leagues, "pool cards," which allowed bettors to gamble on a slate of games, became popular although not generally legal. Following in the footsteps of its casino businesses, Nevada officially legalized sports gambling in 1949, but major casinos didn't join until Stardust opened a sports book in 1976.

The main impetus that led to the establishment of large, commercial sports books at Nevada casinos was the US elimination of a 10 percent tax on sports gambling in 1974. This tax law change led to an increase in the sports gambling handle in Nevada from $825,767 in 1973 to $3,873,217 in 1974 and $26,170,328 in 1975 (*NFL v. Delaware*, 1977). Of course, major casinos could not ignore this surge in this particular gambling activity and most followed the lead of Stardust after 1976. By 2012, over $3.44 billion was wagered at 182 sports betting locations throughout the state (UNLV, 2013).

In other states, Montana legalized pool cards beginning in 1974. The Delaware Lottery offered NFL parlay tickets in 1976 and won a court case against the NFL and its allies for the right to offer the game. Nevertheless, the Delaware sports lottery folded after one year because the fixed-odds nature of the tickets couldn't guarantee the statutory tax contribution required under the state's lottery law. The Oregon Lottery offered NFL parlay tickets from 1998–2007 and NBA parley tickets in 1998 and 1999 (although the NBA ticket did not include games featuring the local NBA team, the Portland Trailblazers). The state yielded to pressure from the NCAA in 2007 and terminated its sports lottery in exchange for the NCAA lifting its ban on hosting college basketball tournament games in the state.

With the Professional and Amateur Sports Protection Act of 1992 (PASPA), the federal government banned sports gambling in all states except those with existing legalized sports gaming, which included Nevada, Oregon, Montana, and Delaware. The act bans other lottery associations from basing games on sports outcomes, prohibits sports books at casinos outside of these states, and prohibits sports gambling at tribal casinos since the federal government has the ultimate jurisdiction over civil laws on Native American reservations.

Since the passage of PASPA, the Montana Lottery has expanded into sports gambling with the introduction of Fantasy NFL and Fantasy NASCAR games in 2008. It should be noted that these games do not command a high level of player interest, generating weekly handles of just $2,500 per week for NASCAR and $5,000 per week for the NFL (Montana Lottery, 2013.) The Delaware Lottery reintroduced NFL parlay lottery tickets in 2009 but lost a court case later that year that would have allowed the state's lottery association to sell tickets with single game bets. A favorable ruling in the case, in effect, would have allowed the Delaware Lottery to create a fully functional sports book.

Other states have recently begun to challenge PASPA's virtual nationwide ban on sports gaming. New Jersey passed a law that would have allowed sports books at Atlantic City casinos in 2012, but the law was challenged by the major professional sports leagues and the NCAA. Preliminary court rulings have upheld PASPA, denying New Jersey the right to legalize sports gambling, but the state has appealed and the legal process is ongoing as of 2013. Should New Jersey ultimately prevail, it is extremely likely that multiple states, including California, would quickly consider legalizing general sports gambling within their own borders, and multiple state lottery associations could choose to follow Montana and Delaware in offering lottery games based on sports outcomes.

In summary, as of 2013, lotteries and casinos are widespread throughout the country with most states having legal access to one or both types of gaming. Sports gambling in the US is much more restricted. Only Nevada operates full sports books while lottery associations in Montana and Delaware offer limited types of sports gambling. The Oregon Lottery has the right to operate limited sports gambling but has given up their sports lottery operations over a dispute with the NCAA. States are currently challenging the nationwide ban on sports gambling with New Jersey at the forefront. In terms of lottery management, the modern history of lotteries in the US has been that of the state operation and management of lotteries, but there has been recent movement towards the privatization of state lotteries. Illinois privatized its lottery in 2011, followed by Indiana in 2012 and New Jersey in 2013. A privatization scheme in Pennsylvania was rejected in 2013. The next section of this chapter addresses the questions of whether privatization is an effective method of increasing lottery revenues and whether it should be encouraged.

2.5   PRIVATIZATION OF STATE LOTTERIES

Standard economic theory generally states that free markets lead to optimal allocations of resources, suggesting that government intervention in the marketplace through the control of firms is unlikely to lead to improvements in societal welfare. Furthermore, since government firms do not operate by the same profit incentives that motivate private business owners, there is again concern that state-owned enterprises will fail to achieve the efficiency and productivity of which private firms are capable. On a grand scale, the economic success of western capitalistic nations compared to the economic stagnation experienced by the socialist former Soviet Bloc countries clearly highlighted the efficiency advantages of privately owned firms. The trend around the world over the past several decades has been one of reduced state-ownership of companies.

Of course, in cases where market failure exists, private firms are less likely to provide optimal outcomes. State-owned enterprises may provide relief in these cases. In many circumstances involving market failures, it is easy to find examples of state-owned enterprises selling goods and services to the public often in direct competition with private for-profit or private non-profit firms. With respect to public goods, governments often provide public hospitals, parks, and schools. When natural monopolies exist, governments may directly sell goods like municipal water or electricity as opposed to allowing a highly regulated monopoly to exist. When firms sell products with significant negative externalities, government control of the retail establishment may reduce the likelihood of a profit-seeking firm selling more than the societally efficient level of production. For example, liquor stores in many states and cities in the US are government owned. Of course, state ownership is not the only solution to the problem of firms selling products with negative externalities. Most liquor stores in the US are not state-owned enterprises but are instead private firms subject to strict government regulation.

With the privatization of lotteries, private firms are granted local monopolies, and maximization of revenue may not by societally optimal, particularly with respect to concerns when gaming becomes problematic or the distributional impact of government revenue generation. As a case in point, in Camelot's failed bid to win the contract for Illinois' lottery in 2011, the company planned to increase annual per capita lottery ticket sales in the state from $171 in 2010 to $292 in 2016 and in particular to raise annual sales on instant games from $92 to $161 per person (Illinois Lottery, 2010). While increasing ticket sales is unquestionably good from a revenue generation or profit maximization perspective, there is a real public policy question about raising government revenue in this manner. Given the fact that lottery players are disproportionally poor (especially those who play instant games), encouraging the consumption of a product that, on average, makes the poor poorer in order to supplement the incomes of the poor and provide funding for other state programs seems questionable at best.

Other questions also exist. Is sufficient innovation possible in the lottery industry to warrant introduction of a middleman who will take a portion of the profits? Privatization often succeeds in increasing profits by cutting costs, but the administrative costs of most state lotteries are only about 5 percent of revenues, limiting the efficiency gains that would be possible. Since most of the revenue gains from privatization would come from expanding revenues rather than cutting costs, there is a real question of whether gambling expansion is socially desirable. Often projections of increased revenue are driven by the introduction of video lottery terminals, internet gaming, or expanded advertising, all of which could be done without privatization of the lottery. Finally, it is important to ask whether states can write contracts that prevent privatization of profits when privatized lotteries do well, but socialization of losses when lotteries fail to meet expectations.

2.6 MODEL AND METHODOLOGY

In order to test the effect of privatizing a lottery, regression analysis will be performed on state-level data over time to determine the impact of state-level economic and demographic data on the level of transfers that a state lottery generates for the government. Previous contributions to the lottery literature have suggested many demographic and economic variables to explain the level of lottery sales in a state. Selecting from those variables, the current study will use population, income level, and the unemployment rate of a state to explain the level of transfers that a state lottery generates for the state government. Lottery sales and lottery transfers are directly related to one another since more lottery sales will lead to more dollars transferred to the government. Because of the direct relationship between the two, it is reasonable to assume that any demographic or economic variables that affect lottery sales would have a similar effect on transfers to the government, even though the dollars transferred will be lower than lottery sales due to prize payouts and commissions. Transfers are the preferred variable for the current study because of the prediction that privatization can generate more revenues to the state. The corollary to that prediction is that the revenues transferred should be higher, not that sales dollars are necessarily higher, although higher sales are certainly one way to generate more transfers.

There is a rich lottery literature with a variety of contributions that test the impact of demographic and economic variables on lottery sales, either within single states or across numerous states. Considering only the variables used in the current model, the empirical results from these studies on population are consistent; however, there are mixed empirical results on unemployment rates and income. A number of studies, including Clotfelter and Cook (1989), Ashley et al. (1999) and Frees and Miller (2004) find that population has a positive impact on state lottery sales. Regarding the unemployment rate, Mikesell (1994) and Scott and Garen (1994) both find that a higher unemployment has a positive impact on state lottery sales. However, DeBoer (1990) finds that unemployment rates in New York do not significantly impact lottery sales and Blalock et al. (2007) find a negative relationship between unemployment rates and sales. Theoretically, one might expect a positive relationship between unemployment rates and lottery sales if lottery sales are regressive in nature and purchased relatively more by people who feel they have few economic alternatives of earning income or wealth in other ways. Blalock et al. (2007) predict that a positive relationship between unemployment rates and lottery sales is an affirmation of prospect theory, "that individuals become more risk loving when they suffer a financial shock," even though that particular study does not support the theory empirically (Blalock et al., 2007, pp. 560–61). It may also be that lottery ticket sales are a normal good and, as opportunities to earn income decline due to higher unemployment rates, so too do state lottery sales, predicting a negative relationship between unemployment rates and sales.

The regressive nature of lottery sales along with the question of whether lotteries are normal goods applies equally to the results regarding state income and income per capita on sales and sales per capita in the lottery literature. The general results are that while lottery sales are regressive in nature, implying that lower income households tend to spend a higher percentage of their income on lottery products than higher income households, they also tend to be normal goods, implying that sales dollars increase with higher incomes.[1] This finding, however, is not consistent across the literature, with some studies finding the opposite results or no impact of income on lottery sales (in dollars or in per capita dollars, depending on the study).

Three different models are proposed and tested, using some combination of the variables previously described. The goal of privatization is to increase revenue transfers from the state's lottery games. Furthermore, tests on both of the dependent variables (change in transfers and change in transfers per capita) indicate that the variables have unit roots. Thus, rather than using transfers or transfers per capita as the dependent variables, the models will use change in transfers and change in transfers per capita as the dependent variables to correct for the unit roots and to emphasize that transfers are expected to increase when the lottery is run by a private firm rather than by a state agency. If individuals in the state are to become better off through management by a private firm, then transfer dollars per capita should rise as well.

The following models are tested empirically:

1. Change in Transfers$_{it}$ = b_0 + b_1Change in Income$_{it}$ + b_2Change in Unemployment$_{it}$ + b_3Change in Population$_{it}$ + b_4Privatization Dummy$_{it}$ + α_i + T_t + ε_{it}
2. Change in Transfers$_{it}$ = b_0 + b_1Change in Income$_{it}$ + b_2Change in Unemployment$_{it}$ + b_3Privatization Dummy$_{it}$ + α_i + T_t + ε_{it}
3. Change in Transfers Per Capita$_{it}$ = b_0 + b_1Change in Income Per Capita$_{it}$ + b_2Change in Unemployment$_{it}$ + b_3Privatization Dummy$_{it}$ + α_i + T_t + $\varepsilon_{it.}$

Data for the variables represent the time period from 2005 to 2012. Revenue transfers to the state that are generated by the lottery are based on a lottery's fiscal year, which is typically from July to June with data provided by state lottery association websites. Population data is provided by the Annual Estimated Populations Table as of 1 July at the end of each fiscal year for each state, as provided by the US Census Bureau. Personal income data for each state is provided by the Bureau of Economic Analysis and state unemployment rates are provided by the Bureau of Labor Statistics.

The privatization dummy is set equal to one if a state has ceded control of its lottery to a private management firm. Since the data set only includes observations until 2012, in effect, this analysis will only capture the effects of the first year of Illinois privatization. In other words, the number of private state-year observations is only one at the time of writing.

It should be noted that the initial year of Northstar's operation of the Illinois Lottery is best described as problematic. The company promised $851 million in ticket sales, but only delivered $757 million, The company blamed foot-dragging by the state government in their promise to introduce expanded VLT gaming, but the firm was ultimately fined $20 million for failing to meet its revenue targets (Garcia 2013). As an aside, the actual revenues generated nearly exactly matched the projections made by Camelot in their failed bid to operate the lottery.

For each of these equations, initial regressions will be run on the data first without inclusion of state fixed effects (α_i) or time effects (T_t) and then subsequently a second set of regressions will be run including both state fixed effects and time effects. Given the discussion in the previous paragraphs, change in income (per capita) is expected to have a positive impact on change in transfers (per capita), based on the assumption that lottery products are normal goods. Change in unemployment could have either a positive or negative impact on change in transfers (per capita) depending on whether the regressive nature of lotteries or risky behavior of lower income individuals is more predominant than the nature of lotteries as normal goods. Change in population is expected to have a positive impact on change in transfers, as more individuals in a state would provide a larger market for lottery sales. If privatization is successful in generating more income for a state, then the privatization dummy should have a positive impact on change in transfers (per capita).

2.7   RESULTS

Table 2.1 provides summary statistics for the variables used in the model, while the results of the regression analyses are provided in Tables 2.2 and 2.3. Overall, the results reveal that the only variables with a statistically significant impact on the change in transfers of lottery revenue are the change in state income and the change in the unemployment rate. In each of the two regressions without state fixed effects or time effects, change in income has a positive and significant effect on change in transfers, but this same relationship does not hold true on a per capita basis (see Table 2.3). The coefficients in these two regressions are 0.0006 and 0.0007, indicating that an added $100 dollars of income increases lottery transfers by approximately $0.06–0.07 to the state. The change in the unemployment rate is the most consistently significant variable, however. In five of the six regression results, the change in unemployment provides a negative and statistically significant coefficient, confirming that lotteries appear to be normal goods, providing declining transfers to state governments as unemployment rates increase. The coefficient on change in unemployment is −3.750 for change in transfers without state fixed effects, between −6.582 and −6.615 for change in transfers with state fixed effects and equal to 1.548 or 1.392 for change in transfers per capita (with and without state fixed effects, respectively). For interpretation purposes, this indicates that a one percentage point increase in unemployment tends to reduce transfers to the state by 3.75 million dollars or by 1.39 dollars per capita when state effects are not included. The impact increases when state and time effects are included, indicating that the impact of changing unemployment on changes in government transfers from lotteries is even greater when other differences among states over time are held constant. The coefficient on

Table 2.1   Summary statistics

Variable	Mean	Std Dev.	Min.	Max.
Transfers (in millions)	412.87	482.57	5.72	3,049.15
Transfers Per Capita	74.21	81.84	6.62	375.06
Income	260,419.80	291,407.30	19,976.50	1,669,594.00
Income Per Capita	38,737.31	7,223.57	25,979.79	73,343.84
Population	6,635,578.00	7,044,558.00	567,136.00	38,041,430.00
Unemployment Rate	6.34	2.27	2.79	13.24
Change in Transfers (in millions)	11.78	45.16	−161.15	382.77
Change in Transfers Per Capita	1.11	8.60	−81.38	53.45
Change in Income	9,137.51	16,704.94	−38,637.00	95,531.00
Change in Income Per Capita	1,152.35	1,274.81	−1,950.90	5,253.33
Change in Population	55,559.35	93,302.61	−273,963.00	581,457.00
Change in Unemployment Rate	0.38	1.27	−2.37	4.78

Table 2.2   Regression results (dependent variable: change in transfers)

	No fixed effects		With fixed effects	
Constant	8.357**	7.964**	11.684**	12.458***
	(3.269)	(3.224)	(5.687)	(3.631)
Change in Income	0.0007***	0.0006***	0.0002	0.0002
	(0.0002)	(0.0002)	(0.0002)	(0.0002)
Change in Unemployment	−3.276	−3.750*	−6.582***	−6.615***
	(2.268)	(2.176)	(2.370)	(2.358)
Change in Population	−0.00003		0.00001	
	−0.00003		(0.00008)	
Privatization Dummy	21.267	22.703	28.92	28.552
	(43.826)	(43.752)	(45.869)	(45.734)
N	300	300	300	300
F-statistic	6.05***	7.89***	1.42*	1.44**
Prob > F	0.0001	0.000	0.0525	0.0463

Note: *** Significant at 1% level; ** significant at 5% level; * significant at 10% level.

Table 2.3   Regression results (dependent variable: change in transfers per capita)

	No fixed effects	With fixed effects
Constant	1.983**	2.077**
	(0.911)	(0.986)
Change in Income Per Capita	−0.0003	−0.0003
	(0.0005)	(0.0006)
Change in Unemployment	−1.392***	−1.548***
	(0.534)	(0.568)
Privatization Dummy	1.717	2.235
	(8.516)	(9.219)
N	300	300
F-statistic	3.26**	0.95
Prob > F	0.0220	0.5730

Note: *** Significant at 1% level; ** significant at 5% level; * significant at 10% level.

population is never statistically significant and is very close to zero. Four of the six regressions have significant F-statistics, indicating that all of the coefficients are not equal to zero, all four of these models having change in transfers as the dependent variable rather than changes in transfers per capita.

The lack of any significant results for the model using transfers per capita as a dependent variable are not necessarily surprising, especially for the state fixed effects model. Since transfers and population tend to be growing over time within states, dividing transfers by population should reduce much of the variability in the dependent variable when using panel techniques, and much of the remaining variability across states are additionally going to be attributed to the state fixed effects.

Of particular interest in this study is the lack of any measurable effect of privatization on transfers of lottery revenue as measured by the privatization dummy variable. Granted, the model is only able to account for one year of privatization in the state of Illinois so the results are very preliminary. However, given the supposedly superior efficiencies of private firms relative to government bureaucracies and the assumed ability to be more innovative and creative in their promotion of the lottery, one would at least expect some additional transfers of lottery dollars to the Illinois government relative to the other state governments for the 2012 fiscal year. The coefficient on the Illinois dummy is positive in all six regressions; however, the standard error is large enough to make all of the positive coefficients not statistically different from zero. This should give pause to those touting the merits of privately administered lotteries and also provide support for current and potentially future lawsuits in states like Pennsylvania and Ohio that have been and are likely to be filed to prevent the state from turning over lottery operations to a private company.

On the other hand, since the unemployment rate in Illinois actually increased from 2011 to 2012 from 9.0–9.4 percent, and given the negative coefficient on the unemployment rate in all of the models, this indicates that things actually could have been much worse for the Illinois government in terms of transfers received from lottery sales. While the Illinois Lottery fell far short of the lofty promises made by Northstar, the actual revenues generated were slightly higher than would have been predicted given the state of the Illinois economy (although, naturally, care must be taken not to place too much confidence in statistically insignificant coefficients). Using the (non-statistically significant) point estimates on the privatization dummy for the six models tested, the Illinois Lottery in 2012 generated between $21.2 million and $28.9 million more than would have been predicted based on Illinois' historical experience and its economic climate during that year. Combine these potential gains with the additional $20 million fine the state collected from Northstar due to the company's failure to meet its revenue projections, and a case can be made that privatization has actually been quite a positive experience for the state.

2.8   CONCLUSION AND FUTURE RESEARCH

State-run lotteries offer products to consumers that add to the variety of other gambling options in the United States. Growth in the lottery industry is discussed in relation to the growth of some of these other options, with a particular focus on sports gambling. As states continue to seek additional ways to increase state transfers from lottery sales, many states are considering the option of privatizing their lottery operations in order to gain from the efficiencies and innovations of a privately operated company. As demonstrated in this chapter, however, states should be cautious about assuming that privately run companies can offer substantial gains in transfer dollars and they may struggle to meet their stated sales goals. While the chapter is preliminary in that there is only one year and one state with a full year of privatized operations, the empirical models do indicate that economic variables such as state unemployment rates and state income provide statistically significant predictors of changes in state transfer revenues while privatization of lotteries, based on the limited available data, do not have a significant impact. As states such as Indiana and New Jersey join the ranks of states choosing to privatize their lottery operations, the data set can be expanded to include more observations for privately run state lotteries and the results offered by the expanded model will provide further conclusions on this controversial issue.

NOTE

1. Studies that confirm either or both of these implications include Brinner and Clotfelter (1975), Clotfelter and Cook (1989), Frees and Miller (2004) and Blalock et al. (2007).

REFERENCES

American Gaming Association (2013), "2013 AGA Survey of Casino Entertainment," http://www.americangaming.org.

Ashley, Terry, Yi Liu and Semoon Chang (1999), "Estimating Net Lottery Revenues for States," *Atlantic Economic Journal* **27** (2): 170–78.

Baumann, Robert and Victor A. Matheson (2013), "Estimating Economic Impact Using Ex Post Econometric Analysis: Cautionary Tales," in Plácido Rodríguez, Stefan Kesenne and Jaume García (eds), *The Econometrics of Sport*, Cheltenham, UK and Northampton, MA, USA: Edward Elgar, pp. 169–188.

Benjamin, Gerald (2013), "If the New York State Constitution Bans Gambling, Why is there So Much Opportunity to Gamble in New York?," http://effectiveny.org/professors-corner/casino-gambling/if-new-york-state-constitution-bans-gambling-why-there-so-much-opp, accessed May 23, 2013.

Blalock, Garrick, David R. Just and Daniel H. Simon (2007), "Hitting the Jackpot or Hitting the Skid: Entertainment, Poverty, and the Demand for State Lotteries," *American Journal of Economics and Sociology* **66** (3): 545–70.

Brinner, Roger E. and Charles T. Clotfelter (1975), "An Economic Appraisal of State Lotteries," *National Tax Journal* **28** (4): 395–404.

Clotfelter, Charles T. (1979), "On the Regressivity of State-Operated Numbers Games," *National Tax Journal* **32** (4): 543–48.

Clotfelter, Charles T. and Philip J. Cook (1989), *Selling Hope*, Cambridge, MA: Harvard University Press.

DeBoer, Larry (1990), "Lotto Sales Stagnation: Product Maturity or Small Jackpots?," *Growth and Change* (Winter 1990): 73–7.

Dunstan, Roger (1997), "Gambling in California," California Research Bureau, working paper CRB-97-003.

Emiston, Kelly D. (2006), "A New Perspective on Rising Nonbusiness Bankruptcy Filing Rates: Analyzing the Regional Factors," *Federal Reserve Bank of Kansas City Economic Review* Q2: 55–83.

Frees, Edward W. and Thomas W. Miller (2004), "Sales Forecasting Using Longitudinal Data Models," *International Journal of Forecasting* **20** (1): 99–114.

Garcia, Monique (2013), "Private Firm Running Illinois Lottery Fined $20 Million for Falling Short on Sales," *Chicago Tribune*, March 18, 2013.

Humphreys, Brad and Victor Matheson (2013), "Booms, Busts, and Gambling:

Can Gaming Revenues Reduce Budget Volatility?," in Robert Ascah and David Ryan (eds), *Boom and Bust Again*, Alberta, Canada: University of Alberta Press, pp. 267–284.

Illinois Lottery (2010), "Camelot Illinois Public Hearing," http://www.illinoislot tery.com/content/dam/ill/documents/subsections/Management/IL_Lottery_Pub lic_Hearing_Presentation.pdf, posted September 8, 2010.

Jamestown-Yorktown Foundation (2013), "The Virginia Company of London," http://www.historyisfun.org/pdf/Laws-at-Jamestown/VA_Company.pdf, accessed May 23, 2013.

LaMarra, Tom (2013), "Total Handle Up for First Time Since 2006," http://www.bloodhorse.com/horse-racing/articles/75370/total-handle-up-for-first-time-since-2006, posted January 5, 2013.

Louisiana Lottery Corporation (2013), "Lottery History," http://www.louisianalot tery.com/index.cfm?md=pagebuilder&tmp=home&cpid=68, accessed May 22, 2013.

Matheson, Victor A. and Kent R. Grote (2008), "U.S. Lotto Markets," in Donald B. Hausch and William T. Ziemba (eds), *Handbook of Sports and Lottery Markets*, New York: North Holland, pp. 503–24.

Mikesell, John L. (1994), "State Lottery Sales and Economic Activity," *National Tax Journal* **47** (1): 165–71.

Montana Lottery (2013), "How is Montana Sports Action Played?," http://mon tanalottery.com/msaFAQ, accessed May 23, 2013.

Nash, Betty Joyce (2009), "Sport of Kings: Horse Racing in Maryland," *Region Focus*, Federal Reserve Bank of Richmond, Spring 2009, 37–9.

National Football League vs. Delaware (1977), United States District Court, D. of Delaware, 435 F. Supp. 1372, decided August 11, 1977.

National Indian Gaming Commission (2012), "Gaming Revenue Reports," http://www.nigc.gov/Gaming_Revenue_Reports.aspx, accessed May 23, 2013.

Scott, F. and J. Garen (1994), 'Probability of Purchase, Amount of Purchase, and the Demographic Incidence of the Lottery Tax', *Journal of Public Economics*, 54 (1): 121–43.

University of Nevada, Las Vegas (UNLV) (2013), "Nevada Sports Betting Totals: 1984–2012," UNLV Center for Gaming Research, http://gaming.unlv.edu/reports/NV_sportsbetting.pdf, accessed May 23, 2013.

3. Price setting and competition in fixed odds betting markets

Xiaogang Che, Arne Feddersen and Brad R. Humphreys

3.1 INTRODUCTION

Betting on sports takes many forms. In general, most sports betting is pari-mutuel or fixed odds betting. Some high scoring North American sports like basketball and (American and Canadian) football have point spread betting, which resembles fixed odds betting in terms of key economic features.

In pari-mutuel betting, the bookmaker earns profits by taking a percentage of the total amount bet on the event, and distributing the remainder to the bettors with winning bets. This form of betting commonly takes place in horse racing, and in certain other forms of sports betting, like the popular Spanish football pool la Quiniela and the Football Pools in the UK.

In fixed odds betting, the bookmaker earns profits by setting the odds on discrete outcomes – home win/draw/away win in sports with draws and home win/away win in sports with no draws – in a way that if an equal amount of money is wagered on each possible outcome, the money wagered on losing bets exceeds the money wagered on winning bets. This system of setting odds on the outcome of sporting events as a way to generate positive profits for bookmakers is called "over-round". Bookmakers are free to set any over-round they wish. The larger the over-round charged by a bookmaker, the larger the bookmaker's profits, if money is wagered equally on all possible outcomes. In this sense, the over-round is the price that bettors must pay to wager on a particular outcome in a sports betting market.

A substantial literature exists on the determination of over-round in fixed odds betting markets. Most of this literature focuses on individual bookmakers, and how their profits can be maximized given the characteristics of bettors and the teams involved in the game or match. This chapter focuses on a related topic, the change in over-round over time in fixed odds betting markets. Levitt (2004) observed that the commission charged by bookmakers in point spread betting, which is analogous to the price of a bet, and the over-round charged by bookmakers on fixed-odds bets, is remarkably stable over time among Las Vegas sports books. Bookmakers do not appear to compete on the basis of the commission charged, or on over-round. Kuypers (2000) similarly noted, in a seminal study of over-round, that over-round in fixed odds betting markets in the UK was "remarkably constant at around 11.5%" throughout the 1990s (p. 1355).

This chapter documents the over-round charged by two large European bookmakers based in the UK, William Hill and Ladbrokes, from the 2004–05 football season to the 2011–12 football season in the English Premier League (EPL), and how this over-round changed in response to increased competition in the sports betting market. A clear decline can be seen in the average over-round charged by these two bookmakers over time. The average over-round charged fell from about 12–15 percent in betting on EPL football matches in 2004–05 to under 10 percent, and in some cases to as low as 5 percent, in 2011–12. This decline in over-round can be interpreted as a decline in prices set by bookmakers, and can be explained by entry of new online bookmakers into this market, the expansion of other betting markets like Betfair, and the increasing popularity of online gambling throughout this period.

Figure 3.1 gives the basic facts. The graph shows the average over-round charged by two large UK-based bookmakers, William Hill and Ladbrokes, as well as the average over-round charged by four online bookmakers

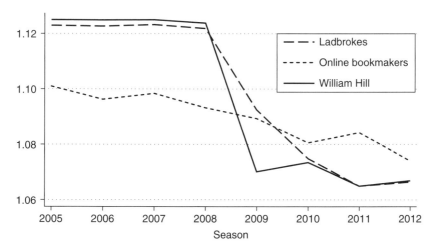

Figure 3.1   Changes in over-round on EPL betting

(Bet365, Bwin, Interwetten, and Sportingbet) on EPL matches, over eight seasons. Many of the online bookmakers began operation in the late 1990s or early 2000s, and experienced increases in betting volume over the period. William Hill and Ladbrokes operated both betting shops and online book-making operations over this period. Early in the period Ladbrokes and William Hill charged larger over-round on EPL matches than the online bookmakers. Later in the period, as the popularity and adoption of online betting increased, the over-round charged by William Hill and Ladbrokes declined sharply. We attribute this decline to be a result of increased competition in the sports betting market. In addition, a third major player in the sports betting market, Betfair, also expanded its operations over this period. Betfair is a betting exchange market, and not a bookmaker.

3.2 UNDERSTANDING AND CALCULATING OVER-ROUND

Bookmakers in fixed odds betting markets earn profits through over-round, which can be interpreted as their commission charged to bettors (Pope and Peel, 1989). Given balanced betting, the higher the over-round on a match, the greater the bookmaker profit.

Over-round can be easily calculated from either fractional or decimal odds. Fractional odds are quoted by UK bookmakers and used in horse race betting around the world. Decimal odds are typically quoted by continental European bookmakers. Fractional odds are also called British or UK odds. Fractional odds show the net total paid to the bettor on a winning bet relative to the amount wagered.

For example, 4/1 fractional odds mean that a bettor makes a 40 unit return on a 10 unit wager. 1/4 fractional odds mean that a bettor makes 2.50 units on a 10 unit wager. Winning bettors always receive the original wager back, so on a 4/1 fractional odds wager a winning bettor receives a total of 50 units (40 units plus the original 10 unit stake). Fractional odds of 1/1 are called even money or even odds.

Decimal odds are quoted by bookmakers in continental Europe, Australia and Canada. Decimal odds are also referred to as European or continental odds. Decimal odds are equal to the fractional odds converted to decimal values plus one. The "plus one" accounts for the amount wagered. For fractional odds (x/y), the decimal odds equivalent is (x/y) + 1. Even (1/1) odds in decimal form are (1/1) + 1 = 1 + 1 = 2. 4/1, fractional odds in decimal form are (4/1) + 1 = 4 + 1 = 5. 1/4 and fractional odds in decimal form are (1/4) + 1 = 0.25 + 1 = 1.25.

A simple example can illustrate how over-round is calculated and how bookmakers in fixed odds betting markets earn profits. Consider the information below on the "Manchester Derby" match in EPL played between Manchester United and Manchester City Football Club in October 2011, a match in this sample. The match was played at Old Trafford, home of Manchester United, so Manchester United was the home team. Manchester United were nearly an even odds favorite in the match; Man City were heavy underdogs.

Match Outcome	Decimal Odds
Home Win	2.1
Draw	3.3
Away Win	3.6

Suppose three bettors wager a given amount on the three outcomes of the Man U/Man City Derby, each to win 100 units. Bettor 1 wagers on Man U to win, and risks 47.60 units to win 100 units (47.60 x 2.1 = 100). Bettor 2 wagers on a draw and risks 30.30 units to win 100 units (30.30 x 3.3 = 100). Bettor 3 wagers on Man City to win and risks only 27.80 units to win 100 units (27.80 x 3.6 = 100). The bookmaker collects 47.60 + 30.30 + 27.80 = 105.70 units and pays the winner 100 units, keeping 5.70 units in profit for a return of 5.7 percent. The over-round in this case is 1.057.

3.3   LITERATURE REVIEW

A number of models describing how bookmakers set fixed odds in sports betting markets have been developed. Pope and Peel (1989) developed a simple model that assumed profit maximizing bookmakers set fixed odds on outcomes in a sporting event based on the perceived *a priori* probability that a specific outcome will occur. This model also assumed that different bookmakers would offer different odds, but no bookmaker would set odds in a way to systematically have a lower over-round than competing bookmakers.

Kuypers (2000) developed a model of a single bookmaker setting odds on a football match emphasizing informational efficiency in betting markets where both bookmakers and bettors have full information about the sporting event. The model explicitly accounted for the way bettors react to the odds posted by bookmakers, based on their perceived outcome of the sporting event. This model emphasized the importance of the behavior of bettors, in that some bettors might exhibit systematic biases for betting on specific teams. These bettors would be unaffected by the odds offered on their favorite team.

Makropoulou and Markellos (2011) developed a model of the determination of optimal fixed odds set by a bookmaker given information uncertainty. This model emphasized that information could become available after the bookmaker posted the odds on the sporting event. It also included the idea that bookmakers must post odds on sporting events before bettors make bets. In this model, bookmakers charge an over-round to offset their informational disadvantage, in that bettors can wait to see if new information becomes available after the odds are posted.

Franck et al. (2011) developed a complete formal model of a profit maximizing bookmaker setting fixed odds in the presence of bettors with bias like in the model by Kuypers (2000) and unbiased bettors. This model emphasizes how odds offered will change depending on the number of biased and unbiased bettors in the market. This study also notes that bookmakers appear to attract large numbers of bettors without reducing the price charged for making bets, despite the emergence of a number of new opportunities to bet on sporting events like Betfair and the World Bet Exchange.

All these papers focus on decisions about odds setting made by individual profit maximizing bookmakers and the informational efficiency of the odds set by bookmakers. Little research in sports economics has focused on changes in over-round charged by bookmakers over time in sports betting markets. Most prior research has focused on understanding how and why bookmakers set odds, and how these odds relate to the actual outcomes of sporting events; little research has focused on the structure of the bookmaking market and how performance in this market is affected by the expansion of betting markets over time.

3.4   MARKET STRUCTURE AND PRICE SETTING

A substantial literature in industrial organization addresses how changes in the structure of specific industries, in the form of expansion of existing firms or the entry of new firms, affects economic decisions like price setting and output determination. Economic models of industry structure make clear predictions about how prices will change as the degree of competition increases in an industry.

When a single monopoly firm exists in an industry, that firm charges a price higher than would be charged if competing firms were present in the market. Under duopoly, firms may collude to continue to charge the monopoly price. In a duopoly, the prices charged by the two firms will be positively correlated if they coordinate their behavior. In the absence of coordinated behavior, the price charged by each will drop.

The entry of additional firms in a market will continue to reduce the price charged for the good or service produced. The limiting case is a perfectly competitive market with many producers of identical goods; in this case, the price charged will equal the marginal cost of production.

Empirically, the entry of new firms is associated with lower prices in many industries. Siegfried and Evans (1994) survey a large number of empirical studies of firm entry into industries and find evidence that entry leads to lower prices. Incumbent bookmakers like William Hill and Ladbrokes face competition from both online bookmakers and betting exchanges.

Koning and van Velzen (2009) document the increase in the number of online betting exchanges that came into existence during the 2000s, beginning with Betfair which was founded in 2000. By 2009, Koning and van Velzen (2009) report, Betfair was the largest online betting company in the UK. These betting exchanges offer lower prices to bettors than traditional bookmakers, since bettors can either back (or buy) or lay (or sell) bets on outcomes in sporting events at prices of their choosing. In traditional sports betting markets offered by bookmakers, bettors always back propositions and bookmakers always lay propositions. Betting exchanges match individual bettors who want to back or lay a bet on a given outcome, and then charge each a small commission for the exchange.

In addition to the explosion of betting exchanges like Betfair in the 2000s, this period also saw an increase in the availability of online bookmakers. Online bookmakers offer fixed odds betting as traditional bookmakers do.

The bookmakers analyzed here, Ladbrokes, William Hill, Bet365, Bwin, Interwetten and Sportingbet, were all accepting online bets in 2005. Bet365 is a UK-based online bookmaker that started operation in 2000. Bwin is a Gibraltar-based online bookmaker that started operation in 1997 in Austria. Sportingbet is a UK-based online bookmaker that started operation in 1997. Interwetten is a Gibraltar-based online bookmaker that started operation in 1990 in Austria. Ladbrokes is a UK-based bookmaker founded in 1886. It operates betting shops and online bookmaking and began offering online sports betting in the 1990s. Ladbrokes operates about 2,000 licensed betting shops in the UK. William Hill is a UK-based bookmaker that began operation in 1934 and operates betting shops and online bookmaking; it began offering online bookmaking in the 1990s. William Hill operates about 2,300 licensed betting shops in the UK. Since both Ladbrokes and William Hill started operation at least 50 years earlier than the listed online bookmakers and operate betting shops, we view them as competitors in a duopoly.

We analyze the price, in the form of over-round, set by bookmakers because we have data on their betting odds for the entire period from 2004–05 to 2011–12. However, competition increased in sports betting markets during this period, including the expansion of betting exchanges like Betfair and increased use of on-line bookmakers; all firms in the industry faced increasing competition over this period. Again, economic models predict that the entry of new firms in an industry that produces similar goods or services to existing firms will reduce the price charged by all firms in the industry.

Our empirical analysis is based on three assumptions about outcomes, in terms of price setting, in the sports betting market on matches played in the EPL over the seasons from 2004–05 to 2011–12 seasons. First, Ladbrokes and William Hill can be thought of as duopolists over the period. Both operate large numbers of betting shops as well as online betting operations. The betting shops compete with each other for customers. Second, the expansion of online bookmakers like Bwin and Bet365, provided bettors with an alternative to placing bets with William Hill and Ladbrokes, and may represent important competitors. However, these online bookmakers require setting up online accounts, access to a computer connected to the internet, and a certain amount of technological knowledge. Because of this, bets placed at online bookmakers may be imperfect substitutes for betting shops operated by Ladbrokes and William Hill.

Third, the emergence of Betfair represents increased competition for both Ladbrokes and William Hill. While placing wagers with Betfair also requires setting up an online account and engaging in online transactions, Betfair offers many more forms of sports betting and types of bets on football matches than traditional bookmakers, since bettors can both back and lay any proposition on Betfair. The ability to lay bets, and the small fixed commission charged by Betfair, could be quite attractive to bettors, making this option a close substitute for both types of bookmaker-based sports betting.

3.5   EMPIRICAL ANALYSIS

3.5.1   Econometric Model

We analyze variation in over-round on bets placed on EPL football matches at William Hill, Ladbrokes, over-round set by the four online bookmakers discussed above, and the relationship between over-round set by these bookmakers and economic activity associated with Betfair.

The unit of observation is an individual football match i played in season s at time t. The betting odds data come from the website www.football-data.co.uk, a popular football betting odds data repository which collects information on match outcomes and betting odds offered by various bookmakers. Our data set contains information on 2,930 football matches played in the EPL over the seasons from 2004–05 to 2011–12.

We estimate a linear reduced-form empirical model explaining observed variation in the over-round set by William Hill on football matches. This model takes the form:

$$ORWH_{ist} = \alpha_s + \alpha_m + \alpha_d + \beta_{1LB}ORLB_{ist} + \beta_2 OROL_{ist} + \gamma BFR_s + \varepsilon_{ist}$$
$$(3.1)$$

where $ORWH_{ist}$ is the over-round set by William Hill on EPL match i played in season s at time t, $ORLB_{ist}$ is the over-round set by Ladbrokes on EPL match i played in season s at time t, $OROL_{ist}$ is the average over-round set by the four online bookmakers (Bet365, Bwin, Interwetten, and Sportingbet) on EPL match i played in season s at time t, and BFR_s is a measure of the effect of the presence of the Betfair betting exchange on traditional bookmaker-set football betting markets in season s. Matches are identified by the month and day of week when they occurred. α_s, α_m, and α_d are vectors of fixed effects indicator variables that capture unobservable heterogeneity at the season (s), month (m) and day of week (d) level.

ε_{ist} is an unobservable equation error that captures all other factors that affect variation in the over-round set by William Hill on EPL football matches. We assume that ε_{ist} is a mean zero random variable that has standard deviation σ_{ist} that can vary across matches and seasons, so we use the standard "White–Huber sandwich" correction for heteroscedasticity. We also assume that σ_{ist} may be correlated within seasons due to unobservable factors affecting the football betting market, and cluster correct the estimated standard errors from Equation (3.1).

α_s, α_m, α_d, β_{1LB}, β_2 and γ are unobservable parameters to be estimated. We estimate these parameters using the Ordinary Least Squares (OLS) estimator. Since Equation (3.1) contains dummy variables, this is technically the OLS Dummy Variable (OLSDV) estimator.

β_{1LB} captures the relationship between over-round set by William Hill on football matches and over-round set by Ladbrokes on the same football match. If the two bookmakers are coordinating in a duopoly market, then the estimated parameter will be significant and positive, as both bookmakers will set similar over-round on different matches. If the two bookmakers are competing for customers on a price basis, the estimated parameter on this variable will be significant and negative, as William Hill would tend to set lower over-round on matches that Ladbrokes has set a higher over-round on.

The parameter β_2 captures the relationship between over-round set on EPL matches by the other four online bookmakers and the over-round set by William Hill on the same football matches. If the parameter estimate is significant and negative, the online bookmakers are competing with William Hill for customers in the sports betting market, leading to lower prices in the market. If the parameter estimate is not different from zero, these online bookmakers are not competing with William Hill, so no downward pressure on prices exists in the market.

The parameter γ captures the effect of Betfair on over-round set by William Hill on football matches. We do not have information on odds that were prevailing on Betfair on football matches, or any other match-level data from Betfair. Recall that bettors can either back or lay positions on Betfair. As a proxy variable for the influence of Betfair on traditional bookmaking markets, we use annual real revenue in thousands of 2012 Pounds Sterling reported by Betfair as a proxy for the effect of Betfair on traditional bookmakers. We deflate nominal reported Betfair revenue by the Retail Price Index (RPI) produced by the UK Office for National Statistics.

We estimate a similar model to explain observed variation in over-round set by Ladbrokes. This model takes the form:

$$ORLB_{ist} = \alpha_s + \alpha_m + \alpha_d + \beta_{1WH}ORWH_{ist} + \beta_2OROL_{ist} + \gamma BFR_s + \varepsilon_{ist} \tag{3.2}$$

The difference between this model and Equation (3.1) is that the dependent variable in Equation (3.2) is the over-round set by Ladbrokes, where in Equation (3.1) the dependent variable is the over-round set by William Hill, and the respective explanatory variable here is also reversed. The parameter β_{1WH} captures the relationship between over-round set by Ladbrokes on football matches and over-round set by William Hill on the same football match. Like in Equation (3.1), if the two bookmakers are coordinating firms in a duopoly market, then the estimated parameter will be significant and positive, as both bookmakers will set similar over-round on different matches. If the two bookmakers are competing for customers on a price basis, the estimated parameter on this variable will be significant and negative, as Ladbrokes would tend to set lower over-round on matches that William Hill has set a higher over-round on.

Both Equations (3.1) and (3.2) could suffer from a number of well-known econometric problems. In Equation (3.1), the over-round set by Ladbrokes could be correlated with unobservable factors that affect the

Table 3.1   Summary statistics

	Mean	Std dev.
Over-round Ladbrokes	1.098	0.029
Over-round William Hill	1.096	0.030
Over-round online bookmakers	1.090	0.009
Betfair revenues (1000s)	204,636	151,176
Observations	2,930	

over-round set by William Hill on a football match, ε_{ist}. If this is the case, then $ORLB_{ist}$ is endogenous in Equation (3.1), and OLS estimates of the parameters of this model could be biased and inconsistent. The same argument applies to Equation (3.2) for the variable $ORWH_{ist}$. Unfortunately, we lack access to an instrument that varies at the match level, so we cannot use the Instrumental Variables (IV) in this case. Strictly speaking, our results are only valid if no correlation exists between unobservable factors affecting the over-round set by one bookmaker and the actual over-round set by the other bookmaker.

3.5.2   Summary Statistics

Table 3.1 contains summary statistics for the key variables in Equations (3.1) and (3.2). We analyze data from almost 3,000 EPL football matches. The average over-round on EPL football matches set by Ladbrokes over the sample period was 1.098, indicating an average profit of 9.8 percent on each football match in the sample.

The average over-round on EPL football matches set by William Hill was slightly lower, at 1.096, suggesting an average profit of 9.6 percent for this bookmaker. The average over-round set by the other four online bookmakers for these matches, 1.090, was even lower suggesting lower profits on EPL matches for these four bookmakers.

Betfair's revenues grew substantially over the period in inflation-adjusted terms. Betfair commenced business in 2000 and earned only £480,000 revenue in 2001. This grew steadily as Betfair's operations grew, and by 2012 annual revenues were £389 million. Note that Betfair's fiscal year runs from May to April, so their annual revenues roughly match the EPL's season.

Table 3.2   *OLS regression results (dependent variable is William Hill's over-round)*

	(1)	(2)	(3)
Over-round Ladbrokes	0.183**	0.186**	0.186**
	(3.72)	(4.02)	(4.02)
Over-round online	–	0.362	0.362
		(2.03)	(2.03)
Betfair revenue	–	–	−0.016***
			(−9.84)
Observations	2,930	2,930	2,930
R^2	0.864	0.865	0.865

Notes: t statistics in parentheses; * $p < 0.05$; ** $p < 0.01$; *** $p < 0.001$.

3.5.3   Regression Results: William Hill Model

Table 3.2 contains results from estimating Equation (3.1) using OLS. The dependent variable for this model is over-round set by William Hill on EPL matches. This model contains indicators for the season, the month of the season and the day of the week to capture unobservable heterogeneity in EPL football betting markets. The estimates of these fixed effect parameters are not reported. All estimated standard errors are corrected for heteroscedasticity and cluster-corrected at the season level.

Model (1) in Table 3.2 contains only the fixed effects terms and Ladbrokes over-round on each match. The parameter estimate on over-round set by Ladbrokes is positive and statistically different from zero. The over-round set by these two bookmakers on specific football matches is positively correlated even when controlling for unobservable heterogeneity. One explanation for this correlation is that the two bookmakers are coordinating their price setting, which can occur in a duopoly.

Model (2) in Table 3.2 adds the average over-round set by the other four online bookmakers. The over-round set by these other bookmakers is not correlated with the over-round set by William Hill on these EPL matches. This suggests that the other bookmakers are not competing directly with William Hill for customers on a price basis.

Model (3) in Table 3.2 adds a variable reflecting Betfair's influence in sports betting markets, total revenue earned by Betfair, to Equation (3.1). The parameter on this variable is negative and significantly different from zero. Over this period, as Betfair grew, and became more prominent in the football betting market, over-round set by William Hill declined. This can reflect competitive effects of Betfair expansion on prices charged to bettors

Table 3.3 OLS regression results (dependent variable is Ladbrokes'
over-round)

	(4)	(5)	(6)
Over-round William Hill	0.285*	0.291*	0.291*
	(3.37)	(3.29)	(3.29)
Over-round online		−0.293	−0.293
		(−0.92)	(−0.92)
Betfair revenue			−0.017***
			(−7.80)
Observations	2930	2930	2930
R^2	0.772	0.773	0.773

Notes: t statistics in parentheses; * $p < 0.05$; ** $p < 0.01$; *** $p < 0.001$.

by William Hill if Betfair, unlike other traditional online bookmakers, was viewed as a competitor by William Hill. In that case, William Hill could respond to the increased presence of Betfair in sports betting markets by lowering prices charged to bettors.

3.5.4   Regression Results: Ladbrokes Model

Table 3.3 contains results from estimating Equation (3.2) using OLS. The dependent variable for this model is over-round set by Ladbrokes on EPL matches. This model contains indicators for the season, the month of the season, and the day of the week to capture unobservable heterogeneity in EPL football betting markets. The estimates of these fixed effect parameters are not reported. All estimated standard errors are corrected for heteroscedasticity and cluster-corrected at the season level.

Model (4) in Table 3.2 contains only the fixed effects terms and William Hill's over-round on each match. The parameter estimate on over-round set by William Hill is positive and statistically different from zero, like the parameter in Table 3.2. Again, these two firms could be engaged in cooperative behavior in a duopoly. Model (5) in Table 3.2 adds the over-round for the other four online bookmakers. The parameter estimate on this variable is again not statistically different from zero. Over-round set by Ladbrokes on EPL matches is not associated with the over-round set by online bookmakers. They may not be competing on a price basis for customers.

Model (6) in Table 3.2 adds a variable reflecting Betfair's influence in sports betting markets, total revenue earned by Betfair, to Equation (3.2). The parameter on this variable is again, like the case for William Hill, negative and significantly different from zero. Over this period, as Betfair grew and became more prominent in the football betting market, over-round set by Ladbrokes declined. This can reflect competitive effects of Betfair expansion on prices charged to bettors by Ladbrokes, if Ladbrokes responded to the increased presence of Betfair in sports betting markets by lowering prices charged to bettors.

3.6   CONCLUSIONS

Football betting markets have undergone substantial changes in the last 15 years. Much of this change was driven by changes in technology, in particular the emergence of online betting as an alternative to traditional forms of sports betting that takes place at betting shops, horse racing tracks or other venues. Economic models predict that entry by new firms into existing markets can have a number of effects on the incumbent firms in these markets and the entrants. One effect of increased competition due to entry is lower prices paid by consumers.

Levitt (2004) observed an absence of such competitive effects in point spread betting markets in the United States, where the commission charged to bettors has not changed over a long period of time. While existing research on price setting in fixed odds betting markets has received considerable attention, little research has focused on the effects of the entry of new firms on over-round, the commission charged to bettors in these markets, over time even though many new entrants emerged in these markets.

We analyze changes in over-round set by two large UK-based bookmakers, William Hill and Ladbrokes, that have large numbers of betting shops and take bets online and over the telephone. These two bookmakers faced substantial competition from new entrants, in the form of online bookmakers that used the same business model, and betting exchange markets like Betfair, that allow bettors to both back and lay any position on a sporting event and also operate online. The evidence generated suggests that over-round set by William Hill and Ladbrokes declined substantially as Betfair expanded, but the expansion of online bookmakers does not appear to have led William Hill and Ladbrokes to reduce their over-round. Some new entrants had an impact on the prices charged by William Hill and Ladbrokes over the period 2004–12, while other entrants did not. We also develop evidence that William Hill and Ladbrokes may engage in cooperative pricing practices, since the prices charged by these two bookmakers show substantial positive association over thousands of EPL football matches.

These conclusions have some important caveats. Our regression results may suffer from endogeneity problems if unobservable factors that affect the over-round set by Ladbrokes are correlated with over-round set by William Hill, and vice versa. If this is the case, then our OLS results may not reflect the actual underlying economic relationship between over-rounds set by the two bookmakers, since OLS will be inconsistent and possibly biased. We lack access to a good instrument to control for this, so our results must be viewed with some caution.

The results suggest some potential future research areas. First, finding an instrument to control for the endogeneity problem in this setting would represent an improvement in the results. Some match-level characteristics exist, including variables reflecting participant effort and referee calls during football matches. Some of these variables may be reasonable instruments. Second, the results suggest that the emergence of Betfair had an impact on prices charged by William Hill and Ladbrokes, but other online bookmakers did not, based on prices charged by online bookmakers. This suggests that betting exchanges, but not other online bookmakers, represent important sources of competition for traditional bookmakers. Future research could explore why consumers find betting exchanges to be closer substitutes for wagering at betting shops than online bookmakers.

REFERENCES

Franck, Egon, Erwin Verbeek and Stephan Nüesch (2011), "Sentimental preferences and the organizational regime of betting markets", *Southern Economic Journal* **78** (2): 502–18.

Koning, Ruud H. and Bart van Velzen (2009), "Betting exchanges: the future of sports betting?", *International Journal of Sport Finance* **4** (1): 42–62.

Kuypers, Tim (2000), "Information and efficiency: an empirical study of a fixed odds betting market", *Applied Economics* **32** (11): 1353–63.

Levitt, Steven D. (2004), "Why are gambling markets organised so differently from financial markets?", *The Economic Journal* **114** (495): 223–46.

Makropoulou, Vasiliki and Raphael N. Markellos (2001), "Optimal price setting in fixed-odds betting markets under information uncertainty", *Scottish Journal of Political Economy* **58** (4): 519–36.

Pope, Peter F. and David A. Peel (1989), "Information, prices and efficiency in a fixed-odds betting market", *Economica* **56** (223): 323–41.

Siegfried, John J. and Laurie Beth Evans (1994), "Empirical studies of entry and exit: a survey of the evidence", *Review of Industrial Organization* **9** (2): 121–55.

4. Evaluating probabilities for a football in-play betting market

Stephen Dobson and John Goddard

4.1 INTRODUCTION

In financial economics, considerable effort has been devoted to investigation of the adjustment of the market prices of financial assets to the arrival of relevant information or news. Under the semi-strong form efficient markets hypothesis (EMH), asset prices should reflect all publicly available information. The event study is the most widely used method of investigation of the semi-strong form EMH in respect of financial markets. An event study examines the change in price of an asset over an event window, during which news that was relevant to the valuation of the asset reached the market. Commonly, the change in price is measured relative to some benchmark, reflecting the price change that would have been expected in the absence of the news.

Practical difficulties associated with event studies arise from uncertainty over the precise time at which market participants became aware of the news, and ambiguity surrounding the definition of a suitable benchmark. News that is specific to a company, or to the industry in which the company operates, might reach company or industry insiders before it is received by the wider investor community, creating difficulties for the researcher in defining the appropriate timeline for the event window. Benchmark definition is a ubiquitous problem for empirical research based on the capital asset pricing model, since the magnitude of any measured price reaction depends fundamentally on the choice of benchmark. The observation that any test for informational efficiency is also a test for the validity of the chosen benchmark has been termed the joint-hypothesis problem.

This chapter reports a preliminary empirical investigation of the semi-strong form EMH for an in-play sports betting market. The subject of the empirical investigation is the Betfair market for in-play betting on the outcomes of English Premier League (EPL) professional football matches. An empirical model for the incidence and timings of goals and player dismissals, described in detail by Dobson and Goddard (2011), is used to obtain probabilities for match outcomes, conditional upon the state of the match (goals already scored and dismissals already having occurred) at any stage of the match. Comparisons are drawn between the probabilities obtained from the model with the probabilities implied by high-frequency Betfair in-play betting odds data for the same outcomes. Similarity between the two sets of probabilities would be interpreted as evidence in support of the semi-strong form EMH. On the contrary, differences between the two sets of probabilities would be contrary to the conditions for semi-strong form informational efficiency.

The Betfair in-play betting market appears to be a promising venue for the empirical study of semi-strong form market efficiency. With reference to the practical difficulties associated with event studies cited above, the timing of major news events expected to prompt a significant adjustment to the betting odds for the match result, either a goal being scored or a player being dismissed, is known to the nearest minute. By their nature, news of these events does not leak to any market participant before the event takes place; but instantaneous reporting through a range of online and traditional broadcast media ensures that any market participant can easily track such events within a few seconds of their occurrence. Accordingly, the usual difficulties surrounding the identification of the precise time at which market participants became aware of the news do not arise.

The rest of the chapter is structured as follows. Section 4.2 provides a review of previous literature. Section 4.3 describes a procedure for the computation of in-play probabilities for match outcomes, based on a simulation model calibrated using estimated hazard functions for the in-play arrivals of goals and player dismissals. Section 4.4 describes the Betfair in-play betting odds data, and draws comparisons with the probabilities obtained from the simulation model. Finally, Section 4.5 summarizes and concludes.

4.2   LITERATURE

The efficient markets hypothesis (EMH) was first introduced by Fama (1970), and its typology identifies three levels of informational efficiency in respect of financial markets. In a weak form efficient market, asset prices reflect any information that is contained in their own past history. In a semi-strong form efficient market, asset prices reflect all publicly available information. In a strong form efficient market, asset prices reflect all information, including insider or private information. The earliest modern event studies, devised to test the semi-strong form EMH by analysing the price adjustment in response to some unanticipated event of relevance to the valuation of the underlying asset, are attributed to Ball and Brown (1968) and Fama et al. (1969). Kothari and Warner (2005) identify 565 papers reporting event studies published in five leading finance and business journals between 1974 and 2000. Brown and Warner (1985) is an influential early contribution to a burgeoning parallel literature on event study methodology, reviewed by MacKinlay (1997) and Corrado (2011).

Key studies of the informational efficiency of sports betting markets include Dowie (1976), Ali (1977), Asch et al. (1984) and Shin (1991) for racetrack betting; and Pankoff (1968), Gandar et al. (1988), Golec and Tamarkin (1991), Brown and Sauer (1993) and Woodland and Woodland (1994, 2001) for various North American major league sports. Sauer (1998) reviews the earlier literature. Several informational efficiency studies of betting markets for English football examine fixed-odds betting, in which the betting prices or odds are fixed by the bookmakers several days before the match takes place. In the first published study, Pope and Peel (1989) investigate the efficiency of the prices set by four national high-street bookmakers, using regressions of match outcomes against implicit bookmaker probabilities. Cain et al. (2000) report evidence of favourite–longshot bias in the fixed-odds betting markets for match results and correct scores. Several other studies test for violations of weak-form or semi-strong form EMH conditions by investigating the profitability of betting rules based on comparisons between bookmakers' fixed odds, and probabilities generated from forecasting models (Dixon and Coles, 1997; Dixon and Pope, 2004; Goddard and Asimakopoulos, 2004; Forrest et al., 2005; Graham and Stott, 2008). Recently, Franck et al. (2013) report evidence of inter-market arbitrage opportunities, based on comparisons between bookmaker odds and Betfair prices.

Sentiment bias is examined in several recent sports betting market studies. Bettors might tend to form biased assessments of the probabilities for matches involving the teams they support. Profit-maximizing bookmakers might exploit sentiment bias by offering reduced odds on outcomes for which their clients' subjective probabilities are above the correct probabilities. Alternatively, bookmakers might offer more favourable odds for bets on wins by popular teams, in an attempt to attract larger betting volumes at reduced margins. Evidence in support of this latter hypothesis is reported by Forrest and Simmons (2008) for Scottish and Spanish football, and by Franck et al. (2011) for English football. Page (2009) finds no evidence of optimistic bias in the form of more favourable odds being offered to bettors located in the team's home country in international and European club football.

The development of the internet has facilitated the growth of online in-play betting markets on sporting events. For major league baseball, Sauer et al. (2010) apply a method originally developed by Lindsey (1961) to evaluate the probability of winning a match conditional on a number of parameters that define the current state of the match. The win probabilities are derived from empirical frequency distributions of the number of runs scored per innings. Price changes in the in-play betting market are found to correspond closely to changes in the evaluated win probabilities. In an early study of in-play betting on football, Fitt et al. (2006) examine the valuation of in-play spread bets. Arrivals of goals and corners are modelled as Poisson processes, with arrival rates that are assumed not to change over the course of the match. For matches played during the 2004 European Championships, the spreads quoted by online bookmakers appear to be consistent with the theoretical valuations. Fitt (2009) derives formulae for the fair values of a number of match results and goals-based spread bets.

Croxson and Reade (2014) use Betfair in-play football betting odds data to test the semi-strong form efficiency hypothesis, by focussing on goals scored during the five-minute period of play immediately before the half-time interval. If the market takes time to adjust fully to the news content of the arrival of a goal, and in the absence of a benchmark model for the evaluation of the relevant probabilities, it would be difficult to separate the effect on the odds of a goal scored from the regular drift in the odds that occurs as play continues and the match proceeds towards its conclusion. For goals scored immediately before half-time, this difficulty is eliminated, because there should be no drift in the odds during the 15-minute half-time interval while play is suspended. The empirical investigation suggests there is no systematic movement in the betting odds over the half-time interval.

Choi and Hui (2012) also use Betfair in-play football betting odds data to test the behavioural hypothesis that market traders tend to under-react to news that is expected and over-react to surprise news. They study the adjustment of the betting odds to the first goal scored in each match, measuring the goal's surprise news content using the difference between the odds for a win by the scoring team, and the odds for a win by the team that conceded, that were available immediately before the goal was scored. Based on the probabilities implied by the betting odds available two minutes after each goal was scored, the expected number of wins by scoring teams is greater than the observed number when the first goal was expected; but less then the observed number when the first goal was a surprise.

4.3   COMPUTATION OF IN-PLAY MATCH OUTCOME PROBABILITIES

This section describes the simulation procedure employed to calculate in-play match outcome probabilities, with which the Betfair implied probabilities will be compared. Empirical hazard functions for the arrival rates of goals scored and red cards by the home and away teams are estimated, using data from all English Premier League and Football League matches played during the eight football seasons from 2001/02 to 2008/09 inclusive. The hazard function covariates include all observable factors that are expected to influence the respective arrival rates of goals and red cards. These include linear and quadratic terms in a measure of the relative quality of the two competing teams, based on the Betfair betting prices for the match result prior to the start of the match; a linear term for the number of minutes of the match currently elapsed, allowing for the tendency for the incidence of goals and cards to increase over the duration of the match; and dummy variables indicating the current goal difference between the two teams, and any difference between the numbers of players on the pitch owing to red cards already incurred.

In order to calculate in-play match outcome probabilities at any stage of any match played during the 2009/10 or 2010/11 seasons, we begin by identifying the parameter set that defines the state of the match at the point at which the probabilities for the final outcome are required. The current state of the match is defined by the relative team quality measure, the time elapsed in minutes, the current goal difference and the current difference, if any, between the numbers of players of the two teams currently on the pitch. The remaining duration of the match, from the point at which the probabilities are required until the end of the match, can be simulated by applying random numbers to the estimated hazard function arrival rate equations, and keeping count of the totals of (simulated) goals scored and red cards incurred by each team as the simulated match develops. The outcome of the match (goals scored by both teams) on completion of 90 minutes' play is recorded. For each required set of probabilities the simulation procedure is repeated 5,000 times. The model probability for any outcome (match result, correct score or total goals) is the ratio of the number of simulated occurrences of the required outcome to the number of repetitions.

4.4   IN-PLAY BETTING ODDS DATA

This section describes the Betfair in-play betting odds data and presents some comparisons between the match result probabilities implied by the betting odds, and the simulation model probabilities generated in accordance with the procedure described in the previous section.

The online betting exchange Betfair operates by pairing a backer, who wishes to bet on an outcome at a specified price, with a layer, who wishes to offer the bet at a price specified by the backer. Betfair commission rates are typically lower than the margins built into the traditional betting firms' odds. Downloads of historical data for Betfair in-play betting odds on English Premier League matches were obtained from *Fracsoft*. This database provides the three most competitive prices at which other Betfair members were willing to accept bets at all stages of each match, and the three most competitive prices at which other Betfair members were willing to place bets. Let $\theta_{H,t}$, $\theta_{D,t}$ and $\theta_{A,t}$ denote the best available decimal odds at which bets on home win, draw and away win outcomes can be placed after t minutes, such that a unit stake placed on a home win result returns $\theta_{H,t}$ (including return of stake) if the bet wins. The implied Betfair home-win probabilities are:

$$\pi_{j,t} = (1/\theta_{j,t})/\{(1/\theta_{H,t}) + (1/\theta_{D,t}) + (1/\theta_{A,t})\} \text{ for } j=\text{H,A,D}. \quad (4.1)$$

Let $p_{H,t}$, $p_{D,t}$ and $p_{A,t}$ denote the match result probabilities obtained from the simulation model, computed in accordance with the procedure outlined in Section 4.3. Direct comparisons between $\pi_{j,t}$ and $p_{j,t}$ (for $j=\text{H,A,D}$) can shed light on the existence and extent of mispricing. Figures 4.1 to 4.4 compare the evolution of the Betfair implied probabilities and the model probabilities over the 90-minute duration of four representative matches from the 2010/11 season. Newcastle vs. Manchester United, played on 13 November 2010, resulted in a 0–0 draw, with no players from either team dismissed. Arsenal vs. Tottenham, played on 20 November 2010, resulted in a 2–3 away win, with no dismissals. Arsenal, the pre-match favourite, raced into a two-goal lead as early as the 27th minute. The odds for a home win shortened from 1.76 at the start of the match to 1.07 at half-time. Tottenham then scored three second-half goals, each of which produced a successively larger adjustment to the probabilities and odds. Sunderland vs. Birmingham, played on 14 August 2010, followed a similar pattern in terms of scores, with Sunderland taking a two-goal lead in the 56th minute, and Birmingham scoring two late goals to force a 2–2 draw. A Sunderland player was dismissed in the 44th minute, causing the home win probability to decrease sharply shortly before half-time. Finally, Everton vs. Aston

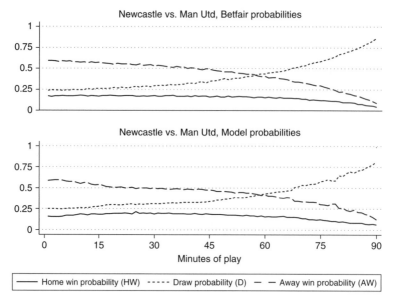

Figure 4.1   Betfair implied probabilities and model probabilities, Newcastle United vs. Manchester United, 13 November 2010

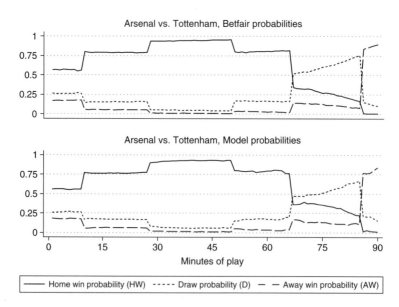

Figure 4.2   Betfair implied probabilities and model probabilities, Arsenal vs. Tottenham Hotspur, 20 November 2010

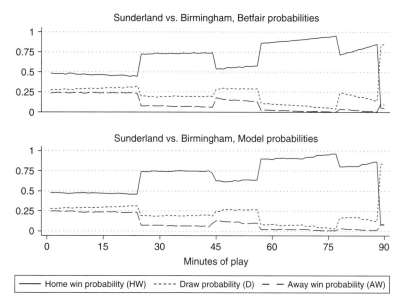

Figure 4.3   Betfair implied probabilities and model probabilities, Sunderland vs. Birmingham City, 14 August 2010

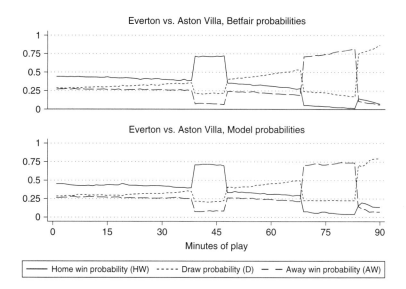

Figure 4.4   Betfair implied probabilities and model probabilities, Everton vs. Aston Villa, 2 April 2011

Villa, played on 2 April 2011, finished as a 2–2 draw, with no players dismissed. Everton took a 1–0 lead in the 38th minute, Aston Villa then took a 1–2 lead with goals in the 47th and 68th minutes, before Everton equalized in the 83rd minute. The plots indicate that the betting market and the simulation model provide a similar, but not identical, appraisal of the match result probabilities. The shapes of the plots are broadly similar in all cases, but small divergences exist between the model probabilities and the implied Betfair probabilities, suggesting that there might be some informational inefficiencies in the betting odds.

In attempting to formulate an in-play betting strategy, it may be especially interesting to focus on bets that could be placed one minute after the occurrence of an event that should have caused a significant adjustment to the betting odds: either a goal, or a player dismissal. Goals and dismissals create significant movements in the betting odds and implied probabilities conditional on the current state of the match. If the market sometimes or often fails to achieve the correct price adjustment immediately, betting prices that were available immediately after such an event should cause a significant movement in the betting odds and implied probabilities should be a strong candidate for the identification of mispricing and informational inefficiencies. To investigate this hypothesis further, we also examine bets that were available at certain observation points, located at the end of 10, 20, 30, 40, 55, 65, 75 or 85 minutes of play, in any case where no goal had been scored and no dismissal had occurred during the 10-minute passage of play immediately preceding the observation point.

Figures 4.5 and 4.6 illustrate the relationship between the adjustments in the simulation model probabilities and the adjustments in the implied Betfair probabilities for win–draw–lose match results in response to goals scored by the home and away teams, for all betting opportunities that qualify for inclusion in the sample on the criteria described above. The changes in probabilities are calculated over the three-minute interval (t–2, t+1) where t denotes the minute in which the goal was scored. Accordingly, Figures 4.5 and 4.6 show scatter plots of $(\pi_{i,t+1} - \pi_{i,t-2})$ on the vertical axis against $(p_{i,t+1} - p_{i,t-2})$ on the horizontal. The plots are conditional on the difference in scores immediately prior to each goal.

The location of the values of $(\pi_{i,t+1} - \pi_{i,t-2})$ and $(p_{i,t+1} - p_{i,t-2})$ on the scale $(-1,+1)$ is heavily dependent on the current difference in scores. For example, a goal scored by the home team has a larger effect on the home win probability if the scores are level (prior to the goal being scored) than it does if the home team is already leading, or if the home team is trailing. A goal scored by the home team has a large positive effect on the draw probability if the home team is trailing by one goal, and a large negative effect if the scores are level. If the changes in Betfair probabilities mirror the

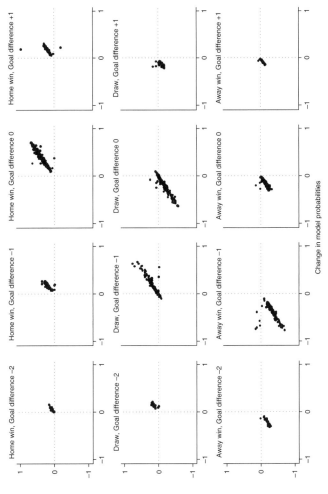

Note: Figure 4.5 shows the scatter plot of the change in simulation model match result probability between minutes $t-2$ and $t+1$, for goals scored in minute t by the home team, conditional on the goal difference immediately prior to the goal having been scored. The horizontal axis shows the change in the model match result probability, and the vertical axis shows the change in the Betfair implied match result probability.

Figure 4.5   Changes in model and Betfair implied match result probabilities following goal scored by home team, conditional on goal difference immediately prior to goal

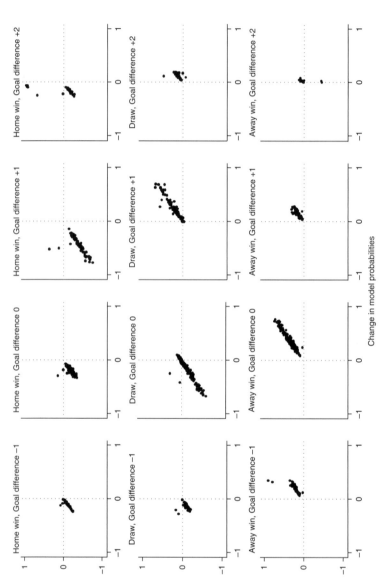

Note: Figure 4.6 shows the scatter plot of the change in simulation model match result probability between minutes $t-2$ and $t+1$, for goals scored in minute t by the away team, conditional on the goal difference immediately prior to the goal having been scored. The horizontal axis shows the change in the model match result probability, and the vertical axis shows the change in the Betfair implied match result probability.

Figure 4.6   Changes in model and Betfair implied match result probabilities following goal scored by away team, conditional on goal difference immediately prior to goal

changes in the simulation model probabilities, then all points should lie on a 45-degree line; any divergence from this line suggests mispricing. While the large majority of points are located close to the 45-degree line, there are large divergences in some individual cases, suggesting that the market does not always adjust rapidly and correctly (within one minute) to news of goals or dismissals.

In order to investigate our hypothesis of mispricing further, Table 4.1 reports average Betfair implied probabilities conditional on the number of minutes elapsed (in 15-minute bands) and the current scores of the home and away teams, for selected correct scores bets (1–0, 2–0, 0–1, 1–1, 2–1, 0–2, 1–2, 2–2), calculated over all sample betting opportunities that were available one minute after a goal was scored. Naturally, the conditioning on the current score has a more pronounced effect on the conditional probabilities as the number of minutes elapsed increases and the probability that the final score will correspond to the current score also increases. For example, the average probabilities of a 1–1 draw conditional on current scores of {1–0, 0–1 and 1–1} are 0.097, 0.136 and 0.089, respectively, for bets placed one minute after a goal scored during the first 15 minutes of play; and 0.090, 0.199 and 0.682 for bets placed one minute after a goal scored during the final 15 minutes of play.

Table 4.2 reports the average probabilities generated by the simulation model, conditional on the number of minutes elapsed (in 15-minute bands) and the current scores of the home and away teams, for selected correct scores bets (1–0, 2–0, 0–1, 1–1, 2–1, 0–2, 1–2, 2–2), calculated over the same set of betting opportunities, available one minute after a goal was scored, as reported in Table 4.1. A direct comparison between corresponding probabilities in Tables 4.1 and 4.2 provides an indication of possible mispricing in the Betfair correct scores odds. In general, the two sets of average probabilities seem to correspond closely. The correlation between the 7,597 individual Betfair implied probabilities from which the averages reported in Table 4.1 are computed, and the corresponding simulation model probabilities (Table 4.2), is 0.957. One possible exception to the pattern of similarity between the two sets of probabilities occurs during the latter stages of matches, when the Betfair implied probabilities for outcomes that involve no further change in the score (short-odds bets) appear to be consistently lower than the model probabilities; and the Betfair implied probabilities for outcomes that involve a further change in the score (long-odds bets) appear to be consistently higher than the model probabilities. This pattern may be a manifestation of favourite–longshot bias in the correct scores betting market, leading to violation of the semi-strong form EMH.

Table 4.3 reports average Betfair implied probabilities conditional on

The economics of sports betting

Table 4.1   *Average Betfair implied probabilities conditional on the number*
              of minutes elapsed and the current scores of the home and away
              teams, for selected correct scores bets, calculated over sample
              betting opportunities that were available one minute after a goal
              was scored

Final score	Current score	Minutes elapsed					
		1–15	16–30	31–45	46–60	61–75	76–90
1–0	1–0	.089	.115	.184	.346	.448	.642
2–0	1–0	.137	.158	.183	.213	.246	.202
	2–0	.118	.131	.170	.321	.456	.656
0–1	0–1	.088	.120	.183	.339	.468	.668
1–1	1–0	.097	.110	.142	.154	.145	.090
	0–1	.136	.140	.170	.194	.228	.199
	1–1	.089	.122	.189	.295	.458	.682
2–1	1–0	.120	.120	.125	.106	.069	.046
	2–0	.086	.125	.110	.160	.129	.122
	0–1	.093	.099	.079	.077	.061	.061
	1–1	.106	.147	.175	.206	.210	.215
	2–1	–	.105	.168	.298	.476	.646
0–2	0–1	.097	.130	.156	.180	.168	.152
	0–2	.100	.117	.173	.297	.434	.702
1–2	1–0	.054	.055	.057	.039	.032	.019
	0–1	.135	.126	.123	.105	.081	.043
	1–1	.103	.111	.157	.183	.173	.143
	0–2	.127	.152	.155	.173	.151	.104
	1–2	.091	.138	.182	.272	.472	.615
2–2	1–0	.068	.059	.050	.033	.017	.010
	2–0	.027	.055	.049	.054	.031	.028
	0–1	.093	.076	.059	.041	.024	.015
	1–1	.132	.127	.130	.111	.079	.040
	2–1	–	.094	.105	.192	.196	.134
	0–2	.096	.121	.077	.068	.040	.010
	1–2	.114	.156	.171	.225	.216	.190
	2–2	–	.134	.087	.257	.434	.618

Note: The averages do not include permutations of current score and final score for which
there were few observations in the sample, or for which the probabilities were negligibly
small.

the number of minutes elapsed (10, 20, 30, 40, 55, 65, 75 or 85) and the
current scores of the home and away teams, for selected correct scores
bets (0–0, 1–0, 2–0, 0–1, 1–1, 2–1, 0–2, 1–2, 2–2), calculated over sample
betting opportunities that were available at points in the match when a 10

Table 4.2   *Average simulation model probabilities conditional on the number of minutes elapsed and the current scores of the home and away teams, for selected correct scores bets, calculated over sample betting opportunities that were available one minute after a goal was scored*

Final score	Current score	Minutes elapsed					
		1–15	16–30	31–45	46–60	61–75	76–90
1–0	1–0	.085	.113	.171	.314	.426	.683
2–0	1–0	.121	.148	.172	.204	.225	.172
	2–0	.083	.123	.157	.302	.445	.679
0–1	0–1	.082	.126	.176	.302	.446	.685
1–1	1–0	.091	.099	.135	.168	.135	.092
	0–1	.123	.140	.164	.202	.218	.172
	1–1	.097	.125	.181	.301	.470	.709
2–1	1–0	.120	.118	.124	.100	.060	.021
	2–0	.060	.099	.107	.150	.131	.088
	0–1	.093	.080	.075	.061	.042	.020
	1–1	.114	.151	.168	.202	.208	.148
	2–1	–	.116	.168	.313	.493	.672
0–2	0–1	.087	.123	.147	.172	.153	.095
	0–2	.083	.105	.168	.289	.427	.705
1–2	1–0	.048	.047	.052	.040	.021	.007
	0–1	.116	.126	.122	.104	.061	.017
	1–1	.111	.109	.142	.160	.149	.103
	0–2	.129	.158	.156	.196	.158	.106
	1–2	.107	.135	.193	.279	.478	.671
2–2	1–0	.064	.053	.048	.026	.010	.003
	2–0	.024	.051	.043	.045	.026	.009
	0–1	.085	.072	.057	.033	.015	.003
	1–1	.129	.125	.130	.102	.066	.021
	2–1	–	.080	.103	.154	.186	.132
	0–2	.098	.129	.075	.069	.028	.009
	1–2	.132	.133	.171	.235	.200	.155
	2–2	–	.137	.113	.293	.487	.693

Note: See note to Table 4.1.

minutes' passage of play had just been completed without any goal having been scored or player having been dismissed. Table 4.4 reports the corresponding average probabilities generated by the simulation model. Similar patterns emerge from the comparison between Tables 4.3 and 4.4. However it is interesting to note that the correlation between the 40,839 individual

Table 4.3   *Average Betfair implied probabilities conditional on the number of minutes elapsed and the current scores of the home and away teams, for selected correct scores bets, calculated over sample betting opportunities that were available after a 10-minute passage of play with no goals scored or players dismissed*

Final score	Current score	Minutes elapsed							
		10	20	30	40	55	65	75	85
0–0	0–0	.091	.115	.149	.195	.315	.425	.557	.731
1–0	0–0	.119	.142	.165	.191	.215	.214	.194	.161
	1–0	–	.102	.135	.177	.283	.385	.514	.705
2–0	0–0	.088	.095	.097	.097	.079	.061	.039	.033
	1–0	–	.143	.157	.180	.211	.217	.205	.155
	2–0	–	.083	.133	.180	.262	.374	.524	.714
0–1	0–0	.092	.105	.124	.138	.162	.168	.157	.123
	0–1	–	.108	.134	.179	.280	.385	.524	.709
1–1	0–0	.125	.128	.128	.126	.096	.071	.048	.034
	1–0	–	.106	.135	.148	.166	.178	.166	.152
	0–1	–	.147	.160	.178	.200	.204	.195	.163
	1–1	–	.118	.142	.182	.286	.401	.532	.706
2–1	0–0	.084	.078	.069	.058	.034	.020	.014	.043
	1–0	–	.121	.124	.119	.102	.084	.055	.033
	2–0	–	.091	.096	.115	.134	.156	.142	.107
	0–1	–	.094	.088	.083	.074	.057	.040	.039
	1–1	–	.149	.153	.171	.197	.203	.196	.151
	2–1	–	–	–	.156	.243	.355	.494	.703
0–2	0–0	.058	.058	.059	.054	.048	.040	.030	.026
	0–1	–	.113	.132	.154	.178	.183	.165	.136
	0–2	–	.111	.129	.163	.273	.375	.511	.714
1–2	0–0	.065	.059	.052	.043	.026	.018	.013	.023
	1–0	–	.054	.066	.064	.053	.046	.037	.039
	0–1	–	.123	.126	.124	.104	.081	.052	.033
	1–1	–	.097	.128	.148	.181	.185	.168	.138
	0–2	–	.116	.158	.185	.189	.193	.181	.144
	1–2	–	–	.114	.193	.258	.356	.492	.699
2–2	0–0	.045	.037	.029	.021	.012	.012	.036	.018
	1–0	–	.060	.058	.051	.032	.022	.013	.027
	2–0	–	.051	.045	.045	.049	.044	.029	.024
	0–1	–	.081	.072	.059	.041	.023	.014	.026
	1–1	–	.137	.134	.126	.105	.079	.054	.036
	2–1	–	–	–	.087	.104	.153	.148	.141
	0–2	–	.065	.107	.122	.077	.063	.042	.032
	1–2	–	–	.135	.151	.211	.231	.220	.166
	2–2	–	–	–	.182	.232	.371	.502	.675

Note: See note to Table 4.1.

Table 4.4 *Average simulation model probabilities conditional on the number of minutes elapsed and the current scores of the home and away teams, for selected correct scores bets, calculated over sample betting opportunities that were available after a 10-minute passage of play with no goals scored or players dismissed*

Final score	Current score	Minutes elapsed							
		10	20	30	40	55	65	75	85
0–0	0–0	.091	.114	.147	.191	.310	.416	.564	.759
1–0	0–0	.124	.143	.163	.186	.212	.210	.186	.122
	1–0	–	.108	.138	.181	.304	.410	.554	.751
2–0	0–0	.086	.091	.090	.089	.069	.050	.027	.008
	1–0	–	.141	.154	.175	.205	.205	.184	.112
	2–0	–	.121	.137	.178	.290	.400	.549	.751
0–1	0–0	.093	.104	.119	.132	.156	.160	.145	.095
	0–1	–	.110	.144	.188	.303	.409	.554	.750
1–1	0–0	.126	.130	.131	.128	.104	.078	.044	.012
	1–0	–	.102	.128	.142	.165	.169	.152	.111
	0–1	–	.145	.160	.177	.203	.208	.194	.134
	1–1	–	.122	.150	.189	.308	.419	.558	.757
2–1	0–0	.082	.076	.068	.057	.031	.017	.006	.001
	1–0	–	.122	.126	.121	.098	.073	.041	.011
	2–0	–	.107	.098	.116	.135	.154	.133	.081
	0–1	–	.094	.087	.081	.066	.049	.031	.010
	1–1	–	.152	.155	.173	.198	.199	.180	.119
	2–1	–	–	–	.181	.295	.403	.548	.751
0–2	0–0	.054	.054	.055	.051	.043	.035	.020	.006
	0–1	–	.103	.126	.145	.170	.170	.144	.094
	0–2	–	.117	.125	.162	.290	.393	.538	.743
1–2	0–0	.062	.056	.050	.042	.024	.014	.005	.001
	1–0	–	.048	.058	.055	.042	.033	.021	.007
	0–1	–	.124	.126	.123	.099	.073	.042	.011
	1–1	–	.104	.130	.144	.170	.171	.152	.099
	0–2	–	.132	.164	.200	.205	.216	.195	.137
	1–2	–	–	.160	.205	.295	.397	.540	.745
2–2	0–0	.041	.034	.026	.019	.007	.003	.001	.000
	1–0	–	.058	.056	.046	.025	.014	.005	.001
	2–0	–	.043	.042	.042	.042	.035	.019	.005
	0–1	–	.080	.068	.056	.031	.017	.006	.001
	1–1	–	.147	.134	.128	.103	.078	.044	.011
	2–1	–	–	–	.091	.111	.155	.143	.111
	0–2	–	.066	.117	.131	.076	.063	.037	.010
	1–2	–	–	.156	.143	.219	.233	.218	.143
	2–2	–	–	–	.190	.287	.418	.543	.758

Note: See note to Table 4.1.

Betfair implied probabilities from which the averages reported in Table 4.3 are computed, and the corresponding simulation model probabilities (Table 4.4), is 0.984, higher than the correlation between the probabilities that comprise Tables 4.1 and 4.2. This finding is consistent with our hypothesis that the betting market may perform better at identifying the 'true' probabilities after a passage of play during which there has been no significant disturbance to the probabilities owing to a goal or a dismissal, than it does immediately after such a disturbance has just occurred.

4.5 CONCLUSION

This chapter reports a preliminary empirical investigation of the semi-strong form EMH for an in-play sports betting market. The subject of the empirical investigation is the Betfair market for in-play betting on the outcomes of English Premier League professional football matches during the football seasons of 2009/10 and 2010/11. An empirical model for the incidence and timings of goals and player dismissals is used to obtain probabilities for match outcomes, conditional upon the state of the match at any stage. A number of comparisons are drawn between the probabilities obtained from the model with the probabilities implied by high-frequency Betfair in-play betting odds data for the same outcomes. During the latter stages of matches, the Betfair implied probabilities for correct score outcomes that involve no further change in the score (short-odds bets) appear to be consistently lower than the model probabilities; and the Betfair implied probabilities for outcomes that involve a further change in the score (long-odds bets) appear to be consistently higher than the model probabilities. This pattern, consistent with the presence of favourite–longshot bias, may reflect a form of semi-strong form informational inefficiency in the correct scores betting market. Discrepancies between the Betfair implied probabilities and the simulation model probabilities are generally rather small, but appear to be larger in the immediate aftermath of a goal or a player dismissal than they are after stable passages of play during which no large adjustments to the betting odds have occurred.

REFERENCES

Ali, M.M. "Probability and utility estimates for race track bettors." *Journal of Political Economy* **85** (1977), 803–815.

Asch, P., B.G. Malkiel and R.E. Quandt. "Market efficiency in race track betting." *Journal of Business* **57** (1984), 157–175.

Ball, R. and P. Brown. "An empirical evaluation of accounting income numbers." *Journal of Accounting Research* **6** (1968), 159–177.

Brown, S.J. and J.B. Warner. "Using daily stock returns: the case of event studies." *Journal of Financial Economics* **8** (1985), 205–258.

Brown, W.O. and R.D. Sauer. "Does the baseball market believe in the hot hand: a comment." *American Economic Review* **83** (1993), 1377–1386.

Cain, M., D. Law and D. Peel. "The favourite–longshot bias and market efficiency in UK football betting." *Scottish Journal of Political Economy* **47** (2000), 25–36.

Choi, D. and S.K. Hui. "The role of surprise: understanding over- and underreactions using in-play soccer betting." Mimeo, Hong Kong University of Science and Technology and Stern School of Business, New York University (2012).

Corrado, C.J. "Event studies: a methodology review." *Accounting and Finance* **51** (2011), 207–234.

Croxson, K. and J.J. Reade. "Information and efficiency: goal arrival in soccer betting." *Economic Journal* **124** (2014), 62–91.

Dixon, M.J. and S.G. Coles. "Modelling association football scores and inefficiencies in the football betting market." *Applied Statistics* **46** (1997), 265–280.

Dixon, M.J. and P.F. Pope. "The value of statistical forecasts in the UK association football betting market." *International Journal of Forecasting* **20** (2004), 697–711.

Dobson, S. and J. Goddard *The Economics of Football*, 2nd edn. Cambridge: Cambridge University Press (2011).

Dowie, J. "On the efficiency and equity of betting markets." *Economica* **43** (1976), 139–150.

Fama, E.F. "Efficient capital markets: a review of theory and empirical work." *Journal of Finance* **25** (1970), 383–417.

Fama, E.F., L. Fisher, M.C. Jensen and R. Roll. "The adjustments of stock prices to new information." *International Economic Review* **10** (1969), 1–21.

Fitt, A.D. "Markowitz portfolio theory for soccer spread betting." *IMA Journal of Management Mathematics* **20** (2009), 167–184.

Fitt, A.D., C.J. Howls and M. Kabelka. "Valuation of soccer spread bets." *Journal of the Operational Research Society* **57** (2006), 975–985.

Forrest, D., J. Goddard and R. Simmons. "Odds-setters as forecasters: the case of English football." *International Journal of Forecasting* **21** (2005), 551–564.

Forrest, D. and R. Simmons. "Sentiment in the betting market on Spanish football." *Applied Economics* **40** (2008), 119–126.

Franck, E., E. Verbeek and S. Nuesch. "Sentimental preferences and the organizational regime of betting markets." *Southern Economic Journal* **78** (2011), 502–518.

Franck, E., E. Verbeek and S. Nuesch. "Inter-market arbitrage in betting." *Economica* **80** (2013), 300–325.

Gandar, J.M., R.A. Zuber, T. O'Brien and B. Russo. "Testing rationality in the point spread betting market." *Journal of Finance* **43** (1988), 995–1008.

Goddard, J. and I. Asimakopoulos. "Modelling football match results, and the efficiency of fixed-odds betting." *Journal of Forecasting* **23** (2004), 51–66.

Golec, J. and M. Tamarkin. "The degree of inefficiency in the football betting market: statistical tests." *Journal of Financial Economics* **30** (1991), 311–323

Graham, I. and H. Stott. "Predicting bookmaker odds and efficiency for UK football." *Applied Economics* **40** (2008), 99–109.

Kothari, S.P. and J.B. Warner. "Econometrics of event studies." In B. Eckbo Espen (ed.) *Handbook of Corporate Finance: Empirical Corporate Finance.* Handbooks in Finance Series, Elsevier, North-Holland (2005).

Lindsey, G.R. "The progress of the score during a baseball game." *Journal of the American Statistical Association* **56**(295) (1961), 703–728.

MacKinlay, A.C. "Event studies in economics and finance." *Journal of Economic Literature* **35** (1997), 13–39.

Page, L. "Is there an optimistic bias on betting markets?" *Economics Letters* **102** (2009), 70–72.

Pankoff, L.D. "Market efficiency and football betting." *Journal of Business* **41** (1968), 203–214.

Pope, P.F. and D.A. Peel. "Information, prices and efficiency in a fixed odds betting market." *Economica* **56** (1989), 323–341.

Sauer, R.D. "The economics of wagering markets." *Journal of Economic Literature* **36** (1998), 2021–2064.

Sauer, R.D., J.K. Waller and J.K. Hakes. "The progress of the betting in a baseball game." *Public Choice* **142** (2010), 297–313.

Shin, H.S. "Optimal betting odds against insider traders." *Economic Journal* **101** (1991), 1179–1185.

Woodland, L.M. and B.M. Woodland. "Market efficiency and the favourite-longshot bias: the baseball betting market." *Journal of Finance* **49** (1994), 269–279.

Woodland, L.M. and B.M. Woodland. "Market efficiency and profitable wagering in the National Hockey League: can bettors score on longshots?" *Southern Economic Journal* **67** (2001), 983–995.

5. Forecasting football match results: are the many smarter than the few?*

Jaume García, Levi Pérez and Plácido Rodríguez

5.1 INTRODUCTION

Forrest and Simmons (2000) reported empirical evidence consistent with the general opinion in the forecasting literature that predictions from statistical models are better than predictions by experts when forecasting football match results using data from English football. In a more recent paper Forrest et al. (2005), also using data from the English football, concluded that "a much more detailed benchmark statistical model proves to be far from dominant over the views of a group of experts". They also concluded that "the performance of these experts has improved in a number of dimensions through a period when an intensification of competitive pressure in bookmaking has made the consequences of poor forecasting performance increasingly costly". In particular in both papers the authors were looking at the odds from several bookmakers (experts). In this chapter we complement the analysis of experts' performances by paying attention to bettors' behaviour. In this case, the focus is on bettors' choices and impressions before the games, employing data from Spanish football pools (La Quiniela); a long-odds high-prize pari-mutuel betting medium based on correctly forecasting the outcome in a number of football games. The main target is to test whether forecasting by experts (bookmakers) differs (better/worse) from that done by the 'crowd' (football pools bettors).[1] According to the wisdom-of-crowds hypothesis (Surowiecki, 2004), La Quiniela bettors, who are likely to be football fans, should collectively forecast optimally. So, one could expect that the many (La Quiniela bettors) may make better predictions than the few (bookmakers).

The sample database includes decimal odds on full time results (home win, draw, away win) set by nine bookmakers – Bet365 (B365), Bet & Win (BW), Gamebookers (GB), Interwetten (IW), Ladbrokes (LB),

Sportingbet (SB), Stan James (SJ), VC Bet (VC) and William Hill (WH) –
for 2,280 Spanish First Division matches (top professional football division in Spain) for the seasons from 2005/06 to 2010/11. Betting odds for
the same matches are estimated from information on the number of tickets
containing a particular given final result from La Quiniela. First, a descriptive comparison of the odds offered by the bookmakers is carried out in
order to test whether their distributions are similar. An additional analysis
of the coefficients of correlation between the odds of a particular outcome
for pairs of bookmakers (including La Quiniela) is performed next.

Since the main characteristics of a bet differ due to take-out and over-
round,[2] alongside the previously mentioned study, an inquiry into the total
take-out rate the bookmakers return offers the possibility of evaluating
the presence of the favourite long-shot bias (on average, bettors tend to
undervalue high-probability events and overvalue low-probability ones) in
the betting market for Spanish football. Evidence of higher take-out rates
for low-probability events may corroborate the existence of this
statistical bias.

A further test of the accuracy of probability forecasts is finally developed by using a modified version of the "Brier scores" (Forrest et al.
2005) and a set of ordered Logit regressions by bookmakers (including La
Quiniela) where the dependent variable is the final result of any match.
The empirical findings should bring evidence whether experts (bookmakers) are better at forecasting football results than the "crowd" (football
pools bettors).

The chapter is organized as follows. The next section describes the
football betting market in Spain focusing on the main features of the La
Quiniela game. Later, a descriptive analysis of the odds offered by the
bookmakers and those estimated in the case of La Quiniela is developed.
The take-out rates and the favourite long-shot bias are then discussed.
The analysis of the forecasting performance is considered in the following
section. Finally, a summary of the more relevant conclusions is presented.

5.2   THE FOOTBALL BETTING MARKET IN SPAIN

Legal sports betting in Spain was largely limited to people gambling on
the outcome of professional football matches through football pools. Since
the introduction of La Quiniela in the season 1946–47 the pools have long
occupied a predominant place in the Spanish gambling market. For many
years La Quiniela was the only football betting game available in Spain,
but recently the pools' industry has experienced several changes and even
the introduction of a new product in 2005: El Quinigol.[3] In 2008 several

bookmakers were awarded the first licences to operate sports betting in some Spanish regions opening up a completely new football betting market. However, it should be noted that online gambling in Spain was not regulated until 2011, so Spaniards could bet on football on the Internet for some years before that and most bookmakers used to accept bets on Spanish football matches.

5.2.1 The Spanish Football Pools: La Quiniela

As explained in Forrest and Pérez (2013), the term "football pools" could be applied to pari-mutuel wagering concerning the outcomes of football matches. More specifically it refers to a long-odds high-prize betting product where players have to correctly guess the results of a long list of football results to win a share of the jackpot.

In particular, La Quiniela (commercial name for Spanish football pools) consists of a ticket or coupon (betting slip) that includes a list of 15 football matches (mainly from the Spanish First Division[4]). Players must forecast the result of each match, home win, draw or away win. Those who correctly guess the 15 results win a share of the jackpot pool. If there is no winner of the jackpot, the amount devoted to this first prize category rolls over to the next fixture. There are also minor prizes for those who correctly guess a lower number of results. The entry fee has been €0.50 since the 2003/04 season and the take-out rate is 45 per cent. La Quiniela is operated by Sociedad Estatal Loterías y Apuestas del Estado (SELAE) – the same state-owned entity that runs national lottery games in Spain.

The main aggregate figures of the game (over the sample period) are shown in Table 5.1. Some empirical evidence about the determinants of the demand for La Quiniela can be found in García and Rodríguez (2007) and García et al. (2008).

Table 5.1   La Quiniela aggregate figures, 2005–11 (in millions)

	Mean	Max.	Min.	S.D.
. . . per season				
Tickets or coupons sold	83.31	69.04	90.90	7.22
Bets placed	994.49	1,114.78	762.59	118.99
Bets placed/coupon ratio	11.91	12.66	11.05	0.58
Fixtures	51.29	62	41	7.99
. . . per fixture				
Tickets or coupons sold	1.66	2.04	1.26	0.29
Bets placed	19.83	24.08	13.87	3.98

Table 5.2   Odds descriptive statistics by season (excluding La Quiniela)

	Home win		Draw		Away win	
	Mean	S.D.	Mean	S.D.	Mean	S.D.
2005/06	2.225	0.972	3.368	0.509	4.010	2.202
2006/07	2.319	1.123	3.415	0.575	4.074	2.415
2007/08	2.290	0.982	3.423	0.577	4.105	2.543
2008/09	2.314	1.076	3.510	0.635	4.154	2.622
2009/10	2.550	1.800	3.840	1.174	4.635	3.937
2010/11	2.643	2.204	3.942	1.327	4.752	4.054
Total	2.391	1.450	3.584	0.893	4.290	3.071

5.2.1.1 Odds descriptive analysis

The odd $Q_{i,j}^k$ is the amount of money a particular bookmaker i will return for a bet of one unit for the event k in game j. In the case of football matches the events are: (H) home win, (D) draw and (A) away win.[5] In this chapter we use a panel data set composed of the odds corresponding to the matches of the Spanish First Division offered by nine bookmakers for the 2005/06 season until the 2010/11 season. The bookmakers are: Bet365 (B365), Bet & Win (BW), Gamebookers (GB), Interwetten (IW), Ladbrokes (LB), Sportingbet (SB), Stan James (SJ), VC Bet (VC) and William Hill (WH). In Table 5.2 we provide some basic statistics (mean and standard deviation) of the odds of the three events corresponding to the six seasons we consider aggregated across bookmakers.

We can distinguish two different periods in terms of values of the average odds and their variability. In the first four seasons the odds look very similar (around 2.3 for the home win, 3.4 for the draw and 4.1 for the away win) and, if any, there is an almost negligible positive trend. In contrast, in the last two seasons the average odds significantly increase for the three events and also its variability. These particular increases in both statistics are associated with the substantial increase in the odds of those games where either *FC Barcelona* or *Real Madrid CF* are involved, which corresponds to situations where the odds are very high depending on whether these teams are the home team or the visitor. The maximum odds for a home win move from 9 in the first four seasons to 19 in the last two when they are the away teams, for an away win from 22 to 43 when they are the home teams, and for a draw from 8 to 14. This is a consequence of the dominating role of these two clubs in the Spanish League during this period. In fact, if we look at the evolution of the competitive balance in the Spanish League, the coefficient of variation of the number of points in the final standings changes from 0.27, in the first four seasons of the period we

consider, to 0.34 in the last two, mainly as a consequence of the performance of both clubs. That means that when posting the odds bookmakers
took into account the abovementioned dominance of these two clubs.[6]

As mentioned in the previous section, information from traditional
football pools in Spain (La Quiniela), provided by SELAE (the Spanish
National Lottery Agency), is used to approximate the implicit odds of the
previously mentioned three events (football match results) by using a corollary of the constant expected return model, establishing that the relative
bet on one event should be equal to the probability of that event and the
odds should be the inverse of that probability.[7] In the case of La Quiniela
we use the number of tickets detailing a particular event for a given match
(T_j^k) to calculate the associated odds ($Q_{LQ,j}^k$):[8]

$$Q_{LQ,j}^k = \cfrac{1}{\cfrac{T_j^k}{\sum_{l=H,D,A} T_j^l}} \qquad k = H, D, A \qquad (5.1)$$

In Table 5.3 we report the some basic statistics (mean and standard
deviation) for the estimated odds for La Quiniela. The first thing we should
mention is that we observe the same pattern across seasons as we did
when discussing the odds for the bookmakers. The last two seasons in our
sample show odds that are substantially higher than those in the previous
seasons. On the other hand, if we compare these figures with those in Table
5.2 we can observe that the odds are higher in the case of La Quiniela than
for the considered bookmakers, this difference being more relevant for the
draw and the away win events than for the home win. This is a consequence
of the fact mentioned in note 9 that the odds do not include the take-out
rate in the case of La Quiniela. If we recalculate the odds for the nine
bookmakers not considering the take-out rates, the odds for La Quiniela

Table 5.3   Odds descriptive statistics of La Quiniela by season

	Home win		Draw		Away win	
	Mean	S.D.	Mean	S.D.	Mean	S.D.
2005/06	2.615	1.511	4.256	1.854	5.865	4.214
2006/07	2.560	1.322	4.130	1.397	5.365	3.274
2007/08	2.558	1.346	4.292	1.584	5.431	3.457
2008/09	2.547	1.384	4.366	1.555	5.385	3.432
2009/10	2.794	2.017	4.872	2.481	6.172	4.717
2010/11	2.864	2.332	5.025	2.735	6.322	5.115
Total	2.657	1.703	4.495	2.027	5.755	4.108

Table 5.4   Odds descriptive statistics by bookmaker

	Home win		Draw		Away win	
	Mean	S.D.	Mean	S.D.	Mean	S.D.
B365	2.454	1.551	3.690	0.946	4.508	3.440
BW	2.397	1.427	3.623	0.955	4.229	2.791
GB	2.422	1.443	3.600	0.864	4.332	3.012
IW	2.336	1.254	3.463	0.702	4.117	2.624
LB	2.334	1.379	3.512	0.810	4.122	2.722
SB	2.376	1.385	3.574	0.829	4.189	2.830
SJ	2.423	1.560	3.648	0.994	4.583	3.660
VC	2.412	1.593	3.627	1.002	4.364	3.403
WH	2.363	1.420	3.520	0.869	4.158	2.947

are still significantly higher in the case of the draw and away win events. This could be explained by the fact that the information available for La Quiniela corresponds to tickets including a particular result for a match instead of bets, given that each ticket can have a different number of bets with a particular result.[9]

In Table 5.4 we present the basic statistics of the odds for each of the bookmakers, the second dimension of our panel data set.[10] The differences among bookmakers both in terms of the average values and the standard deviations do not seem to be very important; although the degree of similarity is greater for the home win odds than for the draw and the away win odds. It is also worth mentioning that the variability of the odds is substantially higher in the case of the away win odds as a consequence of the odds for those games where the home team is clearly the favourite, as in the case of *FC Barcelona* and *Real Madrid CF*. Also the standard deviations are more dissimilar in the case of the visitor's odds, ranging from 2.6 (IW) to 3.7 (SJ). In addition, we can identify the bookmaker B365 as the one with the highest odds for the three events, whereas IW and LB are on the opposite side in this classification with the corresponding implications in terms of the take-out rates, as will become evident in the next section.

We have proceeded to make a formal comparison of the average odds for the different bookmakers and different events by testing whether the average odds are statistically the same by using t-tests to compare averages for pairs of bookmakers.[11] In Table 5.5, for each bookmaker we report the number of tests for which the null hypothesis of equality of the means is rejected.[12] In that sense, and corroborating the previous comments about the different patterns of the odds means depending on the event we consider, the number of rejections is higher in the case of a draw (16 pairs out

Table 5.5 *Number of odds paired t-tests for which H_0 is rejected (5 per cent)*

Bookmaker	Home win	Draw	Away win	Total
B365	0	2	3	5
BW	0	3	2	5
GB	0	3	2	5
IW	1	5	3	9
LB	0	4	3	7
SB	0	3	2	5
SJ	0	5	4	9
VC	1	5	5	11
WH	0	2	0	2
Total	1	16	12	29

of 36) and is also relevant for the away win (12 out of 36). In total we reject the null hypothesis in 29 out of the 108 pair comparisons (27 per cent). When looking at the detail from the bookmakers, we can identify three cases (IW, SJ and VC) where the number of rejections is above one third of the pair comparisons. These are cases associated either with high odds (SJ and VC) or low odds with the smallest variability (IW).[13]

One way of analysing whether the differences between odds averages respond more to differences in level (intercept different from zero) than to differences in the pattern (slope coefficient different from 1) is by looking at the coefficients of correlation between the odds of a particular event for pairs of bookmakers. The correlation matrices for the three events are reported in Tables 5.6a–c.[14] In this case we included La Quiniela (L-Q) in this analysis because, although the level of its odds cannot be compared to those of the other bookmakers, the coefficient of correlation is capturing patterns no matter the level of the odds.

According to the figures in these tables there is strong evidence of similar patterns for the odds of the nine bookmakers in our data set. All the coefficients of correlations for the three events are higher than 0.95 with the exception of the coefficients associated to bookmaker LB in the case of draw, but even in this case the coefficients are higher than 0.90, still a very high degree of positive correlation. On the other hand, the coefficients of correlation in which La Quiniela is involved are smaller than the previous ones but still quite high, and are above 0.85 with just two exceptions in the case of a draw. As mentioned above, that could be a consequence of having information on the number of tickets for each particular event but not the exact number of bets.

Table 5.6a   Odds correlation matrix (home win)

	B365	BW	GB	IW	LB	SB	SJ	VC	WH	L-Q
B365	1.0000									
BW	0.9885	1.0000								
GB	0.9932	0.9912	1.0000							
IW	0.9817	0.9844	0.9848	1.0000						
LB	0.9807	0.9794	0.9824	0.9752	1.0000					
SB	0.9907	0.9892	0.9929	0.9841	0.9829	1.0000				
SJ	0.9888	0.9844	0.9876	0.9812	0.9864	0.9858	1.0000			
VC	0.9900	0.9852	0.9900	0.9841	0.9815	0.9866	0.9884	1.0000		
WH	0.9898	0.9788	0.9840	0.9763	0.9770	0.9818	0.9896	0.9859	1.0000	
L-Q	0.9185	0.9323	0.9212	0.9287	0.9183	0.9231	0.9170	0.9168	0.9075	1.0000

Table 5.6b   Odds correlation matrix (draw)

	B365	BW	GB	IW	LB	SB	SJ	VC	WH	L-Q
B365	1.0000									
BW	0.9727	1.0000								
GB	0.9822	0.9802	1.0000							
IW	0.9610	0.9618	0.9658	1.0000						
LB	0.9364	0.9383	0.9536	0.9242	1.0000					
SB	0.9732	0.9739	0.9799	0.9634	0.9375	1.0000				
SJ	0.9557	0.9583	0.9641	0.9432	0.9482	0.9513	1.0000			
VC	0.9681	0.9635	0.9708	0.9546	0.9379	0.9567	0.9542	1.0000		
WH	0.9608	0.9573	0.9686	0.9413	0.9579	0.9476	0.9610	0.9555	1.0000	
L-Q	0.8720	0.8692	0.8810	0.8865	0.8341	0.8824	0.8381	0.8532	0.8492	1.0000

Table 5.6c   Odds correlation matrix (away win)

	B365	BW	GB	IW	LB	SB	SJ	VC	WH	L-Q
B365	1.0000									
BW	0.9712	1.0000								
GB	0.9832	0.9744	1.0000							
IW	0.9688	0.9723	0.9706	1.0000						
LB	0.9659	0.9715	0.9701	0.9651	1.0000					
SB	0.9809	0.9816	0.9841	0.9755	0.9749	1.0000				
SJ	0.9682	0.9738	0.9720	0.9622	0.9706	0.9743	1.0000			
VC	0.9797	0.9622	0.9786	0.9611	0.9580	0.9698	0.9660	1.0000		
WH	0.9696	0.9587	0.9637	0.9447	0.9593	0.9622	0.9657	0.9620	1.0000	
L-Q	0.8695	0.8979	0.8769	0.8891	0.8935	0.8941	0.8756	0.8572	0.8539	1.0000

5.2.1.2 Take-out rates (overround) and the favourite long-shot bias

We can calculate the implied probabilities ($P_{i,j}^k$) for each of the three events from the corresponding odds ($Q_{i,j}^k$) according to the following expression:

$$P_{i,j}^k = \frac{1}{Q_{i,j}^k} \quad k = H,D,A \quad i = B365,BW,GB,IW,LB,SB,SJ,VC,WH \quad (5.2)$$

where, in general:

$$\sum_{l=H,D,A} P_{i,j}^l > 1 \quad (5.3)$$

and the total take-out rate (r_i), the bookmaker's return, is:

$$r_i = \left[\frac{1}{N} \sum_j \sum_{l=H,D,A} P_{i,j}^l \right] - 1 \quad (5.4)$$

where N is the number of games, and r_i deconstructed into the contributions of each event:

$$r_i = r_i^H + r_i^D + r_i^A \quad (5.5)$$

In Table 5.7 we report the aggregate take-out rates for all the seasons included in the panel data set and the contribution of each event to the total. We can identify a clear pattern: the overall take-out rate is decreasing with time. In the period we consider, this rate moves from 10.7 per cent in the 2005/06 season to 7.4 per cent in the 2010/11 season, with an overall 9.5 per cent for the whole period. As mentioned above, we can deconstruct this take-out rate into the three components: 1.7 percentage points correspond to the home win bets, 4.9 points to the draw event and 2.8 points to the away win. This means that odds are not approximating the three events equally well. The difference between the observed frequencies and those implied by the odds are more important for the draw and the visitor's

Table 5.7 Average take-out rates by season

Season	Home win	Draw	Away win	Total
2005/06	0.075	0.025	0.006	0.107
2006/07	0.042	0.041	0.023	0.106
2007/08	0.014	0.070	0.017	0.101
2008/09	0.009	0.073	0.011	0.094
2009/10	−0.014	0.024	0.077	0.087
2010/11	−0.023	0.063	0.034	0.074
Total	0.017	0.049	0.028	0.095

Table 5.8   Average take-out rates by bookmaker

Bookmaker	Home win	Draw	Away win	Total
B365	0.010	0.042	0.020	0.072
BW	0.018	0.047	0.030	0.095
GB	0.011	0.047	0.023	0.081
IW	0.019	0.057	0.030	0.106
LB	0.026	0.053	0.035	0.114
SB	0.018	0.049	0.032	0.100
SJ	0.016	0.046	0.019	0.081
VC	0.019	0.047	0.029	0.095
WH	0.019	0.054	0.035	0.109
Total	0.017	0.049	0.028	0.095

win results. On the other hand, this pattern for the deconstruction of the overall rate is not uniform through the seasons. The part of the take-out rate associated with the home win is decreasing through the season. It accounted for almost 75 per cent of the total figure in the 2005/06 season and it is even negative for the last two seasons. This is compensated by an increase in the participation of the other two events in the overall figure and the draw seems to have, in general, the largest contribution.

When looking at the take-out rates by bookmakers in Table 5.8 we observe that in all cases the aggregate pattern of the draw having the largest contribution and the home win the smallest one is repeated. At the same time the aggregate rates show a substantial heterogeneity, moving from 7.2 per cent for B365 to 11.4 per cent for LB. In general, this difference in terms of the aggregate figures is uniformly distributed among the different types of events. B365 shows the smallest contributions for all three results and LB has the largest ones with the exception of the draw event.

The evidence of the take-out rates for the nine bookmakers and six seasons we are considering in this chapter allows us to analyse to what extent the favourite long-shot bias is present in the betting market for Spanish football. This bias is characterized by a systematic pattern in which bettors tend to undervalue events that are characterized by a high probability and overvalue those with a low probability.[15] As mentioned by Rossi (2011), there are several potential explanations behind the favourite long-shot bias: the concavity of the bettors' utility function, bettors' loss aversion, bettors' different weighting of gains and losses, biases in bettors' subjective probabilities, a supply side explanation of asymmetric information among traders or more casual evidence as the example of match rigging in the Italian football discussed by Rossi (2011). The existence of

this type of bias has been tested for several sports, in particular horserac-
ing, with different conclusions, although its existence seems to be quite
common.[16]

To provide evidence of the existence of this type of bias in the Spanish
football betting market, we follow the approach by Rossi (2011) and we
define three sets of games for each type of event (home win, draw and away
win) according to the values of the implied probabilities ($P_{i,j}^k$) coming from
the observed odds (low, medium and high implied probabilities). For each
bookmaker in each season we have 380 observations (odds) for each event.
We include the 30 observations with the smallest probabilities in the "low"
group, the 30 with the highest probabilities in the "high" group and the
remaining in the "medium" group.[17] We perform the analysis in two different ways: aggregating the odds (and implied probabilities) by season and
aggregating by bookmakers.[18] If there is evidence of the favourite long-shot
bias we should be finding that the take-out rates are higher for the subsets
with low probabilities than for the one associated to the highest probabilities.

In Tables 5.9a–c we report the take-out rates by season for the three
events and the three sets according to the values of the implied probabilities. The evidence is mainly in favour of the existence of this type of
favourite long-shot bias. The take-out rate is higher in the "low" group
than in the "high" group for the home win (Table 5.9a) and the draw (Table
5.9b) events but not in the case of the away win event (Table 5.9c). In fact,
the take-out rates for the "high" group in Table 5.9a are even negative for
the last seasons and the pattern has been reversed compared to what we
had in the first two seasons in our data set. Of course, the pattern is not
completely uniform and there are some seasons with some peculiar evidence, as it is the case of the 2008/09 season for the draw event, in which
the take-out rates are very high for all three groups and smaller in the
"low" group compared to that of the "high" group against the evidence
for the whole period. Finally, the evidence for the away win event should

Table 5.9a   Take-out rates for subgroups by season (home win)

Season	Low	Medium	High
2005/06	0.028	0.082	0.046
2006/07	−0.002	0.043	0.063
2007/08	−0.051	0.032	−0.105
2008/09	0.063	0.007	−0.024
2009/10	0.098	−0.020	−0.077
2010/11	0.050	−0.030	−0.006
Total	0.031	0.019	−0.018

Table 5.9b   Take-out rates for subgroups by season (draw)

Season	Low	Medium	High
2005/06	0.064	0.018	0.051
2006/07	0.058	0.040	0.020
2007/08	0.142	0.064	0.044
2008/09	0.077	0.067	0.129
2009/10	0.104	0.013	0.056
2010/11	0.063	0.063	0.052
Total	0.085	0.044	0.059

Table 5.9c   Take-out rates for subgroups by season (away win)

Season	Low	Medium	High
2005/06	0.005	0.003	0.036
2006/07	−0.019	0.021	0.076
2007/08	0.054	−0.004	0.196
2008/09	0.030	0.020	−0.116
2009/10	0.069	0.085	−0.013
2010/11	−0.036	0.037	0.077
Total	0.017	0.027	0.043

be qualified because the aggregated pattern is mainly due to two seasons (2007/08 and 2010/11), whereas in two other seasons (2008/09 and 2009/10) the pattern of the take-out rates is what we would expect in the presence of favourite long-shot bias.

In Tables 5.10a–c we report the take-out rates by bookmakers for the three events and the three sets according to the values of the implied probabilities. The evidence is clearer than that from the previous analysis by season, but goes in the same direction. For the home win and draw events the implications of the favourite long-shot bias are satisfied (higher take-out rates for the "low" group than for the "high" group) for all bookmakers and even for the home win event the take-out rates of the "high" group are all negative. On the other hand, for the away win event the take-out rates are higher in the "high" group, with the exception of the bookmaker IW, which has the largest rate in the "low" group and is higher than that of the "high" group. Consequently, we can conclude that there is substantial evidence of the existence of favourite long-shot bias in the Spanish football betting market, but more research should be devoted to taking into account the specific characteristics of the odds distributions.

Table 5.10a   Take-out rates for subgroups by bookmaker (home win)

Bookmaker	Low	Medium	High
B365	0.027	0.010	−0.008
BW	0.026	0.020	−0.010
GB	0.027	0.012	−0.021
IW	0.055	0.021	−0.043
LB	0.037	0.028	−0.012
SB	0.026	0.020	−0.010
SJ	0.021	0.018	−0.013
VC	0.028	0.022	−0.022
Total	0.031	0.019	−0.018

Table 5.10b   Take-out rates for subgroups by bookmaker (draw)

Bookmaker	Low	Medium	High
B365	0.070	0.038	0.050
BW	0.090	0.041	0.067
GB	0.100	0.040	0.073
IW	0.085	0.052	0.081
LB	0.092	0.048	0.071
SB	0.083	0.044	0.066
SJ	0.090	0.042	0.036
VC	0.066	0.047	0.027
Total	0.085	0.044	0.059

Table 5.10c   Take-out rates for groups by bookmaker (away win)

Bookmaker	Low	Medium	High
B365	0.012	0.019	0.042
BW	0.024	0.028	0.056
GB	−0.002	0.025	0.033
IW	0.028	0.032	0.012
LB	0.016	0.035	0.059
SB	0.023	0.031	0.058
SJ	0.016	0.018	0.041
VC	0.020	0.029	0.039
Total	0.017	0.027	0.043

5.3   ANALYSIS OF THE FORECASTING PERFORMANCE

There have been several papers in the literature trying to analyse whether the forecasts of the results of professional sports games by experts are better than those based on statistical models, i.e. whether experts process the information included in the models in a similar way, adding some specific information not captured by the observed variables.[19] Forrest et al. (2005) perform a similar exercise but using published odds on football games as proxies for the experts' views. The evidence from these studies is mixed in the sense that it is not clear that forecasts by experts are worse than those obtained from a statistical model.

In this section, following an approach similar to that used by Forrest et al. (2005), we try to bring evidence about the extent to which forecasts based on football fans' bets on La Quiniela are better than those based on the odds from different bookmakers. We use two approaches to measure the forecasting performance of bookmakers (through odds) and bettors of La Quiniela: one based on the use of a modified version of the Brier scores and the second one based on a probabilistic model where implied frequencies (from the bookmakers' odds) and observed frequencies (La Quiniela) are used as explanatory factors of the result of a football match.

The Brier score (BS), introduced by Brier (1950) when verifying weather forecasts, is basically the mean square error associated with the forecast of whether a particular result k happens in match j (R_j^k), where k is either a home win, a draw or an away win, by using a specific predictor. In our case we use the implied probabilities from the odds of the different bookmakers ($P_{i,j}^k$) except for La Quiniela where we use the observed frequencies associated with each particular result. The three Brier scores we can define for each predictor (bookmaker) and each season have the following definition:

$$BS_i^k = \frac{\sum_{j=1}^{N}(R_j^k - P_{i,j}^k)^2}{N}$$

$$k = H,D,A \quad i = B365,BW,GB,IW,LB,SB,SJ,VC,WH,LQ \quad (5.6)$$

where R_j^k is a 0–1 variable associated with a particular result k in match j and N is the number of matches. By definition the original Brier scores take values between 0 (perfect forecast) and 1 (worst forecast).

We propose a modified version of the Brier scores which takes into account the fact that the variance of the errors is not constant but depends on $P_{i,j}^k$. We weight each error by the inverse of its standard deviation, to allow for the possibility of giving more weight to those errors associated to forecasts ($P_{i,j}^k$) close to either 1 or 0, i.e. without too much uncertainty. The modified version of the Brier score (*MBS*) is the following:

$$MBS_i^k = \frac{\sum_{j=1}^{N} \frac{(R_j^k - P_{i,j}^k)^2}{P_{i,j}^k(1 - P_{i,j}^k)}}{N} \qquad (5.7)$$

In Tables 5.11a–c we report the values of the modified Brier scores for the three events by season and bookmaker, including La Quiniela. The forecasts by experts seem to improve through seasons, in particular for the home win event, although the evidence is a bit more erratic in the case of a draw. There is also a strange result, which applies to all, in the 2009/10 season, with very low values of the modified Brier score. On the other

Table 5.11a Modified Brier scores for forecasting performance (home win)

Bookmaker	2005/06	2006/07	2007/08	2008/09	2009/10	2010/11
B365	0.968	1.018	0.991	0.959	0.937	0.951
BW	0.961	1.031	1.005	0.973	0.941	0.946
GB	0.962	1.019	0.991	0.959	0.936	0.947
IW	0.955	1.017	0.986	0.949	0.935	0.953
LB	0.964	1.013	0.996	0.965	0.940	0.951
SB	0.968	1.019	0.995	0.962	0.937	0.951
SJ	0.969	1.022	0.996	0.954	0.936	0.952
VC	0.958	1.008	0.993	0.962	0.934	0.953
WH	0.960	1.012	1.024	0.959	0.933	0.948
L-Q	1.102	1.132	1.074	1.034	1.043	1.048

Table 5.11b Modified Brier scores for forecasting performance (draw)

Bookmaker	2005/06	2006/07	2007/08	2008/09	2009/10	2010/11
B365	1.008	0.966	0.887	0.873	0.979	0.876
BW	1.007	0.975	0.874	0.875	0.985	0.870
GB	0.998	0.963	0.876	0.866	0.968	0.867
IW	0.994	0.947	0.873	0.856	0.974	0.865
LB	1.009	0.964	0.885	0.876	0.972	0.868
SB	1.002	0.971	0.884	0.868	0.980	0.876
SJ	1.000	0.971	0.874	0.866	0.977	0.876
VC	1.015	0.970	0.882	0.874	0.968	0.878
WH	0.993	0.958	0.866	0.873	0.973	0.858
L-Q	1.122	1.016	0.948	0.896	1.086	0.949

*Table 5.11c   Modified Brier scores for forecasting performance (away
              win)*

Bookmaker	2005/06	2006/07	2007/08	2008/09	2009/10	2010/11
B365	1.061	1.034	1.098	1.006	0.762	1.033
BW	1.060	1.047	1.087	1.005	0.764	0.982
GB	1.068	1.022	1.078	0.995	0.764	0.985
IW	1.026	1.035	1.069	1.002	0.761	0.976
LB	1.063	1.025	1.089	0.991	0.764	0.979
SB	1.054	1.018	1.079	0.984	0.759	0.973
SJ	1.068	1.042	1.106	1.036	0.778	1.013
VC	1.048	1.007	1.086	0.984	0.766	1.048
WH	1.040	1.011	1.083	0.990	0.764	0.984
L-Q	1.328	1.264	1.276	1.169	0.904	1.249

hand, forecasts from bookmakers seem to work better than those from
the observed frequencies in La Quiniela, in particular for the away win
event.[20]

To corroborate the evidence from the modified Brier scores we estimate
a model for each bookmaker where the dependent variable is the result of
a football game and the explanatory variables are the implied probabilities
or the observed frequencies of the results. Given that each football match
has three possible results,[21] we define as our dependent variable (Y_j) a qualitative variable with three possible values (3 = home win; 2 = draw; 1 =
away win) that are subject to a specific "order". This is why for each bookmaker we use an ordered Logit model that has the following definition:[22]

$$L_j^* = X_j'\beta + \varepsilon_j$$
$$Y_j = 1 \quad if \quad L_j^* < \mu_1$$
$$Y_j = 2 \quad if \quad \mu_1 \leq L_j^* < \mu_2$$
$$Y_j = 3 \quad if \quad \mu_2 \leq L_j^* \tag{5.8}$$

where X_j' is the vector of explanatory variables, which in our case includes
the odds associated with the home win and the draw, but not the away win
odds to avoid multicollinearity problems; β, μ_1 and μ_2 are parameters to be
estimated and ε_j is the error term capturing unobserved factors affecting
the result of a match and it is assumed to have a logistic distribution.[23]

In Table 5.12 we report some statistics for the goodness of fit of the
ordered models estimated for the different bookmakers. The base model
includes the odds associated with the home win and the draw, and we also
estimate a model including season dummies. We use the same sample for

Table 5.12   Explanatory power of the ordered Logit models by bookmaker

Bookmaker	Base model		Base model + season dummies	
	Log L	Pseudo-R^2	Log L	Pseudo-R^2
B365	−2,077.54	0.070	−2,071.99	0.073
BW	−2,083.90	0.068	−2,078.11	0.070
GB	−2,080.05	0.069	−2,074.09	0.072
IW	−2,081.01	0.069	−2,076.05	0.071
LB	−2,087.07	0.066	−2,081.36	0.069
SB	−2,080.29	0.068	−2,077.37	0.070
SJ	−2,081.70	0.069	−2,076.51	0.071
VC	−2,076.85	0.071	−2,071.79	0.073
WH	−2,080.47	0.069	−2,075.75	0.071
L-Q	−2,104.66	0.058	−2,098.82	0.061

all the bookmakers and since the dependent variable is the same for all the models we can compare the non-nested specifications with the values of the log likelihood function, which is equivalent to using the Akaike Information Criterion, given that the number of parameters to be estimated is the same for all the models (bookmakers).

We can point out the following pieces of evidence from the statistics in Table 5.12. First, corroborating what we obtained when using the modified Brier scores, the fit of the model using frequencies from La Quiniela (log L = −2104.7) is worse than that of the other models using odds by bookmakers (log L higher than −2087.07 in all the cases). This finding is also verified if we look at the values of the pseudo-R^2. As usual with microdata, these values are small but we can appreciate a difference between bookmakers' models and the model using information from La Quiniela.[24] Second, the basic results are qualitatively the same if we include a set of season dummies to control the time effect. The null hypothesis of the coefficients of these dummies being equal to zero is rejected in all cases at a 10 per cent significance level, and at 5 per cent for some, but not all, the cases. The predictive power of the different bookmakers looks very similar, although VC and B365 seem to perform better than the others.

We also estimated ordered Logit models for the different seasons in our data set aggregating the information from the different bookmakers. The results are reported in Table 5.13 and they allow us to identify a clear trend in terms of the predictive performance of the estimated models. A substantial increase in the value of the pseudo-R^2 can be identified for the last two seasons in the sample (10.5 per cent on average) compared with the performance in the previous four (around 5 per cent on average).[25]

Table 5.13   Explanatory power of the ordered Logit models by season

Season	Pseudo-R^2
2005/06	0.046
2006/07	0.041
2007/08	0.035
2008/09	0.076
2009/10	0.109
2010/11	0.100

Bookmakers seem to learn about the determinants of the result of a match and this information is incorporated into the odds proposed.

5.4   CONCLUDING REMARKS

Overall, the empirical analysis of information and forecasting performance on Spanish football betting odds suggests that experts (bookmakers) seem to be better at estimating football results than the "crowd" (football pools bettors).

By comparing the odds offered by the nine bookmakers in our data set, their distributions seem quite similar in their first two moments. However, an additional examination of the coefficients of correlation between the odds of a particular outcome for pairs of bookmakers (including La Quiniela) hints at La Quiniela to be a "different thing". A further study of the probabilities derived from the odds suggests that they do not properly approximate the three possible examined results (home win, draw and away win) in the same way. Even though the predictive power of the different bookmakers looks very similar, the analysis of the forecasting performance through both the calculated values of the modified Brier scores and the goodness of fit of the estimated ordered models shows that forecasts from bookmakers seem to work better than those from La Quiniela bettors. However, the fact that the data correspond to the number of tickets but not exactly to the number of bets could have an influence on the reported evidence.

Notwithstanding, global explanatory power improves as time goes by, perhaps as a consequence of the existence of a learning process.

Substantial evidence of the existence of favourite long-shot bias in the betting market for Spanish football is also found.

NOTES

* This study was funded by the Consejería de Economía y Empleo del Principado de Asturias (FC-15-GRUPIN 14-064).

1. On average, more than 1.6 million of La Quiniela tickets/coupons were sold for each fixture during the 2005–11 period. This leads to close to 20 million bets placed on each La Quiniela fixture.

2. The pari-mutuel betting system puts a type of implicit tax on wagering called the take-out. The take-out rate is then the percentage of each betting pool that is withheld by the operator (bookmaker). In fixed odds betting markets a similar term is overround that represents bookmakers' expected profit as shown by Cortis (2015). It is equivalent to a commission and can be calculated as the amount by which the sum of the percentages (relative probabilities) derived from the odds exceeds 100 per cent. Even though these two different terms are not exactly the same, in this chapter we opt to use the take-out rate as the general term.

3. This game's name is derived from the fact that bettors are required to predict the number of goals that will be scored by the teams involved in a particular football match.

4. It should be noted that not all the coupons include Spanish First Division games; occasionally the coupon list of games is composed of Second Division and Second Division B games, national teams or even teams from other European leagues such as the *English Premier League*. In addition, some specific fixtures in the pools referring to European Champions League or other international competitions have also been introduced.

5. This is in contrast to what happens in the English football betting market where the odds are quoted as *a* to *b* for each particular event. This means that a bet of *b* in a particular event gets a return of *a* if the event occurs.

6. See the presentations in the *1ª Conferència Acadèmica Ernest Lluch d'Economia i Futbol* (Fundació Ernest Lluch and FC Barcelona, 2013) for the most recent discussion about the competitive balance in the Spanish Football League.

7. See Sauer (1998) for a complete review of the economics of wagering markets.

8. Notice that in this particular case we are calculating a kind of odds which do not include the take-out rate by the bookmaker, as included in the odds offered by the bookmakers (our original data). Consequently, they are higher than those including the take-out rate.

9. In fact, in La Quiniela, as mentioned in the previous section, bets correspond to a set of 15 games, not individual games, and the take-out rate by the public company in charge of La Quiniela is larger than the ones we will observe for bookmakers.

10. The estimated odds for La Quiniela are not included in Table 5.4 given that, as mentioned above, they cannot be properly compared to those of the bookmakers.

11. The tests are performed based on the assumption that the distributions of the odds are homoscedastic.

12. Notice that the figures in the row "Total" are just half of the total number of rejections in each column. This is because each rejection of odds equality within each pair affects two bookmakers.

13. Rossi (2011) also performs an alternative approach based on running the regression of the odds of one event for a particular bookmaker on the odds associated with another bookmaker. The null hypotheses to be tested are: the slope coefficient is equal to one and, the second one, the intercept is equal to zero. In our case that would imply running 36 regressions. All the rejections are associated with the null hypothesis corresponding to the intercept, which gives us evidence of a very high linear correlation between the odds of different bookmakers but with different levels (the intercept is different from zero).

14. Notice that the correlation matrices are symmetric. This is why in Tables 5.6a–c we only report the coefficients of correlation for half of the matrix.

15. See Shin (1991, 1992) for how insider trading affects optimal odds by bookmakers.

16. See Thaler and Ziemba (1988), Vaughan Williams and Patton (1997), Cain et al. (2000), Schnytzer and Weinberg (2008) and Woodland and Woodland (2011), among others, as

17. We use the proportions 30/380 for the size of the extreme groups instead of 1/6 (more or less defined by one standard deviation) used by Rossi because in our case the distributions of the odds by bookmaker and season were not symmetrical, generating some distortion in the analysis. Some further research should be devoted to this asymmetrical distribution issue.
18. In the analysis of the favourite long-shot bias we have not included the bookmaker WH since we miss almost 25 per cent of the observations for the season 2007/08.
19. See Forrest and Simmons (2000) and Boulier and Stekler (2003), among others.
20. As mentioned, information from La Quiniela corresponds to tickets, not to bets, and this could be worsening the forecasting power.
21. This approach is similar to that used by Forrest and Simmons (2008), but they use only home and away win bets and, consequently, they estimate a binary Probit model.
22. See, for instance, Cameron and Trivedi (2005). It is well known that there are no substantial differences between using a Probit or a Logit version of the ordered model. In our case there are no substantial differences depending on the distributional assumptions of the error term, i.e. whether we use a Logit or a Probit ordered mode.
23. Rossi (2011) uses a similar approach but he estimated a multinomial Logit model. We also estimated this alternative model and the results do not change but from the goodness of fit perspective and also the "ordered" nature of the attributes of the dependent variable, the ordered version is preferred.
24. Rossi (2011) reports and emphasizes the high values (above 80 per cent) of the pseudo-R^2 in the multinomial models he estimated. This is very surprising, and doubtful given the usual experience, although this does not invalidate the basic results he reports.
25. In Table 5.13 we do not report the value of the log likelihood given that the sample size is different in each season.

REFERENCES

Boulier, B. and H. Stekler (2003), "Predicting the Outcomes of National Football League Games", *International Journal of Forecasting*, **19**, 257–270.

Brier, G.W. (1950), "Verification of Weather Forecasts Expressed in Terms of Probability", *Monthly Weather Review*, **78**, 1–3.

Cain, M., D. Law and D. Peel (2000), "The Favourite Long-Shot Bias and Market Efficiency in UK Football Betting", *Scottish Journal of Political Economy*, **47**, 25–36.

Cameron, A.C. and P.K. Trivedi (2005), *Microeconometrics. Methods and Applications*, Cambridge University Press, New York.

Cortis, D. (2015), "Expected Values and Variances in Bookmakers Payouts: A Theoretical Approach towards Setting Limits on Odds", *The Journal of Prediction Markets*, **9**, 1–14.

Forrest, D. and L. Pérez (2013), "The Football Pools", in L. Vaughan and D. Siegel (eds) *The Oxford Handbook of the Economics of Gambling*, Oxford University Press: USA, pp. 147–162.

Forrest, D., J. Goddard and R. Simmons (2005), "Odds-Setters as Forecasters: The Case of English Football", *International Journal of Forecasting*, **21**, 551–564.

Forrest, D. and R. Simmons (2000), "Forecasting Sport: The Behaviour and Performance Football Tipsters", *International Journal of Forecasting*, **16**, 317–331.

Forrest, D. and R. Simmons (2008), "Sentiment in Betting Market on Spanish Football", *Applied Economics*, **40**, 19–126.

Fundació Ernest Lluch and FC Barcelona (2013), *L'impacte de la crisi al futbol. Estratègies adaptatives*, First Ernest Lluch Academic Conference on Economy and Football. http://www.fundacioernestlluch.org/files/050-112722-LACRISIALFUTBOLmarca.pdf.

García, J. and P. Rodríguez (2007), "The Demand for Football Pools in Spain: The Role of Price, Prizes and the Composition of the Coupon", *Journal of Sports Economics*, **8**, 334–354.

García, J., L. Pérez and P. Rodríguez (2008), "Football Pool Sales: How Important is a Football Club in the Top Divisions?", *International Journal of Sport Finance*, **3**, 167–176.

Rossi, M. (2011), "Match Rigging and the Favourite Long-Shot Bias in the Italian Football Betting Market", *International Journal of Sport Finance*, **6**, 317–334.

Sauer, R.D. (1998), "The Economics of Wagering Markets", *Journal of Economic Literature*, **36**, 2021–2064.

Schnytzer, A. and G. Weinberg (2008), "Testing for Home Team and Favourite Biases in the Australian Rules Football Fixed-Odds and Point Spread Betting Markets", *Journal of Sports Economics*, **9**, 173–190.

Shin, H.S. (1991), "Optimal Odds against Insider Traders", *Economic Journal*, **101**, 1179–1185.

Shin, H.S. (1992), "Measuring the Incidence of Insider Trading in a Market for State-Contingent Claims", *Economic Journal*, **102**, 426–435.

Surowiecki, J. (2004), *The Wisdom of Crowds*, Doubleday: New York.

Thaler, R.H. and W.T. Ziemba (1988), "Anomalies-parimutuel betting markets: Racetrack and Lotteries", *Journal of Economic Perspectives*, **2**, 161–174.

Vaughan Williams, W.L. and D. Patton (1997), "Why is there a Favourite Long Shot Bias in British Racetrack Betting Markets", *Economic Journal*, **107**, 150–158.

Woodland, L.M. and B.M. Woodland (2011), "The Reverse Favorite–Longshot Bias in the National Hockey League: Do Bettors Still Score on Longshots?", *Journal of Sports Economics*, **12**, 106–117.

6. New empirical evidence on the Tote–SP anomaly and its implications for models of risky choice in gambling markets

Babatunde Buraimo, David Peel and Robert Simmons

6.1 INTRODUCTION

As Thaler and Ziemba (1988) pointed out in an early contribution, wagering markets share many of the characteristics of other asset markets, such as a large number of investors (wagers or bettors) with readily available cheap sources of public information, as well as insiders with private information. Wagering markets also have a simpler structure than is usual in other asset markets in that a wager has a well-defined termination point at which its value becomes certain.

Perhaps the least well-known example of an apparent market anomaly is that suggested by Gabriel and Marsden (1990).[1] In most countries returns to winning bets are determined by pari-mutuel pools where a total pool is shared out among winners in proportion to stakes after the operator has deducted a fixed percentage commission. This type of pari-mutuel betting is prevalent in Europe and North America. However, in the UK there are two parallel betting markets. On-course and off-course bookmakers offer fixed odds while pari-mutuel odds are also available from the pool known as the totalizer or Tote.[2] Gabriel and Marsden examined the returns to winning bets in the two markets during the 1978 British horse racing season and reported the striking finding that average pari-mutuel returns for winning horses exceeded the average returns from bookmakers (at final odds). They suggested that since both betting systems involved similar risks and the payoffs were widely reported, their empirical evidence was consistent with market inefficiency. As Sauer (1998) noted in his survey, this result calls for an explanation.

That is the purpose in this chapter. Employing two data sets we report a new empirical relationship between Tote and starting price (henceforth SP) returns and provide an explanation for the apparent anomaly. For the 1996 season we have 2096 horse races with 19,273 runners[3] with data on bookmakers and Tote odds for both winning and losing horses. This is a unique data set assembled by Bruce and Johnson (2000) in that all previous research, as in Gabriel and Marsden, only had Tote odds for winning horses. Our second data set is a sample of 52,919 horse races over the seasons 2003–12 with 543,048 runners where we have SP for all horses but only Tote data for the winners.[4] This is the largest data set assembled to investigate the relationship between Tote and SP returns.

The rest of the chapter is structured as follows. In section 6.2 we assess the literature on the relationship between Tote and SP. Section 6.3 offers a theoretical exposition of the Tote–SP relationship while section 6.4 reports the empirical results. Section 6.5 offers discussions while the final section (6.6) concludes the chapter.

6.2 NEW ANALYSIS OF THE RELATIONSHIP BETWEEN TOTE AND SP RETURNS

Subsequent to Gabriel and Marsden's study, a number of authors have analysed the relationship between Tote and SP returns solely for winning horses in a variety of different horse racing data sets (Blackburn and Pierson (2003); Cain et al. (2003); Peel and Law (2009)). This research reveals that the relationship between Tote returns and bookmaker returns is more complicated than that implied in the Gabriel and Marsden study. Tote odds are on average higher than bookmaker's odds for longshots but the reverse holds for more favoured horses. However, contrary to the assertion of Gabriel and Marsden, betting with the Tote as opposed to bookmakers is fundamentally different since the bettor is certain of the bookmaker payouts but uncertain of the Tote pay-out. While bettors have some limited information on the pattern of on-course Tote betting via Tote boards in the UK, off-course bettors have no such information and the Tote payout is determined after the race ends, employing the total amounts bet, both off-course and on-course. Of course, if bettors knew both the bookmakers and Tote odds they would receive on a winning bet then any discrepancy in odds would seemingly imply bettor irrationality and market inefficiency.

Tables 6.1 and 6.3 reveal the standard favourite longshot bias in the SP odds of bookmakers in both data sets as documented in numerous other studies of the UK horse race betting market (see e.g. Dowie (1976); Vaughan Williams (1999); and Law and Peel (2002)). In Table 6.2 we are

Table 6.1   All runners in 1996 horse races ranked by SP

SP	Mean SP	Mean Tote	Proportion of Win	Runner	Maximum Tote	Minimum Tote	% Return SP	Return Tote
SP < 1	**0.635**	**0.605**	**0.622**	**304**	**1.4**	**0.1**	**1.70**	**−0.002**
1/1	1.0	0.954	0.487	76	1.6	0.5	−2.63	−4.87
11/8	1.375	1.287	0.410	83	1.9	0.5	−2.71	−6.33
6/4	1.5	1.426	0.318	110	11.6	0.7	−20.46	−22.08
2/1	2.0	1.969	0.312	253	4.7	0.6	−6.32	−7.29
3/1	3.0	2.898	0.239	443	13.3	1.0	−4.29	−6.72
9/2	4.5	4.43	0.158	573	11.7	2	−12.65	−13.80
5/1	5.0	4.99	0.135	728	13.1	2.3	−18.41	−18.54
11/2	5.5	5.55	0.121	454	26.1	2.3	−21.26	−20.39
6/1	6.0	6.16	0.126	773	33	1.7	−11.26	−9.06
10/1	10	11.56	0.074	1037	80	3.1	−18.32	−6.77
20/1	20	28.541	0.0183	1311	156.8	5.8	−61.55	−45.93
33/1	33	55.355	0.0084	1315	600.3	5.6	−71.56	−52.86
50/1	**50**	**75.44**	**0.0042**	**713**	**713.1**	**7.9**	**−78.54**	**−67.83**

Table 6.2   All runners in 1996 ranked by Tote odds

Tote Odds	Mean Tote	Mean SP	% Win	Runners	% Return Tote	% Return SP
Tote < 1	**0.629**	**0.990**	**0.569**	**392**	**−7.33**	**13.20**
1 < 2	1.497	1.862	0.342	1,016	−14.73	−2.26
2 < 3	2.464	2.892	0.251	1,322	−13.00	−2.25
3 < 4	3.448	3.948	0.184	1,250	−18.16	−8.96
4 < 5	7.783	8.091	0.098	1,246	−24.88	−17.91
5 < 6	5.442	5.946	0.124	1,037	−19.86	−13.60
6 < 10	7.783	8.091	0.098	3,207	−14.00	−10.99
10 < 20	14.305	13.611	0.059	4,210	−9.54	−15.70
20 < 33	25.525	22.686	0.026	2,333	−31.78	−39.08
33 < 50	40.351	32.491	0.015	1,429	−39.23	−50.78
50 and over	95.153	47.161	0.008	1,731	−22.23	−61.05

able to examine the favourite longshot bias ranked on tote odds, given that we have Tote data for all runners in this data set. As with US totalizer returns (see e.g. Weitzman (1965); Ali (1977); and Golec and Tamarkin (1998)) we also observe a favourite longshot bias. However, comparison with Table 6.1 shows that the favourite longshot bias is much more pronounced in the bookmaker fixed odds market than in the Tote pari-mutuel market. This implies a crossover point in relative odds, ceteris paribus, where odds are superior in one form of betting.[5]

Table 6.3   All runners from 2003–12

SP	Mean SP	Proportion of Win	Runners	% Return SP
SP < 1	**0.650**	**0.573**	**6,263**	**−7.36**
Evens	1.000	0.471	1,170	−5.81
11–8	1.375	0.402	1,608	−4.52
6–4	1.500	0.364	2,048	−9.06
2–1	2.000	0.302	4,938	−9.48
3–1	3.000	0.227	9,946	−9.31
9–2	4.500	0.166	16,577	−8.73
5–1	5.000	0.146	16,435	−12.20
6–1	6.000	0.122	16,863	−14.82
10–1	10.000	0.075	23,149	−17.32
20–1	20.000	0.035	31,157	−26.40
33–1	33.000	0.017	30,345	−41.51
50–1	50.000	0.010	18,413	−50.70

Table 6.4   1996 winner

SP	Mean SP	Mean Tote	Races	Maximum Tote	Minimum Tote
SP < 1	**0.585**	**0.560**	**189**	**1.4**	**0.1**
1/1	1	0.943	37	1.3	0.5
11/8	1.375	1.244	34	1.9	0.5
6/4	1.5	1.29	35	3.8	0.8
2/1	2	1.914	79	3.3	1
3/1	3	2.840	106	4.6	1.5
9/2	4.5	4.400	91	9.4	2
5/1	5	5.083	99	9.5	2.7
11/2	5.5	5.502	55	9.5	2.9
6/1	6	6.309	98	10.5	2.7
10/1	10	11.442	77	18.8	6.3
20/1	20	24.708	24	53	12
33/1	33	51.700	11	178.6	17
50/1	**50**	**50.267**	**3**	**64**	**31.2**

Tables 6.4 and 6.5 compare average SP and Tote returns for winners in the two data sets. Both reveal a similar crossover point in relative average returns. The maximum and minimum Tote returns associated with the bookmaker odds reveal the uncertainty of return in betting on the Tote rather than at known bookmaker odds, as also noted by Cain et al. (2003).

The economics of sports betting

Table 6.5 Winners from 2003–12 horse races, comparison of mean SP and Tote odds

SP	Mean SP	Mean Tote	Runners	Maximum Tote	Minimum Tote
SP < 1	**0.618**	**0.612**	**3587**	**3.10**	**0.02**
Evens	1.000	0.978	551	2.30	0.10
11–8	1.375	1.304	647	3.00	0.20
6–4	1.500	1.406	745	2.90	0.40
2–1	2.000	1.977	1,490	7.60	0.50
3–1	3.000	2.982	2,255	7.60	0.30
9–2	4.500	4.507	2,751	13.10	1.30
5–1	5.000	5.135	2,405	15.50	1.30
6–1	6.000	6.237	2,052	13.70	0.60
10–1	10.000	11.238	1,740	23.90	2.90
20–1	20.000	24.678	1,092	80.70	5.50
33–1	33.000	41.375	522	107.30	8.50
50–1	50.000	60.124	178	125.20	17.10

6.3 THE TOTE–SP RELATIONSHIP

The relationship between Tote returns on the ith winning greyhound, T_i, and the starting price with the bookmakers of the ith winning horse, SP_i, have been examined in previous researchers (see e.g. Gabriel and Marsden (1990); Blackburn and Pierson (1995); and Cain et al. (2001)) by running the regressions

$$T_i - SP_i = \lambda + \varepsilon_t \qquad (6.1)$$

and

$$T_i = \alpha + \beta SP_i + u_t \qquad (6.2)$$

where T_i is the Tote odds on the ith runner, SP_i is the bookmaker starting price odds on the ith runner, α, β and γ are constants and u_t. and ε_t are error terms. However, these regressions do not reflect the relationship implied from assumptions about how odds are determined in both markets. Given this, we derive a new relationship between Tote and bookmaker returns.

We assume the bookmaker starting price on the ith horse is given by

$$SP_i \equiv \frac{(1 - b_i)}{p_i} - 1 \qquad (6.3)$$

where b_i is the margin of the bookmaker on the ith horse, which could be negative for short priced favourites but is of course generally negative, and p_i is the objective probability of the bookmakers of the horse winning. Though we assume that bookmakers set odds on the basis of the objective probability this is not a necessary feature of our analysis as becomes clearer below. We assume the variable margin b_i occurs as a consequence of insider activity as set out theoretically in a series of papers by Shin (1991, 1992, 1993). Shin assumes that bookmakers act as market makers determining odds in the presence of a percentage of insider traders and a percentage of outsiders. Shin demonstrates that the odds set by bookmakers have to generate enough revenue from outsiders to pay insiders their winnings and that the odds exhibit the favourite longshot bias.

The Tote odds T_i on the ith horse are given by

$$T_i = \frac{(1-t)\sum_{i=1}^{n} s_i}{s_i} - 1 = \frac{(1-t_i)}{p_i^s} - 1 \qquad (6.4)$$

where $p_i^s = \frac{s_i}{\sum_{i=1}^{n} s_i}$ t_i is the constant Tote margin and constant across horses, s_i the stake on the ith runner, p_i^s is the market determined probability of bettors and n the number of runners.

We assume the market determined probability p_i^s is a multiple of the objective probability

$$p_i^s \equiv k_i p_i \qquad (6.5)$$

From manipulation of equations (6.3), (6.4) and (6.5) we can obtain that

$$\frac{T_i - SP_i}{1 + SP_i} = \frac{(1-t) - (1-b_i)k_i}{k_i(1-b_i)} \qquad (6.6)$$

In the models of Weitzman (1965), Ali (1977) and Quandt (1987), employed to explain the favourite longshot bias in US Totalizer betting markets, bettors are assumed to determine their betting wealth and are risk-seeking in all areas of their allocations on the basis of the objective probability. The assumed risk-seeking behaviour creates a favourite longshot bias so that the market determined probability is a biased forecast of the objective probability of a horse winning.

Jullien and Salanié (2000) report that Cumulative Prospect Theory (CPT) of Tversky and Kahneman (1992) provides a good fit for US totalizer data, and Snowberg and Wolfers (2010) also report that a misperception of probability approach is supported by US data over a neoclassical based approach such as that of Ali (1977) or Quandt (1987). In CPT the subjective probability is assumed to be a nonlinear function of the objective probability via a weighting function. This implies that in equation (6.5) k_i is a nonlinear function of the objective probability.

Since the objective probability can be expressed in terms of the SP on the ith horse and the margin on the ith horse from equation (6.3), the right hand side of equation (6.6) is a nonlinear function of SP_i, b_i. We assume that bookmaker margin on the ith horse, due to the presence of insiders in the market, is a positive function of the bookmaker odds, SP_i, consistent with the favourite–longshot bias. We also assume that the margin on a horse, b_i, is positively related to the gross bookmaker margin in a race measured as the over round minus one. The bookmaker's gross margin is a good proxy for the Shin measure of the degree of overall insider dealing in a race (Vaughan Williams and Patton, 1997).

Our assumptions imply that the difference between Tote and bookmaker odds for a particular horse will be a nonlinear function of the bookmaker's odds and the bookmaker aggregate margin in the race.[6] While we experimented with higher order approximations of equation (6.6) a parsimonious empirical representation was provided by a first order Taylor expansion

$$\frac{T_i - SP_i}{1 + SP_i} = \beta_0 + \beta_1 m_i + \beta_2 SP_i + \beta_3 SP_i m_i + \phi_i \tag{6.7}$$

where m_i is the bookmaker aggregate margin, which is equal to the over round minus one and ϕ_i is the error term. Clearly equation (6.7) has a very different form to the regressions reported by Gabriel and Marsden and those reported in previous research.

6.4   REGRESSION RESULTS

We report estimates of equations (6.1), (6.2) and (6.7) in Tables 6.6 to 6.8, employing both OLS with White corrected standard errors and also median quantile estimates given the significant degree of non-normality indicated by the Jarque–Bera test statistic in the least squares regressions. For convenience, we also report estimates of equations (6.1) and (6.2).

The regression results for our new relationship equation (6.7) have the same sign pattern for both data sets and the variables are all significant at normal levels except in the winner-only regressions for the 1996 sample. The regressions reveal that the bookmaker margin, a measure of insider activity in the Shin models, plays an economically and statistically significant role in determining the difference between expected Tote and bookmaker odds. Not surprisingly, as the margin rises Tote odds increase relative to bookmaker odds, ceteris paribus. Estimates of equations (6.1) and (6.2) have

Table 6.6   Models for $T_i - SP_i = \lambda + \varepsilon_t$

	(1) All Horses OLS Horses 1996	(2) All Horses Median Horses 1996	(3) Position = 1 OLS Horses 1996	(4) Position = 1 Median Horses 1996	(5) Position = 1 OLS Horses 2003–12	(6) Position = 1 Median Horses 2003–12
Constant	5.193*** (19.065)	0.400*** (20.730)	0.669*** (6.004)	−0.050*** (−3.064)	0.785*** (44.698)	0.090*** (21.431)
Observations	19,273	19,273	2,096	2,096	52,919	52,919

Notes:
White adjusted *t* statistics in parentheses.
* $p < 0.10$; ** $p < 0.05$; *** $p < 0.01$.

Table 6.7   Models for $T_i = \alpha + \beta SP_i + u_t$

	(1) All Horses OLS Horses 1996	(2) All Horses Median Horses 1996	(3) Position = 1 OLS Horses 1996	(4) Position = 1 Median Horses 1996	(5) Position = 1 OLS Horses 2003–12	(6) Position = 1 Median Horses 2003–12
SP Odds	1.126*** (13.333)	1.192*** (110.39)	1.276*** (16.054)	1.106*** (92.865)	1.180*** (82.053)	1.151*** (946.764)
Constant	3.294*** (3.034)	−0.640*** (12.23)	−0.843*** (−2.445)	−0.318*** (−9.885)	−0.427*** (−5.009)	−0.376*** (−30.166)
Adjusted R^2	0.228			0.693		0.852
Pseudo R^2		0.474		0.652		0.705
Jarque–Bera	2.71e+10		10,072,281		4.0e+07	
Observations	19,273	19,273	2,096	2,096	52,919	52,919

Notes:
White adjusted *t* statistics in parentheses.
* $p < 0.10$; ** $p < 0.05$; *** $p < 0.01$.

the same qualitative pattern as reported in previous research. The positive and significant estimates of the coefficients in equation (6.1) would suggest that Tote odds were superior to bookmakers on average at all odds and this was the basis of Gabriel and Marsden's claim of a market anomaly in their 1978 data set. However, as Table 6.1 and the median estimates in Table 6.8 reveal, this is incorrect and demonstrates how OLS regression methods can be highly influenced by extreme Tote returns relative to SP, and a consequent flawed interpretation can arise. The empirical results also

Table 6.8 *Models for* $\dfrac{T_i - SP_i}{1 + SP_i} = \beta_0 + \beta_1 m_i + \beta_2 SP_i + \beta_3 SP_i m_i + \phi_i$

	(1) All Horses OLS Horses 1996	(2) All Horses Median Horses 1996	(3) Position = 1 OLS Horses 1996	(4) Position = 1 Median Horses 1996	(5) Position = 1 OLS Horses 2003–12	(6) Position = 1 Median Horses 2003–12
SP Odds	−0.012***	−0.0131***	−0.014**	−0.005	−0.002**	−0.001***
	(6.288)	(−11.308)	(−1.97)	(−0.977)	(−2.116)	(−2.625)
SP Odds x	0.085***	0.131***	0.116*	0.063**	0.044***	0.049***
Margin	(10.362)	(21.350)	(3.043)	(2.026)	(9.742)	(23.783)
Margin	0.522***	0.147**	0.069	0.282**	0.443***	0.354***
	(4.844)	(2.164)	(0.342)	(−0.977)	(14.133)	(16.443)
Constant	−0.026	0.047***	−0.051	−0.099***	−0.077***	−0.081***
	(0.949)	(93.950)	(−1.600)	(−5.227)	(−15.285)	(−21.037)
Adjusted R^2	0.039		0.209		0.111	
Pseudo R^2		0.172		0.071		
Jarque–Bera	6.17e+10		47,074		1.4e+05	
Observations	19,273	19,273	2,096	2,096	52,919	52,919

Notes:
White adjusted t statistics in parentheses.
* $p < 0.10$; ** $p < 0.05$; *** $p < 0.01$.

imply a crossover point in the comparison of Tote and SP odds as revealed in Tables 6.6, 6.7 and 6.8. At longer SP odds, the Tote offers superior returns to bookmaker fixed odds on winning bets, given the over round.

6.5 DISCUSSION

We observe from equation (6.6) that only if the bookmaker's margin for each horse was equal to the constant Tote margin (0.16) and the market and objective probabilities coincided would we observe equality of bookmaker and Tote returns. However, bookmakers set odds that reflect the presence of insiders. This creates a favourite–longshot bias that appears from the 1996 data set to be more pronounced in bookmaker odds than in the Tote odds. This result suggests a crossover point in expected relative payouts. Our new regression results show how the bookmaker margin, a proxy for insider activity in the Shin model, impacts on the expected difference in odds as well as the SP.

The regression results we have reported do not appear inconsistent with market efficiency from the perspective of generating systematic abnormal returns based on them. There appears to be no risky betting strategy for betting on Tote or SP that can generate that outcome.

However, the systematic difference between Tote and SP odds does seemingly have an important implication for the different models of risky choice employed to explain wagering at actuarially unfair odds. One suggestion from experimental research is that the heterogeneity of preferences revealed implies that there is no one model of risky choice applicable to all agents (see e.g. Bruhin et al. (2010) and Harrison et al. (2010)). Assuming that bettors are aware that expected Tote and bookmaker odds will differ in a systematic manner, our results appear to have the same implication in a non-experimental setting. It appears that there is no single model of risky choice suggested in the literature to explain betting at actuarially unfair odds that can explain the systematic pattern observed in Tote and SP returns.

For example, CPT (Tversky and Kahneman, 1992) is perhaps the most prominent model of risky choice in experimental work (see e.g. Stott, 2006).[7] In this non-expected utility model, agents who exhibit probability distortion are assumed to be risk-averse over gains. Jullien and Salanié (2000) report that CPT provides significant explanatory power for US horse race pari-mutuel data. However, as noted by Peel and Law (2009), given a choice between the Tote and SP, bettors with CPT preferences will only bet on more favoured horses with the SP (by Jensen's inequality) and will bet on longshots on either the Tote or SP depending on the expected premium they require to compensate for uncertainty.

The Markowitz (1952) model of non-expected utility also has significant empirical support in the literature (see Peel and Law, 2009). In the Markowitz model, agents are initially risk-seeking over gains and then risk-averse. A bettor with Markowitz preferences could, when in the risk-seeking segment of their value function, wager on more favoured horses on either the Tote or SP but would only wager on longshots on the Tote pari-mutuel form.

The agent seeking risk in all areas in the models of Weitzman (1965), Ali (1977) or Quandt (1986) can also wager on favourites on the Tote or SP but will only wager on long shots on the Tote. Similar properties apply to other models of risky choice for betting agents such as Golec and Tamarkin (1998) based on the analysis of Friedman and Savage (1948).

We might assume that any uniformed recreational bettors or fun bettors will allocate their bets randomly (Bruce et al., 2012).

6.6   CONCLUSIONS

The empirical findings that Tote odds are higher on average than book-maker odds and that there is a crossover point in relative odds does not necessarily imply that the betting market is inefficient. The odds from the two markets will only be equal if the bookmaker margin is equal to the constant Tote margins for each runner in a race. However, bookmakers have to determine odds in the presence of insiders and therefore require a variable margin. This creates a favourite–longshot bias that appears more pronounced than that observed in the totalizer market in the UK.

The two betting mediums do not have the same characteristics since the bookmaker odds are certain from the punter's perspective while Tote odds are inherently uncertain. Well-informed punters, who understand that the average odds payouts will differ in a systematic manner, can be assumed to bet on the basis of the extant models of betting at actuarially unfair odds. They will wager on either the Tote or at bookmaker fixed odds depend-ing on the model of risky choice that best describes them. However, there appears to be no single model of risky choice that can explain the system-atic pattern. For instance, the prominent model CPT implies there would only be bets on favourites with bookmakers.

Consequently, consistent with experimental work, the systematic dif-ferences between Tote and bookmaker odds that we find here, both in the descriptive statistics and our regression analysis, might not be best inter-preted as an example of market inefficiency. Instead, the anomalous differ-ences in returns appear to be an example in real betting markets where no single model of risky choice can be applied across agents.

NOTES

1. Two well-known apparent anomalies are the behaviour of the prices of twin shares that often deviate for long periods from their theoretical parity and the closed-end fund anomaly where stock prices often diverge significantly from net asset value. For example, see e.g. De Jong et al. (2009), and Gemmill and Thomas (2002) on closed-end funds.
2. The Tote was Government owned up to 2012 (covering our sample period) but was then sold to a private bookmaker, Betfred, which now offers both fixed-odds and pari-mutuel forms of betting.
3. Our data set is slightly smaller than that of Bruce and Johnson due to removal of races with odds that appeared erroneous (e.g. Tote 0.8, SP = 100).
4. Data kindly provided by Johnnie Johnson (1996) and Flatstats.UK (2003–12).
5. Bruce and Johnson also note this feature of the 1996 data set employing a different form of analysis.
6. It is also the case that if the bookmaker odds are determined by a weighted average of the subjective and objective probability of winning then (6.6) would become a still more complex function of the SP and bookmaker margin. For the 1996 data set the average

margin was 0.226 with a maximum of 0.712 and a minimum of 0.014. For the 2003–12 set the figures were a mean of 0.189, a minimum of 0.0008 and a maximum of 0.601. The Tote margin is a constant 0.16 on each horse.

7. Starmer (2000), in his review of non-expected utility, concluded that if EU theory is to be replaced as the dominant theory of risky choice in economics, the evidence points to Tversky and Kahneman's (1992) Cumulative Prospect Theory (CPT) as being the best candidate.

REFERENCES

Ali, M.M. (1977). Probability and utility estimates for racetrack bettors. *Journal of Political Economy*, **83**, 803–815.

Blackburn, P. and Pierson, J. (1995). Betting at British racecourses: an analysis of semi-strong efficiency between bookmaker and Tote odds, Discussion Paper 95/4, Department of Economics, University of Kent at Canterbury.

Bruce, A.C. and Johnson, J.E.V. (2000). Investigating the roots of favourite–longshot bias: an analysis of decision-making by supply and demand-side agents in parallel betting markets. *Journal of Behavioral Decision Making*, **13**(4), 413–430.

Bruce, A.C., Johnson, J.E. and Peirson, J. (2012). Recreational versus professional bettors: Performance differences and efficiency implications. *Economics Letters*, **114**(2), 172–174.

Bruhin, A., Fehr-Duda, H. and Epper, T. (2010). Risk and rationality: Uncovering heterogeneity in probability distortion. *Econometrica*, **78**(4), 1375–1412.

Cain, M., Law, D. and Peel, D.A. (2001). The incidence of insider trading in betting markets and the Gabriel and Marsden anomaly. *Manchester School*, **69**(2), 197–207.

Cain, M., D. Law and D.A. Peel (2003). The favourite–longshot bias and the Gabriel and Marsden Anomaly: An explanation based on utility theory, in L. Vaughan Williams (ed.), *The Economics of Gambling*, London: Routledge, pp. 2–13.

De Jong, A., Rosenthal, L. and Van Dijk, M.A. (2009). The risk and return of arbitrage in dual-listed companies. *Review of Finance*, **13**, 495–520.

Dowie, J. (1976). On the efficiency and equity of betting markets. *Economica*, **43**, 139–150.

Friedman, M. and Savage, L.J. (1948). The utility analysis of choices involving risk. *Journal of Political Economy*, **56**, 279–304.

Gabriel, P.E., and Marsden, J.R. (1990). An examination of market efficiency in British racetrack betting. *Journal of Political Economy*, **98**, 874–885.

Gemmill, G. and Thomas, D.C. (2002). Noise trading, costly arbitrage, and asset prices: Evidence from closed-end funds. *Journal of Finance*, **57**, 2571–2594.

Golec, J. and Tamarkin, M. (1998). Bettors love skewness, not risk, at the horse track. *Journal of Political Economy*, **106**(1), 205–225.

Harrison, G.W., Humphrey, S.J. and Verschoor, A. (2010). Choice under uncertainty: Evidence from Ethiopia, India and Uganda. *Economic Journal*, **120**(543), 80–104.

Jullien, B. and Salanié, B. (2000). Estimating preferences under risk: The case of racetrack bettors. *Journal of Political Economy*, **108**(3), 503–530.

Law, D. and Peel, D. (2002). Insider trading, herding behaviour and market plungers in the British horse race betting market. *Economica*, **69**, 327–338.

Markowitz, H.M. (1952). The utility of wealth. *Journal of Political Economy*, **60**, 151–54.

Peel, D.A. and Law, D. (2009). A more general non-expected utility model as an explanation of gambling outcomes for individuals and markets. *Economica*, **76**, 251–263.

Peirson, J and Blackburn, P. (2003). 'Betting at British racecourses; A comparison of the efficiency of betting with bookmakers and at the Tote', in L. Vaughan Williams (ed.), *The Economics Gambling*, London and New York: Routledge, pp. 30–42.

Quandt, R.E. (1986). Betting and equilibrium. *Quarterly Journal of Economics*, **101**(1), 201–207.

Sauer, R.D. (1998). The economics of wagering markets. *Journal of Economic Literature*, **36**(4), 2021–2064.

Shin, H.S. (1991). Optimal betting odds against insider traders. *Economic Journal*, **101**, 1179–1185.

Shin, H.S. (1992). Prices of state contingent claims with insider traders, and the favourite–longshot bias. *Economic Journal*, **102**, 426–435.

Shin, H.S. (1993). Measuring the incidence of insider trading in a market for state-contingent claims. *Economic Journal*, **103**, 1141–1153.

Snowberg, E. and Wolfers, J. (2010). Explaining the favourite–longshot bias: Is it risk-love or misperceptions? *Journal of Political Economy*, **118**, 723–746

Starmer, C. (2000). Developments in non-expected utility theory: The hunt for a descriptive theory of choice under risk. *Journal of Economic Literature*, **38**(2), 332–382.

Stott, H.P. (2006). Cumulative prospect theory's functional menagerie. *Journal of Risk and Uncertainty*, **32**, 101–130.

Thaler, R.H. and Ziemba, W.T. (1988). Anomalies: Parimutuel betting markets: Racetracks and lotteries. *Journal of Economic Perspectives*, **2**(2), 161–174.

Tversky, A. and Kahneman, D. (1992). Advances in prospect theory: Cumulative representation of uncertainty. *Journal of Risk and Uncertainty*, **5**(4), 297–323.

Weitzman, M. (1965). Utility analysis and group behavior: An empirical study. *Journal of Political Economy*, **73**(1), 18–26.

Williams, L.V. (1999). Information efficiency in betting markets: A survey. *Bulletin of Economic Research*, **51**, 307–3

Williams, L.V. and Paton, D. (1997). Why is there a favourite–longshot bias in British racetrack betting markets? *Economic Journal*, **107**, 150–158.

7. Market efficiency and the favorite–longshot bias: evidence from handball betting markets

Arne Feddersen

7.1 INTRODUCTION

The analysis of market efficiency has received some attention in economics and finance research. The concept has a long history and has been formalized by Fama (1970). Market efficiency is based on the proposition that a security (stocks, bonds, etc.) fully reflects the available information at any point in time. This also means that no mispriced securities exist and, thus, no strategies can be developed to consistently out-perform the market. Consequently, a market is considered to be efficient if it is impossible to make economic profits by trading on the basis of information included in a defined information set (Jensen, 1978, p. 96) – or as Direr (2013, p. 343) puts it: "Markets are efficient if prices reflect information to the point where the marginal benefit of acting on information does not exceed marginal costs."

Betting markets, due to their similarity with financial markets, their unique characteristics, and data availability, seem to be an interesting field for the analysis of the efficient market hypothesis (Nyberg, 2014). The advantage of betting markets, according to Thaler and Ziemba (1988, p. 162), is that each bet has a well-defined termination point at which its value is realized. Thus, betting markets could be even better suited to the analysis of the efficient market hypothesis than financial markets are (Nyberg, 2014).

In betting markets, the conditions of (weak-form) market efficiency do not hold if the implicit probabilities, which can be generated based on the decimal betting odds published by the bookmakers, do not mirror all relevant and available information at the time the betting odd is published. In such a case, it would be possible to systematically generate economic profits based on more accurate probability forecasts (Nyberg, 2014). However, empirical research has identified a persistent (and unexpected) anomaly, which is known as the favorite–longshot bias. This describes the empirical phenomenon that the returns for betting on favorites are consistently found to be higher than the returns for betting on longshots. Market efficiency, however, would dictate that betting on favorites and betting on longshots is equally profitable (Sobel and Ryan, 2008, p. 138).

The empirical literature on the market efficiency of betting markets can roughly be classified into three categories. First, various tests of the informational efficiency of betting markets have been based on betting rules in order to formulate profitable betting strategies (Direr, 2013; Vlastakis et al., 2009). Second, a related strand of the literature has focused on forecasting match results indirectly by means of statistical modeling of home and away team scores (Dixon and Coles, 1997; Koopman and Lit, 2015; Rue and Salvesen, 2000) or directly by using discrete choice regression models (Forrest and Simmons, 2000; Goddard and Asimakopoulos, 2004; Koning, 2000; Kuypers, 2000). In order to analyze the market efficiency, these forecasts are tested as to whether they yield positive returns when used as the basis of a betting strategy. Third, a direct statistical approach to testing betting market efficiency is based on the examination of whether betting odds are an unbiased estimator of the outcome of a sporting contest (Koning, 2012; Nyberg, 2014; Pope and Peel, 1989).

The focus of this chapter lies exclusively on a regression-based test of market efficiency and, hence, no economic-based tests of the analysis of betting rules have been conducted. In order to contribute to the empirical analysis of the favorite–longshot bias in fixed odds betting on team sports leagues, the dataset consists of games from top-tier handball leagues in Europe. Analyses of the betting market efficiency in European team sports have, so far, been exclusively focused on football (soccer). The dataset used in the empirical analysis contains almost 14,500 handball games played in six top-tier European handball leagues (Spain, Germany, France, Denmark, Poland, and Sweden).

The remainder of this chapter is organized as follows. In Section 7.2, the existing literature on betting market efficiency and the favorite–longshot bias will be summarized. Section 7.3 outlines the empirical strategy and describes the data used in the empirical analysis. The results of the regression tests of the efficiency of fixed odds handball betting markets are reported in Section 7.4. Finally, Section 7.5 concludes the chapter.

7.2   LITERATURE REVIEW

This section gives a brief overview of the literature but for more comprehensive surveys of the relevant literature please refer to Thaler and

Ziemba (1988), Sauer (1998), and Snowberg and Wolfers (2008). To begin with, three different explanations for the favorite–longshot bias can be found (Lahvička, 2014; Makropoulou and Markellos, 2011; Snowberg and Wolfers, 2010). First, (casual) bettors might systematically overestimate the winning probability of longshots, which is exploited by the bookmakers. Second, bookmakers might take advantage of risk-loving bettors by offering lower odds for bets on longshots. Third, bookmakers might offer lower odds for bets on longshots in order to avoid losses due to information asymmetries, which might exist because of better-informed insider bettors or a faster reaction to new information by bettors compared to bookmakers in general (Shin, 1991, 1993).

The favorite–longshot bias has been empirically analyzed in racetrack wagering markets in, for example, the US (Ali, 1977; Asch et al., 1982; Thaler and Ziemba, 1988), the UK (Vaughan Williams and Paton, 1997; Vaughn Williams and Paton, 2001), Germany (Stefan and Martin, 2006), and New Zealand (Gandar et al., 2001a). It has been studied beyond racetrack wagering markets in the betting markets of many other sports, where the majority of studies have been conducted based on data from North American team sports leagues like the National Football League (NFL), the National Basketball Association (NBA), the National Hockey League (NHL), and the National Collegiate Athletic Association (NCAA). These studies include Woodland and Woodland (1994, 2001, 2003, 2015a), Gray and Gray (1997), Metrick (1996), and Gandar et al. (2001b). The phenomenon of the favorite–longshot bias has also been analyzed in European soccer leagues (Cain et al., 2000; Koning, 2012; Nyberg, 2014; Rossi, 2011). Only a few studies can be found for individual sports like tennis (Abinzano et al., 2016; Forrest and McHale, 2007; Lahvička, 2014).

While many of the above-mentioned analyses show evidence for the existence of the favorite–longshot bias, some studies identified the opposite pattern – often referred to as the reverse favorite–longshot bias. Scholarly contributions that show evidence for the reverse favorite–longshot bias include the studies from Busche and Hall (1988) on Hong Kong and Japanese horserace betting, Woodland and Woodland (1994, 2001, 2003, 2015a) on MLB, NFL and NHL betting, as well as Schnytzer and Weinberg (2008) on Australian football betting. Gandar et al. (2001b) show evidence of the reverse favorite–longshot bias, both in the point spread betting market on NBA games and the fixed odds betting market on MLB games. Humphreys et al. (2013) found that bettors in the NFL betting market have clear and predictable tendencies for betting on the best team and, thus, identified significant bettor biases that are both persistent and predictable. The reverse favorite–longshot bias is, according to Woodland and Woodland (2015b), thereby analogous to the sentiment bias where there is a preference towards stronger or more glamorous teams (Feddersen et al., 2016, 2017; Forrest and Simmons, 2008; Franck et al., 2011). In contrast, Sauer (1998) and Johnson and Pawlukiewicz (1992), inter alia, did not find evidence for the favorite–longshot or the reverse favorite–longshot bias in the NFL and NBA over/under betting markets respectively. Finally, evidence for the favorite–longshot bias was also found in laboratory experiments (Hurley and McDonough, 1995; Piron and Smith, 1995). Thus, as Rossi (2011) concludes, it seems like evidence exists that the favorite–longshot bias is a common phenomenon, but not a universal feature of sport betting markets.

7.3   EMPIRICAL STRATEGY AND DATA

Following Koning (2012) and Nyberg (2014), this study tries to test the informational efficiency of the underlying implicit probabilities derived from decimal odds set by bookmakers operating in fixed odds betting markets. The (average) implicit probabilities can, thereby, be obtained as follows (e.g., Feddersen et al., 2017; Forrest and Simmons, 2008):

$$\overline{\theta}_i^j = \frac{1/\overline{d}_i^j}{1/\overline{d}_i^H + 1/\overline{d}_i^D + 1/\overline{d}_i^A} \text{ with } j = H, D, A \tag{7.1}$$

Let $\overline{\theta}_i^j$ denote the implicit probabilities based on average betting odds, where j denotes the three possible outcomes of a given handball game, i – home win (H), draw (D), away win (A). The dataset contains betting odds for a given game offered by up to 17 different bookmakers. However, since the focus of this analysis lies on testing the efficiency of the betting market as a whole, average decimal betting odds have been used. In line with previous research, it is assumed that these average betting odds reflect the market consensus (Koning, 2012; Nyberg, 2014). The average betting odds are calculated as follows:

$$\overline{d}_i^j = \frac{1}{k} \sum_{k=1}^{K} d_{ik}^j \text{ with } j = H, D, A, \tag{7.2}$$

where d_{ik}^j stands for individual betting odds for outcome j, of game i, and bookmaker k and $\overline{d}_i^j$ stands for the average betting odds of outcome j and game i. K is the total number of bookmakers offering betting odds for this particular game.

The dataset consists of almost 14,500 handball games played in six top-tier European handball leagues: Spain, Germany, France, Denmark, Poland, and Sweden. This sample is slightly smaller than the overall number of games played in these leagues during the observation period

Table 7.1   Descriptive statistics

League	Observations	Relative frequencies of game outcomes (in %)		
		Home wins	Draws	Away wins
Spain	2,627	55.96	9.33	34.72
Germany	3,551	56.55	8.39	35.06
France	1,800	55.00	9.50	35.50
Denmark	2,229	53.21	8.52	38.27
Sweden	2,659	57.28	7.97	34.75
Poland	1,592	58.10	6.28	35.62
Full sample	14,458	56.04	8.41	35.55

since valid betting odds could not be obtained for all games. The starting point of the observation period is different for the individual leagues and depends on the general availability of betting odds for each league. Betting odds have been collected starting with 2004/05 for the leagues in Germany and Spain, 2005/06 for the Swedish league, and 2006/07 for the leagues in Denmark, France, and Poland. The observation period ends with the 2015/16 season for all leagues. All necessary information (betting odds and game results) has been collected from http://www.oddsportal.com.

Table 7.1 contains some basic descriptive statistics. The number of observations varies between the different leagues, since (1) the observation period is not identical as mentioned above and (2) the number of teams and thus games per season differs. The number of teams participating in the leagues varies between 18 for Germany, 16 for Spain, 14 for France, Denmark, and Sweden, and 12 for Poland. Thus, the largest subsample with more than 3,500 games is from the German league, while the smallest subsample consists of approximately 1,600 games played in the Polish league. Overall, the full sample contains almost 14,500 handball games.

Additionally, Table 7.1 shows the relative frequencies of the different outcomes for the six leagues. The share of home wins ranges from 53.2% (Denmark) to 58.1% (Poland). Differences can also be found for the share of draws – ranging from 6.3% (Poland) to 9.5% (France) – and the share of away wins – ranging from 34.7% (Spain) to 38.3% (Denmark). Here, it is interesting to note that these relative frequencies are quite different from those obtained for European football. Since team handball is a high-scoring game compared to football, the share of draws in particular is significantly smaller. The average number of goals scored by both teams in a game was 56.2 (standard deviation of 7.2) in the full sample, while the minimum was 32 and the maximum 134. According to Nyberg (2014, p. 27), the share of draws was approximately 27% for the top four tiers of

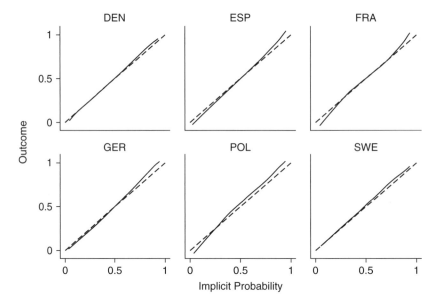

Figure 7.1   *Non-parametric regressions of game outcomes and implicit home win probabilities*

English football during the seasons from 2001/02 to 2012/13. Additionally, the share of home wins was notably higher for handball than for football (approximately 56% vs. 45%) as was the share of away wins (approximately 36% vs. 28%).

7.4 EMPIRICAL ANALYSIS

To provide a first impression of the informational efficiency of the different handball betting markets, Figures 7.1 and 7.2 depict non-parametric regressions for the six leagues. The solid black lines display non-parametric locally weighted regressions based on the *lowess* command in Stata 14. The gray dashed line is the 45-degree line. If the implicit probabilities are unbiased estimators of the likelihood that a particular outcome occurs, the non-parametric regression line should be (almost) identical with the 45° line (Koning, 2012, p. 268). Or, in other words, if the non-parametric regression lines correspond to the 45-degree line, the null hypothesis of informational efficient betting markets cannot be rejected (Nyberg, 2014, p. 19) and no evidence of the existence of the favorite–longshot bias could be found.

Based on Figure 7.1, for all six leagues, there is some visual evidence that

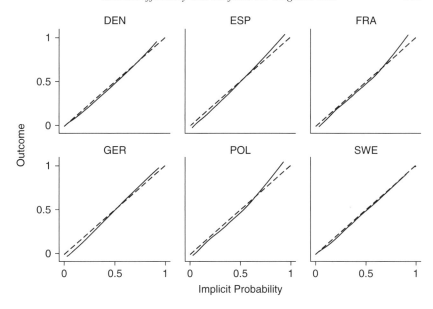

Figure 7.2   Non-parametric regressions of game outcomes and implicit away win probabilities

the non-parametric regression lines do not correspond to the 45-degree line and that – in all cases – the locally weighted regression line lies above the 45-degree line for higher implicit probabilities. This means that home favorites in these leagues won their games more often than indicated by the implicit bookmaker probabilities for a home win. Figure 7.2 reveals similar evidence. Here, the non-parametric regression line, which is based on game outcomes and implicit away win probabilities, also lies above the 45-degree line in five of the six cases. Only in the case of the Swedish league does the solid line appear to correspond with the dashed line quite well. However, Figure 7.2 shows evidence that away favorites also won their games more often than indicated by the implicit bookmaker probabilities for an away win. Overall, it can be stated that both home and away favorites won their games more often than expected based on the implicit probabilities and, thus, that first evidence for the existence of the favorite–longshot bias in handball betting markets exists.

After this first test of the informational efficiency of the handball betting markets, a more formal test – similar to the test in Koning (2012) – was conducted. This test is based on independent Logit regressions for the different leagues and possible game outcomes. These regressions are based on the following Logit model:

$$P(Y_i^j) = \frac{1}{1 + \exp(-\beta_0 - \beta_1 \log(1/\overline{\theta}_i^j - 1))}, \qquad (7.3)$$

where Y_i^j is a binary variable that indicates whether outcome j of game i occurred. For example, if j is equal to H and the home team actual won the game, Y_i^H is equal to one and zero otherwise. Overall, there is a set of three indicator variables (Y_i^H, Y_i^D, Y_i^A), which must sum up to one. The Logit model presented in equation (7.3) uses the implicit probabilities ($\overline{\theta}_i^j$) as the single predictor of the game outcome (Y_i^j). Consequently, the condition for (weak-form) market efficiency reads as follows:

$$H_0: \beta_0 = 0, \beta_1 = -1 \qquad (7.4)$$

The results in Table 7.2 show that the favorite–longshot bias is present in most cases. In this table, the coefficients β_0 and β_1, as well as their respective standard errors (in parenthesis), are given for each league. Furthermore, the table also contains the Wald statistics and the corresponding p-values for the joint test of the null hypothesis.

The null hypothesis of informational efficiency has to be rejected in most of the cases displayed in Table 7.2. For the top-tier handball leagues in Germany and Spain, the null hypothesis is rejected for all three possible match outcomes and at all conventional levels. Concerning the Polish league, the null hypothesis is rejected for bets on both home and away wins, while it cannot be rejected for bets on draws. In the case of the Danish league, the null hypothesis is rejected at the 5% level for bets on draws, while it is rejected only at the 10% level for bets on home wins and away wins respectively. With respect to both the French and the Swedish league, the null hypothesis cannot be rejected for bets on draws but is rejected for bets on home wins and away wins – although on different significance levels. Here, the Wald test is significant at the 5% level for bets on away wins in the French market and home wins in the Swedish market. In contrast, the test is significant at the 10% level for home win bets in France and away win bets in Sweden.

On balance, the findings from the logit regressions confirm the overall impression derived from the non-parametric analysis depicted in Figure 7.1. In summary, it can be stated that there seems to be evidence that the handball betting markets in the analyzed countries are characterized by the existence of the favorite–longshot bias.

Table 7.2   Estimations of individual logit models by leagues

	Home win	Draw	Away win
Spain			
β_0	−0.019	2.106	0.016
(SE)	(0.050)	(0.596)	(0.056)
β_1	−1.243	−1.858	−1.271
(SE)	(0.052)	(0.258)	(0.052)
Wald	22.892	15.293	30.986
(p-value)	(0.000)	(0.000)	(0.000)
Germany			
β_0	0.055	2.236	−0.044
(SE)	(0.043)	(0.598)	(0.046)
β_1	−1.241	−1.901	−1.290
(SE)	(0.042)	(0.251)	(0.044)
Wald	37.228	15.382	50.929
(p-value)	(0.000)	(0.000)	(0.000)
France			
β_0	−0.007	1.128	−0.024
(SE)	(0.056)	(0.781)	(0.062)
β_1	−1.124	−1.420	−1.138
(SE)	(0.061)	(0.332)	(0.061)
Wald	4.757	4.258	6.961
(p-value)	(0.093)	(0.119)	(0.031)
Denmark			
β_0	0.055	2.252	−0.069
(SE)	(0.050)	(0.797)	(0.053)
β_1	−1.102	−1.921	−1.074
(SE)	(0.051)	(0.336)	(0.051)
Wald	5.534	8.572	5.185
(p-value)	(0.063)	(0.014)	(0.075)
Sweden			
β_0	0.095	−0.277	−0.064
(SE)	(0.044)	(0.870)	(0.051)
β_1	−1.098	−0.914	−1.056
(SE)	(0.055)	(0.368)	(0.055)
Wald	9.663	1.158	4.999
(p-value)	(0.008)	(0.561)	(0.082)
Poland			
β_0	0.148	0.852	−0.041
(SE)	(0.061)	(0.986)	(0.068)
β_1	−1.219	−1.424	−1.216
(SE)	(0.068)	(0.400)	(0.068)
Wald	19.124	4.345	13.868
(p-value)	(0.000)	(0.114)	(0.001)

7.5 CONCLUSIONS

This study analyzes the market efficiency of handball betting markets in Europe. It is, thereby, the first study to test the efficient market hypothesis in this team sport. The empirical analysis is based on almost 14,500 handball games played in top-tier handball leagues in Spain, Germany, France, Denmark, Poland, and Sweden. Betting odds have been collected starting from the 2004/05 season and going through to the 2015/16 season, with the beginning of the data availability being different for the individual leagues.

Special focus was put on tests of the so-called favorite–longshot bias in these leagues. The empirical approach followed similar studies by Koning (2012), Goddard and Asimakopoulos (2004), and Nyberg (2014) and, hence, was completely based on regression-based tests of the efficient market hypothesis. Consequently, no economic tests of market efficiency based on betting rules have been conducted. The empirical analysis contains two slightly different approaches. First, non-parametric regressions have been carried out and graphically presented for the six leagues and bets on home wins and away wins respectively. Second, independent logit regressions for each league and each possible outcome (home win, draw, away win) have been conducted based on implicit probabilities, which have been derived from average decimal odds set by different bookmakers.

The key result of this contribution is that there appears to be a favorite–longshot bias in European handball betting markets. This overall conclusion is based on both non-parametric regressions as well as parametric logit regressions, which have been conducted for all three possible outcomes of a handball game. With respect to the logit regressions, in most of the leagues, the null hypothesis of market efficiency was rejected at the 5% level and only in some cases on the 10% level. In contrast, the null hypothesis could not be rejected only with respect to bets on draws in France, Sweden, and Poland. Furthermore, evidence of the existence of a favorite–longshot bias is unambitious with respect to all possible game outcomes for the Spanish and the German league.

REFERENCES

Abinzano, Isabel, Muga, Luis, and Santamaria, Rafael (2016). Game, set and match: The favourite–longshot bias in tennis betting exchanges. *Applied Economics Letters,* **23**(8), 605–608.
Ali, Mukhtar M. (1977). Probability and utility estimates for racetrack bettors. *Journal of Political Economy,* **85**(4), 803–815.
Asch, Peter, Malkiel, Burton G., and Quandt, Richard E. (1982). Racetrack betting and informed behavior. *Journal of Financial Economics,* **10**(2), 187–194.

Busche, Kelly and Hall, Christopher D. (1988). An exception to the risk preference anomaly. *The Journal of Business,* **61**(3), 337–346.

Cain, Michael, Law, David, and Peel, David (2000). The favourite–longshot bias and market efficiency in UK football betting. *Scottish Journal of Political Economy,* **47**(1), 25–36.

Direr, Alexis (2013). Are betting markets efficient? Evidence from European Football Championships. *Applied Economics,* **45**(3), 343–356.

Dixon, Mark J. and Coles, Stuart G. (1997). Modelling association football scores and inefficiencies in the football betting market. *Journal of the Royal Statistical Society: Series C (Applied Statistics),* **46**(2), 265–280.

Fama, Eugene F. (1970). Efficient capital markets: A review of theory and empirical work. *The Journal of Finance,* **25**(2), 383–417.

Feddersen, Arne, Humphreys, Brad R., and Soebbing, Brian S. (2016). Sentiment bias in National Basketball Association betting. *Journal of Sports Economics,* Advance online publication.

Feddersen, Arne, Humphreys, Brad R., and Soebbing, Brian S. (2017). Sentiment bias and asset prices: Evidence from sports betting markets and social media. *Economic Inquiry,* **55**(2), 1119–1129.

Forrest, David and McHale, Ian (2007). Anyone for tennis (betting)? *The European Journal of Finance,* **13**(8), 751–768.

Forrest, David and Simmons, Robert (2000). Forecasting sport: The behaviour and performance of football tipsters. *International Journal of Forecasting,* **16**(3), 317–331.

Forrest, David and Simmons, Robert (2008). Sentiment in the betting market on Spanish football. *Applied Economics,* **40**(1), 119–126.

Franck, Egon, Verbeek, Erwin, and Nüesch, Stephan (2011). Sentimental preferences and the organizational regime of betting markets. *Southern Economic Journal,* **78**(2), 502–518.

Gandar, John M., Zuber, Richard A., and Johnson, R. Stafford (2001a). Searching for the favourite–longshot bias down under: An examination of the New Zealand pari-mutuel betting market. *Applied Economics,* **33**(13), 1621–1629.

Gandar, John M., Zuber, Richard A., and Lamb, Reinhold P. (2001b). The home field advantage revisited: A search for the bias in other sports betting markets. *Journal of Economics and Business,* **53**(4), 439–453.

Goddard, John and Asimakopoulos, Ioannis (2004). Forecasting football results and the efficiency of fixed-odds betting. *Journal of Forecasting,* **23**(1), 51–66.

Gray, Philip K. and Gray, Stephen F. (1997). Testing market efficiency: Evidence from the NFL sports betting market. *The Journal of Finance,* **52**(4), 1725–1737.

Humphreys, Brad R., Paul, Rodney J., and Weinbach, Andrew P. (2013). Bettor biases and the 'home–underdog' bias in the NFL. *International Journal of Sport Finance,* **8**(4), 294–311.

Hurley, William and McDonough, Lawrence (1995). A note on the Hayek hypothesis and the favorite–longshot bias in parimutuel betting. *American Economic Review,* **85**(4), 949–955.

Jensen, Michael C. (1978). Some anomalous evidence regarding market efficiency. *Journal of Financial Economics,* **6**(2), 95–101.

Johnson, Robert S. and Pawlukiewicz, James E. (1992). The efficiency of the over-under betting market for NBA basketball games. *The Journal of Economics,* **18**, 97–100.

Koning, Ruud H. (2000). Balance in competition in Dutch soccer. *Journal of the Royal Statistical Society: Series D (The Statistician)*, **49**(3), 419–431.

Koning, Ruud H. (2012). Regression tests and the efficiency of fixed betting odds. *International Journal of Sport Finance*, **7**(3), 262–274.

Koopman, Siem Jan and Lit, Rutger (2015). A dynamic bivariate Poisson model for analysing and forecasting match results in the English Premier League. *Journal of the Royal Statistical Society: Series A (Statistics in Society)*, **178**(1), 167–186.

Kuypers, Tim (2000). Information and efficiency: An empirical study of a fixed odds betting market. *Applied Economics*, **32**(11), 1353–1363.

Lahvička, Jiří (2014). What causes the favourite–longshot bias? Further evidence from tennis. *Applied Economics Letters*, **21**(2), 90–92.

Makropoulou, Vasiliki and Markellos, Raphael N. (2011). Optimal price setting in fixed-odds betting markets under information uncertainty. *Scottish Journal of Political Economy*, **58**(4), 519–536.

Metrick, Andrew (1996). March madness? Strategic behavior in NCAA basketball tournament betting pools. *Journal of Economic Behavior & Organization*, **30**(2), 159–172.

Nyberg, Henri (2014). A multinomial logit-based statistical test of Association Football betting market efficiency. HECER – Helsinki Center of Economic Research, Discussion Paper No. 380, June 2014.

Piron, Robert and Smith, L. Ray (1995). Testing risklove in an experimental race-track. *Journal of Economic Behavior & Organization*, **27**(3), 465–474.

Pope, Peter F. and Peel, David A. (1989). Information, prices and efficiency in a fixed-odds betting market. *Economica*, **56**(223), 323–341.

Rossi, Marco (2011). Match rigging and the favorite long-shot bias in the Italian football betting market. *International Journal of Sport Finance*, **6**(4), 317–334.

Rue, Havard and Salvesen, Oyvind (2000). Prediction and retrospective analysis of soccer matches in a league. *Journal of the Royal Statistical Society: Series D (The Statistician)*, **49**(3), 399–418.

Sauer, Raymond D. (1998). The economics of wagering markets. *Journal of Economic Literature*, **36**(4), 2021–2064.

Schnytzer, Adi and Weinberg, Guy (2008). Testing for home team and favorite biases in the Australian Rules football fixed-odds and point spread betting markets. *Journal of Sports Economics*, **9**(2), 173–190.

Shin, Hyun Song (1991). Optimal betting odds against insider traders. *The Economic Journal*, **101**(408), 1179–1185.

Shin, Hyun Song (1993). Measuring the incidence of insider trading in a market for state-contingent claims. *The Economic Journal*, **103**(420), 1141–1153.

Snowberg, Erik and Wolfers, Justin (2008). Examining explanations of a market anomaly: Preferences or perceptions? In D.B. Hausch and W.T. Ziemba (eds), *Handbook of Sports and Lottery Markets*, San Diego, CA: Elsevier, pp. 103–136.

Snowberg, Erik and Wolfers, Justin (2010). Explaining the favorite–long shot bias: Is it risk-love or misperceptions? *Journal of Political Economy*, **118**(4), 723–746.

Sobel, Russell S. and Ryan, Matt E. (2008). Unifying the favorite–longshot bias with other market anomalies. In D.B. Hausch and W.T. Ziemba (eds), *Handbook of Sports and Lottery Markets*, Amsterdam: North-Holland, pp. 137–160.

Stefan, Winter and Martin, Kukuk (2006). Risk love and the favorite–longshot bias: Evidence from German harness horse racing. *Schmalenbach Business Review*, **58**(4), 349–364.

Thaler, Richard H. and Ziemba, William T. (1988). Parimutuel betting markets: Racetracks and lotteries. *Journal of Economic Perspectives,* **2**(2), 161–174.

Vaughan Williams, Leighton and Paton, David (1997). Why is there a favourite–longshot bias in British racetrack betting markets? *Economic Journal,* **107**(440), 150–158.

Vaughan Williams, Leighton and Paton, David (2001). Risk, return and adverse selection: A study of optimal behaviour under asymmetric information. In M. Baldassarri, M. Bagella and L. Paganetto (eds), *Financial Markets: Imperfect Information and Risk Management,* New York: Palgrave, pp. 63–81.

Vlastakis, Nikolaos, Dotsis, George, and Markellos, Raphael N. (2009). How efficient is the European football betting market? Evidence from arbitrage and trading strategies. *Journal of Forecasting,* **28**(5), 426–444.

Woodland, Linda M. and Woodland, Bill M. (1994). Market efficiency and the favorite–longshot bias: The baseball betting market. *The Journal of Finance,* **49**(1), 269–279.

Woodland, Linda M. and Woodland, Bill M. (2001). Market efficiency and profitable wagering in the National Hockey League: Can bettors score on longshots? *Southern Economic Journal,* **67**(4), 983–995.

Woodland, Linda M. and Woodland, Bill M. (2003). The reverse favourite–longshot bias and market efficiency in major league baseball: An update. *Bulletin of Economic Research,* **55**(2), 113–123.

Woodland, Linda M. and Woodland, Bill M. (2015a). The National Football League season wins total betting market: The impact of heuristics on behavior. *Southern Economic Journal,* **82**(1), 38–54.

Woodland, Linda M. and Woodland, Bill M. (2015b). Testing profitability in the NBA season wins total betting market. *International Journal of Sport Finance,* **10**(2), 160–174.

8. "Hot arms" and the "hot hand": bettor and sportsbook reaction to team and pitcher streaks in Major League Baseball

Rodney Paul and Andrew Weinbach

8.1 INTRODUCTION

Camerer (1989) and Brown and Sauer (1993) were the first to investigate the "hot hand" hypothesis as it relates to sports betting. The notion behind the "hot hand" is that teams that are on winning streaks become "hot" (or on losing streaks become "cold") and either their performance actually improves (deteriorates) or bettors believe their performance improves (deteriorates), but it actually does not. This distinction creates the empirical need to test for the existence of the "hot hand", if any, and if the "hot hand" is real or a myth.

Studies of the "hot hand" have mainly focused on basketball and football, two sports that use point spreads as the betting "price". This study takes a different angle and studies the "hot hand" in Major League Baseball, a sport that uses odds as the foundation for wagering. Major League Baseball is different from other sports in that teams continually play on consecutive days, with few off-days during the season. In addition, one key player on the field changes from game to game: the starting pitcher. Starting pitchers in Major League Baseball are typically in a five-man rotation, meaning that they typically pitch every fifth day. The pitcher is a key position in baseball, and the quality of the overall team often changes drastically based upon which pitcher is starting, which is easily evidenced by the betting market odds.

Given the importance of the starting pitcher to the betting market, it is also possible that bettors may follow specific pitchers, in addition to or instead of following particular teams. Elite starting pitchers have been shown to be quite popular betting propositions (Paul et al., 2011). The importance of the starting pitcher also allows for the study of the "hot hand" as it relates to a particular player in a sport, as pitchers may become "hot" or "cold" during the season. It is straightforward to apply the testing of the "hot hand" hypothesis to games, and particularly to the starting pitcher, based upon wins or losses in their previous outing(s). Therefore, Major League Baseball provides the opportunity to test both team "hot hand" effects and pitcher "hot hand" effects, which we will refer to as the "hot arm" effect.

If teams or pitchers are on winning streaks and a simple betting strategy of wagering against the "hot" team or pitcher is profitable, this is evidence that supports a mythical "hot hand", where bettors believe that teams become better when they are on winning streaks, but they actually are not. If the betting market is found to be efficient, either there is not a "hot hand" effect or the market correctly prices for any changes in team ability during streaks. There is also the possibility that teams or pitchers become "hot" and the market does not fully incorporate this change in ability. In this case, betting with the streak would reject the null of market efficiency and lead to potential profits.

Testing for the "hot hand" has become a bit more complicated with the rejection of the balanced book hypothesis of wagering. If sportsbook managers take significant positions on individual games where the biases of the betting public are clear and easily predictable, the prices (point spreads and odds) do not reflect the full sentiment of bettors within the market. To allow for further study of this possibility within Major League Baseball, we use detailed data on betting markets from www.sportsinsights. com to examine how streaks (teams and pitchers) impact betting volume, percentage bet on favorites and underdogs, and game odds.

This chapter proceeds as follows. We first examine how prices and quantities in the market change based upon streaks (and other important factors) through a regression model of betting volume, percentage bet on the favorite, and odds. After establishing what the "hot hand" does to these prices and quantities, we then turn our focus to betting simulations to determine if betting with or against streaks was found to be profitable during the 2012 Major League Baseball season. The final section offers a brief discussion of the overall results and concludes this chapter.

8.2   LITERATURE REVIEW

The "hot hand" hypothesis was first applied to sports betting by Camerer (1989) and was soon followed by a subsequent study by Brown and Sauer (1993). These studies analyzed outcomes in NBA betting markets for evidence that teams became "hot" and that betting markets reflect this "hot" behavior. Both focused on a behavioral bias which may exist in financial markets: "hot" teams show improved short-run performance in games, which could lead these teams to both win multiple consecutive games and perform well against the point spread in consecutive games.

The exchange between Camerer (1989) and Brown and Sauer (1993) focused on the distinction between a mythical "hot hand" which exists only in the mind of bettors and an actual "hot hand" reflecting a period of better than average performance by a sports team. Camerer (1989) stated that betting against teams on winning streaks could be profitable, as point spreads may reflect the mythical "hot hand", while game outcomes may or may not reflect an actual "hot hand" effect. Brown and Sauer (1993) countered by demonstrating that both point spreads and game outcomes reflect the "hot hand" but could not reject the Camerer (1989) hypothesis of a mythical "hot hand", or the explanation (under rational expectations) that both team performance and the point spreads reflect streaks. Paul and Weinbach (2005) also analyzed winning and losing streaks in the NBA and found support for the mythical "hot hand" hypothesis in that betting against winning streaks generated excess returns to bettors.

Woodland and Woodland (2000) analyzed winning streaks in the NFL and betting on NFL games. They linked winning streaks by NFL teams to long-term stock market overreaction by investors who take contrarian strategies in terms of buying losers and selling winners (DeBondt and Thaler, 1985). Evidence suggests that these contrarian strategies can yield excess returns due to expectation-based errors made by investors about future earnings (La Porta et al., 1997). Woodland and Woodland (2000) found that betting on or against streaks did not generate excess returns in the NFL betting market. Any real or imagined improvement or decline in team performance embedded in a winning or losing streak appeared to be incorporated into the final point spread. Unlike the earlier evidence from betting on the NBA, simple contrarian betting strategies applied to teams on winning or losing streaks did not earn statistically significant excess returns for bettors.

Paul et al. (2011) and Paul et al. (2013) studied the "hot hand" in the NBA and NFL betting markets using more detailed betting data on betting percentages (percentage bet on the favorite and underdog). In both the NBA and the NFL, the percentage bet on the team on the streak was shown to increase by a positive and significant amount; however, betting against the "hot hand" streak was shown to only win about half the time, and did not offer positive returns to bettors who wagered against these streaks. These studies illustrated that the sportsbook does not behave under the balanced book hypothesis as they take sizeable positions within the market, allowing a large percentage of the bets to accumulate on the best teams, biggest favorites, and teams on streaks. They appear to price as a forecast of game outcomes, however, leaving the null hypothesis of an efficient market unable to be rejected. The betting percentages in both markets, however, clearly illustrate the belief of the betting public in the "hot hand".

8.3 IMPACT OF THE "HOT HAND" AND "HOT ARM" ON BETTING VOLUME, PERCENTAGES, AND ODDS

The "hot hand" is examined in this section as it relates to three specific elements of the sports betting market. "Hot hand" effects on betting volume (the quantity of bets placed in this market), the percentage of bets on the favorite (another quantity-based variable), and the odds themselves (a price) are studied, in order, below.

8.3.1 Betting Volume

The first regression model we estimate uses betting volume as the dependent variable. Betting volume is in terms of the number of bets offshore sportsbooks collected as reported by www.sportsinsights.com. The use of this dependent variable allows for the study of how bettors respond to winning and losing streaks, in addition to other key variables that have been shown to impact betting volume (Paul and Weinbach, 2010; 2012). The independent variables in the regression model include the absolute value of the odds on the game, a dummy for road favorites, home and visiting team win percentages, home and visiting team pitcher win percentages, the day of the week, month of the season, and various measures of team win streak dummy variables.

The absolute value of the odds is included to test if games with larger favorites are more popular with bettors, which has been shown in previous studies of sports betting market volume (Paul and Weinbach, 2010; 2012). Similarly, the road favorite dummy variable is included to note the possibility that bettors prefer to wager on road favorites as they will bet at shorter odds, given the implicit home field advantage in sports such as baseball, which bettors may not fully account for in their wagering decisions. The team and pitcher win percentages are included to account for the quality of the team and starting pitchers for the teams. Day of the week and month of the season dummies are included to differentiate for different days for games, such as weekend games potentially being more popular to bet on due to the opportunity cost of a fan's time, and the month of the season to see if baseball betting is more popular during one part of the season compared to another.

Winning and losing streaks are included as dummy variables by category of streak length. We only consider winning and losing streaks of 2 or more. Categories formed include both winning and losing streaks (for both teams and pitchers) of streaks of lengths of 2+ games, 4+ games, and 6+ games. These streaks allow for the study of the "hot hand" hypothesis in this setting, as it is possible that teams on streaks attract a greater amount of attention from bettors and will increase the betting volume on these games. Given that streaks become more prominent as they continue, the varying lengths of streaks included as independent variables in the regression model allow for an investigation of this issue.

Pitcher streaks are calculated in the same manner as team streaks, in the sense that the pitcher is on a streak if his team wins (loses) consecutive games in which he starts. This is different than wins or losses statistically attributed to pitchers in Major League Baseball, however, as pitchers may receive "no decisions" in games in which they start where either they leave the game when it is tied, do not pitch enough innings to earn a decision, leave the game with their team in the lead but the bullpen eventually loses the game, or leave the game with his team trailing but the team comes back when another pitcher is in the game. There are other ways to measure pitcher quality that may ultimately improve this variable relating to pitcher streaks, such as measuring the actual quality of the start, but for this study we examined pitcher streaks in the same exact way team streaks are calculated, based upon wins or losses during the game in which the pitcher started the game.

Regression results are presented in Table 8.1.

The intercept was shown to be nearly 6,000 bets on a Major League Baseball game during the 2012 season. The absolute value of the odds on the game was shown to have a positive and significant effect on the volume of bets on a game. The bigger the favorite, the more bets on the game. This result is consistent with what has been shown previously in baseball (Paul et al., 2013), the NFL (Paul and Weinbach, 2012), and the NBA and NHL (Paul and Weinbach, 2010). As in the other studies mentioned above, road favorites attracted considerably more betting action as the road favorite dummy was shown to have a positive and significant impact on the volume of bets. Bettors, in particular recreational bettors, likely prefer road favorites, as they do not need to lay as much money on the favorite when wagering on the best teams in the league (as they likely ignore the home field advantage).

Team win percentages, home and road, were both shown to have positive and significant effects on betting volume. Bettors, like fans, prefer to wager

Table 8.1   MLB volume regression: "hot hand" effects

Variable	Coefficient (t-statistic)	Variable	Coefficient (t-statistic)
Intercept	5,966.83*** (7.45)	Home Win Streak 2+	−126.96 (−0.56)
ABS(Odds)	20.87*** (6.88)	Home Win Streak 4+	398.04 (0.96)
Road Favorite Dummy	2,187.84*** (8.56)	Home Win Streak 6+	1,649.57** (1.96)
Home Win %	3,301.11*** (4.13)	Home Loss Streak 2+	94.03 (0.34)
Road Win %	2,204.92*** (3.43)	Home Loss Streak 4+	719.86* (1.71)
Home Pitcher Win %	2,255.85*** (5.39)	Home Loss Streak 6+	−835.44 (−1.03)
Road Pitcher Win %	2,953.19*** (6.39)	Road Win Streak 2+	281.83 (1.05)
Sunday	−92.80 (−0.27)	Road Win Streak 4+	815.98** (2.03)
Monday	2,290.64*** (8.06)	Road Win Streak 6+	−49.19 (−0.06)
Tuesday	337.86 (1.56)	Road Loss Streak 2+	397.71* (1.72)
Thursday	2,173.52*** (6.48)	Road Loss Streak 4+	−438.11 (−1.22)
Friday	483.98* (1.83)	Road Loss Streak 6+	436.44 (0.68)
Saturday	407.54 (1.37)	Home Pitcher WS 2+	465.83** (2.08)
March	−2,581.86** (−1.97)	Home Pitcher WS 4+	−846.99** (−2.26)
April	739.20 (1.62)	Home Pitcher WS 6+	3,224.95*** (4.11)
May	−1,476.80*** (−4.33)	Home Pitcher LS 2+	44.51 (0.19)
July	−970.38*** (−2.69)	Home Pitcher LS 4+	96.91 (0.23)
August	−3,058.98*** (−16.44)	Home Pitcher LS 6+	1,589.06* (1.68)
September	−5,969.98*** (−16.44)	Road Pitcher WS 2+	473.62** (1.98)
October	−6,672.45*** (−9.85)	Road Pitcher WS 4+	1,129.05** (2.46)

Table 8.1   (continued)

Variable	Coefficient (t-statistic)	Variable	Coefficient (t-statistic)
		Road Pitcher WS 6+	−2.93 (−0.01)
		Road Pitcher LS 2+	290.06 (1.28)
		Road Pitcher LS 4+	85.01 (0.85)
R-squared	0.32	Road Pitcher LS 6+	42.21 (0.94)

Notes: Given initial issues with both heteroskedasticity and autocorrelation in the regression model, the results presented below use Newey-West HAC-consistent standard errors and covariances. Statistical significance is noted using * notation with * denoting significance at the 10 percent level, ** denoting significance at the 5 percent level, and *** denoting significance at the 1 percent level.

on games with the best teams. As noted before in the literature, this result supports the notion that much of gambling activity is consumption in nature, as fans tend to wager on the best teams. Pitcher win percentage was also shown to have a positive and significant effect for both home and road pitchers. The better the pitchers in the game, the more bets on the game. This also likely supports the consumption-based motive for gambling on baseball.

There are also consumption-based gambling motives illustrated by the signs and statistical significance of the dummy variables for the days of the week and the months of the season. The days of the week dummies revealed that both Monday and Thursday were shown to have positive and significant effects on betting volume. These two days are "travel days" for Major League Baseball teams, with fewer games being played on these days as some teams travel from one city to another. Given fewer games on the daily schedule, bettors wager more on the individual games played. It is unlikely that they have better information on these games, leading to this result being an impact of consumption-based gambling, as bettors have fewer games to bet. The drop-off late in the baseball season in terms of wagering volume has been shown before (Paul and Weinbach, 2013) and was shown to be due to the start of the NFL and college American Football season in the United States.

In relation to the key variables in this study, the dummy variables related to the "hot hand", many streaks for the home team, road team, home pitcher, and road pitcher, were all shown to have a positive and significant impact on betting volume. Both winning and losing streaks were shown to have an effect on the number of bets placed on a game. It appears that bettors follow streaks, and teams/pitchers that become either "hot" or "cold" tend to receive more bets on their games due to the winning or losing streak they are on.

This result supports the notion of the "hot hand", although it does not distinguish between the "hot hand" being a myth and being real. In either case, winning and losing streaks play a significant role in the popularity of games being bet on in the Major League Baseball wagering market. Other tests, shown below, have more explanatory power when it comes to distinguishing the mythical "hot hand" from real "hot hand" effects.

8.3.2 Betting Percentages

Table 8.2 investigates how the percentage bet on the favorite changes with winning and losing streaks. The dependent variable is the percentage bet on the favorite on the game, taken from the betting percentages shown by www.sportsinsights.com for the 2012 MLB season. The independent variables used are generally the same as in Table 8.1 in the previous section. Expected percentage bet on the favorite is calculated by the closing odds on the baseball game. Under the balanced book hypothesis, the coefficient on this variable should be one.

Given the popularity of road favorites in other studies of betting percentages, it is expected that the road favorite dummy will have a positive and significant impact on the percentage bet on the favorite. Home team and pitcher win percentages should positively impact the percentage bet on the favorites, while road team and pitcher win percentages should negatively impact the percentage bet on the favorite. Days and months are included to determine if there is any seasonable or day-of-the-week pattern to betting percentages.

The "hot hand" dummy variables in terms of winning and losing streaks are included in the regression model. If the betting public believes in the "hot hand", the percentage bet on the favorite should rise with home (team and pitcher) winning streaks and road (team and pitcher) losing streaks and should decline with home (team and pitcher) losing streaks and road (team and pitcher) winning streaks.

In terms of the percentage bet on the favorite, the actual percentage bet on the favorite was shown to exceed the expected percentage bet on the favorite (based on the game odds). Under a balanced book, the coefficient on the expected betting percentage was expected to be one, which can be soundly rejected. The percentage bet on the favorite increases with the magnitude of the favorite. Therefore, stronger teams (and stronger

The economics of sports betting

Table 8.2 *MLB betting percentages regression: "hot hand" effects (dependent variable: percent bet on favorite)*

Variable	Coefficient (t-statistic)	Variable	Coefficient (t-statistic)
Intercept	−24.50*** (−6.95)	Home Win Streak 2+	0.33 (0.47)
ABS (Odds)	1.55*** (30.22)	Home Win Streak 4+	−1.06 (−0.97)
Road Favorite Dummy	13.08*** (14.02)	Home Win Streak 6+	−1.12 (−0.45)
Home Win %	3.22* (1.71)	Home Loss Streak 2+	−0.53 (−0.70)
Road Win %	−8.49*** (−3.44)	Home Loss Streak 4+	0.27 (0.25)
Home Pitcher Win %	1.38 (1.16)	Home Loss Streak 6+	−0.35 (−0.20)
Road Pitcher Win %	−3.41** (−2.53)	Road Win Streak 2+	−0.94 (−1.29)
Sunday	−0.53 (−0.67)	Road Win Streak 4+	0.31 (0.25)
Monday	−0.01 (−0.02)	Road Win Streak 6+	−0.19 (−0.09)
Tuesday	0.05 (0.06)	Road Loss Streak 2+	−0.94 (−1.41)
Thursday	0.27 (0.29)	Road Loss Streak 4+	0.97 (0.87)
Friday	0.35 (0.41)	Road Loss Streak 6+	−0.65 (−0.36)
Saturday	1.15 (1.46)	Home Pitcher WS 2+	1.21* (1.91)
March	−29.56*** (−19.69)	Home Pitcher WS 4+	1.30 (0.32)
April	−1.09 (−1.14)	Home Pitcher WS 6+	−4.15* (−1.81)
May	−0.31 (−0.32)	Home Pitcher LS 2+	0.34 (0.57)
July	0.66 (0.62)	Home Pitcher LS 4+	0.31 (0.24)
August	−0.70 (−0.74)	Home Pitcher LS 6+	0.16 (0.05)
September	−0.01 (−0.02)	Road Pitcher WS 2+	−1.61** (−2.39)
October	1.98 (0.96)	Road Pitcher WS 4+	0.79 (0.63)

Table 8.2 (continued)

Variable	Coefficient (t-statistic)	Variable	Coefficient (t-statistic)
		Road Pitcher WS 6+	0.16 (0.05)
		Road Pitcher LS 2+	0.33 (0.51)
		Road Pitcher LS 4+	−0.64 (−0.48)
R-squared	0.41	Road Pitcher LS 6+	3.48* (1.86)

pitchers on these teams) are definitely favored by bettors and the balanced book hypothesis can be rejected as sportsbooks clearly allow for a greater percentage of bets to accumulate on the favorites than is implied by the balanced book hypothesis.

Road favorites were even more popular, as the odds on the game compared to the same teams and pitchers playing at the favorite team's park are lower (due to the home field advantage), as an additional 13 percent of the betting dollars accumulated on the favorite in these contests. Given that this preference is highly predictable, it again rejects the notion of a balanced book as the sportsbook takes a definite position in these games.

Team quality was also found to be a significant determinant of the percentage bet on the favorite. Higher quality home teams generated a greater percentage of the bets on the favorite. The better the road team, the lower the percentage bet on the favorite. In terms of the pitchers, only the road pitcher was found to have a significant effect on the betting percentages, with higher quality road pitchers accounting for a significant decrease in the percentage bet on the favorite by around 3.5 percent. The days of the week and the months of the year had very little effect on the percentage bet on the favorite. The only exception was the very early season games in March, where a much lower percentage of the bets were made on the favorite.

In terms of streaks, very few effects of team streaks were found on the percentage bet on the favorite. None of the groupings of team win streaks were found to have a significant impact on the betting percentages. In the case of pitcher streaks, however, home team pitcher win streaks of 2 or more were found to lead to a significant increase in the percentage bet on the favorite, while road team pitcher win streaks of 2 or more were found to significantly decrease the percentage bet on the favorite (by a slightly greater amount than the home team pitcher streaks). Similarly, in the case of a long losing streak for the road pitcher (6 or more games), the percentage bet on the favorite rises by nearly 3.5 percent. In the case of long winning streaks for the home pitcher, however, there appears to be a statistically significant belief on the part of bettors of mean reversion. With 6 or more game winning streaks for the home pitcher, the percentage bet on the favorite dropped by over 4 percent. In the case of relatively infrequent, but long winning or losing streaks by pitchers, the evidence of the "hot hand" is mixed in terms of the betting percentages.

8.3.3   Betting Odds

Table 8.3 uses the closing odds on the game as the dependent variable. Games were broken into home favorites and road favorites and studied separately. The regression model is similar to those run above, except the odds are now the dependent variable, with team quality, pitcher quality, days, months, and streak variables included as independent variables.

In relation to the betting odds themselves, the results are mostly as expected in terms of team and pitcher quality. For home favorites (with favorites being a negative number – so a negative coefficient on the variable implies a bigger favorite in that case), the home win percentage was found to be negative and significant (a better home team implies a bigger favorite) and the road win percentage was found to be positive and significant (a better road team means a smaller favorite). Home pitcher win percentage was also found to have a negative and significant impact on the odds, meaning that the best pitchers were also the largest favorites. Road pitcher win percentage was found to be positive, but statistically insignificant.

In terms of road favorites, the home team win percentage and the home pitcher win percentage were found to have statistically significant impacts on the odds, with better home teams and pitchers leading the odds to be smaller on those games. Road team win percentage and road pitcher win percentage were not found to have statistically significant results in relation to betting odds for road favorites.

The days of the week had little to no effect on the betting market odds, but the months of the season did show some statistically significant effects. In the small sample of games in March, the odds on the home favorite were reduced (and statistically significant at the 1 percent level). For road favorites, April games showed a slight decrease in the odds on the favorite. In terms of late season, the odds on both the home and road favorites increased in both August and September. As the season winds down, the odds on the best teams (teams likely to be in playoff contention) appear to rise considerably.

Table 8.3   MLB odds (home and road): "hot hand" effects (dependent variable: odds on game)

Variable	Home Favorite	Road Favorite	Variable	Home Favorite	Road Favorite
Intercept	−144.56***	−134.63	Home Win Streak 2+	1.27	2.16
	(−17.85)			(0.52)	(0.87)
Home Win %	−22.93***	26.88***	Home Win Streak 4+	−1.81	−1.52
	(−2.62)	(3.03)		(−0.50)	(−0.32)
Road Win %	35.87***	−3.83	Home Win Streak 6+	−3.55	4.98
	(2.63)	(−0.49)		(−0.45)	(0.62)
Home Pitcher Win %	−37.67***	17.84***	Home Loss Streak 2+	−0.65	2.92
	(−9.20)	(4.61)		(−0.27)	(1.37)
Road Pitcher Win %	35.14	−20.90	Home Loss Streak 4+	−3.26	0.45
	(7.22)	(−5.32)		(−0.85)	(0.12)
Sunday	−2.23	−3.30	Home Loss Streak 6+	11.54	−7.47
	(−0.77)	(−1.12)		(1.62)	(−1.14)
Monday	1.73	2.12	Road Win Streak 2+	1.27	0.26
	(0.64)	(0.72)		(0.50)	(0.12)
Tuesday	−2.35	0.23	Road Win Streak 4+	0.95	−2.38
	(−0.91)	(0.08)		(0.25)	(−0.63)
Thursday	1.26	−2.45	Road Win Streak 6+	−3.58	7.99*
	(0.40)	(−0.79)		(−0.49)	(1.71)
Friday	2.02	−1.07	Road Loss Streak 2+	−1.33	1.61
	(0.74)	(−0.35)		(−0.60)	(0.72)
Saturday	3.00	−1.74	Road Loss Streak 4+	−11.06***	−4.83
	(1.06)	(−0.64)		(−2.65)	(−0.76)
March	21.47***	−6.20	Road Loss Streak 6+	6.03	−0.76
	(6.23)	(−1.41)		(0.68)	(−0.07)
April	−0.74	5.30*	Home Pitcher WS 2+	1.18	1.15
	(6.22)	(1.70)		(0.56)	(0.43)
May	−1.14	−0.51	Home Pitcher WS 4+	−6.87	0.30
	(−0.39)	(−0.16)		(−1.51)	(0.06)
July	−3.18	0.15	Home Pitcher WS 6+	−7.98	−0.47
	(−0.92)	(0.05)		(−0.97)	(−0.06)
August	−14.58***	−6.32*	Home Pitcher LS 2+	1.82	−4.30**
	(−3.43)	(−1.85)		(0.78)	(−2.11)
September	−15.14***	−9.43**	Home Pitcher LS 4+	−1.63	−0.54
	(−3.49)	(−2.56)		(−0.28)	(−0.11)

Table 8.3   (continued)

Variable	Home Favorite	Road Favorite	Variable	Home Favorite	Road Favorite
October	−11.58	−5.33	Home Pitcher LS 6+	14.51*	−5.47
	(−1.11)	(−0.71)		(1.83)	(−0.91)
			Road Pitcher WS 2+	6.27	−2.80
				(0.52)	(−1.37)
			Road Pitcher WS 4+	2.46	−5.18
				(0.52)	(−1.33)
			Road Pitcher WS 6+	2.41	9.22*
				(0.36)	(1.88)
			Road Pitcher LS 2+	−0.31	1.57
				(−0.13)	(0.70)
			Road Pitcher LS 4+	0.63	−0.46
				(0.12)	(−0.09)
			Road Pitcher LS 6+	−19.52**	8.34
				(−2.26)	(0.72)

Team winning and losing streaks did not impact the betting market odds by a significant margin for either home or road favorites. There were only two exceptions to this. The first exception was for road teams on a 4-or-more-game losing streak in games involving home favorites. In this case, the odds on the favorite increased (statistically significant at the 1 percent level). The other exception involved road favorites in the situation where the road team was on a long winning streak (6 or more). In this case the odds on the road favorite actually declined (a positive coefficient), implying another case where mean reversion appears to be believed in the market.

In relation to pitcher streaks, there were two situations where statistically significant results were found for both home and road pitcher streaks. For home favorites, situations where the home and road pitcher were on long losing streaks were found to have significant results. When the home pitcher was on a 6-or-more-game losing streak, the odds on the favorite were considerably smaller. Likewise, when the road pitcher was on a 6-or-more-game losing streak, the odds on the home favorite increased by a large margin.

For road favorites, with respect to pitcher streaks, when the home pitcher was on a 2-or-more-game losing streak, the odds on the road favorite increased. When the road pitcher was on a 6-or-more-game winning streak however, there again appears to be some belief in mean reversion (belief the streak will end) as the odds on the road favorite decreased in these cases.

Overall, the odds on both home and road favorites responded as expected to team and pitcher quality. There were some impacts of the months of the season as well, as favorites became considerably stronger later in the season (during the push for the playoffs). Some impacts of team and pitcher winning and losing streaks were found, but they were generally sporadic with mostly expected results, although some belief in mean reversion after long streaks appears to exist in the marketplace.

8.4   BETTING SIMULATIONS – TEAM "HOT HAND" AND PITCHER "HOT ARM" EFFECTS

The previous section focused on the change in key variables (volume, betting percentages, odds) when teams and pitchers were on streaks. This section focuses on the returns to simple betting strategies involving these team and/or pitcher streaks for the 2012 Major League Baseball season. The data are arranged and the returns are calculated for strategies of betting with or against the team and/or pitcher on a winning or losing streak. All returns are calculated based upon a $1 bet on the team of interest (either the team on the streak or against the team on the streak).

The returns are organized in a variety of ways to attempt to ascertain whether simple strategies of betting with or against streaks are profitable. The streaks are a bit complicated due to the fact that both teams could be on a winning (losing) streak. In the first structuring of the data for teams and pitchers (Tables 8.4 and 8.6), the betting strategy is initiated when one team/pitcher is on a streak and the other team/pitcher is on the opposite streak (i.e. a team on a winning streak vs. a team on a losing streak). The second grouping of data expands the data set to include games where one team/pitcher is on a longer winning (losing) streak than the other. In this case, it is assumed that the team/pitcher on the longer streak is the one considered to be more "hot" ("cold") and the strategies of betting with or against the streak are generated based upon this team. The last table (Table 8.8) looks at the subset of games where both the team and the pitcher are on winning (losing) streaks.

Tables 8.4 and 8.5 present the results for team streaks. In Table 8.4, results are presented for the home team on a win streak vs. the road team on a loss streak, the home team on a loss streak vs. the road team on a win

Table 8.4　Betting returns – team streaks – team on streak vs. team on opposite streak

Streak	Home Win Streak W–L	Vs. Home Return $1 Bet	Road Loss Streak Road Return $1 Bet	Home Loss Streak W–L	Vs. Home Return $1 Bet	Road Win Streak Road Return $1 Bet	Bet against Streak W–L	Vs. $1 Bet against Streak	Bet with Streak $1 Bet on Streak
6+	10–17	−9.676	11.040	22–25	−2.737	0.3971	39–35	8.303	−9.279
4+	76–73	−13.706	16.4534	73–67	−0.312	−7.077	146–143	16.765	−20.784
2+	324–253	−3.009	−17.106	262–222	14.868	−30.774	561–497	−2.238	−33.783

Table 8.5   Betting returns – team streaks – includes games with teams on shorter streaks

Streak	Bet against Streak vs. Bet on Streak	$1 Bet against Streak	$1 Bet on Streak
6+	52–55	1.471	−5.595
4+	207–198	26.549	−31.377
2+	647–689	−10.968	−29.442

streak, and the final columns combine the two into betting strategies of a bet against the streak and a bet with the streak.

In relation to home win streaks vs. road loss streaks, there is some evidence of a mythical "hot hand" effect in relation to teams on winning streaks as betting against home teams on longer winning streaks (4+ and 6+ games) were found to generate positive returns, with the results of the 4+ game streaks being statistically significant. For 2+ game streaks, returns to both strategies were negative. For situations where the road team was on the win streak, the contrarian strategy of betting on the home team was found to generate positive and significant returns for 2+ game streaks (although longer length streaks did not fare as well as 2 and 3 game streaks). Again, this reveals evidence of profitability of betting against the "hot hand". Combining both situations (last columns in Table 8.4) shows that betting against the streak (against the team with the "hot hand") clearly outperformed the strategy of betting with the streak, as betting against the team on the 4+ and 6+ game streaks earned positive returns for bettors.

Table 8.5 expands the data set to consider games where one team is on a longer winning (losing streak) than the other team, in addition to the games shown in Table 8.4 above where the teams were on opposite streaks.

Expanding the sample yields similar results as a simple strategy of betting against the streak earned positive returns (statistically significant for 4+ game streaks). In 405 games where the streak was 4+ games, betting against this team earned over $26 from a $1 bet for a 6.5 percent return to this strategy. It appears that betting against the team with the "hot hand" yields positive returns for bettors of Major League Baseball.

Tables 8.6 and 8.7 use the same format as above except with the pitcher being on the streak rather than the team. In Table 8.6, home pitchers on win streaks vs. road pitchers on loss streaks, home pitchers on loss streaks vs. road pitchers on win streaks, and strategies of betting against and with the streaks are considered and returns to each strategy are calculated.

Table 8.6 *Betting returns – pitcher streaks – pitcher on streak vs. pitcher on opposite streak*

Streak	Home Win Streak W–L	Vs. Home Return $1 Bet	Road Loss Streak Road Return $1 Bet	Home Loss Streak W–L	Vs. Home Return $1 Bet	Road Win Streak Road Return $1 Bet	Bet against Streak W–L	Vs. $1 Bet against Streak	Bet with Streak $1 Bet on Streak
6+	8–7	−1.760	2.681	4–7	−2.973	0.259	11–15	−0.292	−1.501
4+	42–25	6.349	−7.342	33–34	−3.655	−3.008	58–76	−10.997	3.341
2+	157–100	20.843	−24.082	137–142	−14.316	−4.265	237–299	−38.398	16.578

Table 8.7   Pitcher streaks – includes games with pitchers on shorter streaks

Streak	Bet against Streak vs. Bet on Streak	$1 Bet against Streak	$1 Bet on Streak
6+	26–40	−5.706	1.609
4+	107–146	−23.897	11.118
2+	414–498	−52.565	16.684

The returns for betting on "hot hand" streaks related to pitchers (the "hot arm") reveal the opposite result of what was seen with team streaks. Betting on the home pitcher on a winning streak yielded positive returns for the sample of 2+ and 4+ game streaks (although betting against the home pitcher on a long streak of 6+ led to positive, yet insignificant, results for contrarian bettors). When the road pitcher was on a winning streak, significant positive returns were not seen. However, when combining the sample to strategies of betting against or with streaks, the strategy of wagering with the pitcher on a winning streak yielded positive returns for pitchers on 2+ and 4+ game streaks. It appears that pitchers, unlike teams, may actually get "hot", in that their ability and success may actually increase (decrease) while they are on winning (losing) streaks.

The results of Table 8.6 are reinforced by those in Table 8.7. This table includes teams on lesser streaks of the same type (i.e. one team on a shorter winning streak than the other). The results of betting against the streak and betting with the streak are shown below.

Betting with the pitcher on the streak yielded a positive return in all categories for the 2012 Major League Baseball season. This again illustrates the possibility that pitchers may actually become "hot" (or "cold"), as their performance may actually change, but the betting market does not fully incorporate their improved (or deteriorated) play.

The final table of this section, Table 8.8, incorporates the sample of games where both the team and the pitcher are on the same streak (i.e. both

Table 8.8   Team and pitcher streaks combined

Streak	Bet against Streak vs. Bet on Streak	$1 Bet against Streak	$1 Bet on Streak
6+	19–17	5.299	−5.298
4+	42–38	12.755	−10.511
2+	115–132	−6.6285	−8.820

the team and the pitcher are on winning streaks). The results of betting against or with the streak are shown below.

In the case where both the team and the pitcher are on the same streak, the team effect appears to dominate as betting against the streak (against the "hot hand") yielded positive returns. This is a smaller sample than the others, as it is jointly determined, but during the 2012 season it appears that the team hot streak dominated the pitcher hot streak and contrarian bettors were rewarded when betting against the "hot hand".

Overall, the results of this section show that team streaks in baseball are similar to other sports with respect to the "hot hand". A strategy of wagering against the team on the streak was shown to earn positive returns. On the other hand, when the pitcher is on a streak (a "hot" arm or "cold" arm), the results are the exact opposite, as a strategy of wagering with the streak is shown to be profitable. It appears that with respect to Major League Baseball teams, the mythical "hot hand" appears to be in order. However, in relation to pitchers, their performance may actually improve when on a winning streak (the opposite for losing streaks), with the market not fully capturing this change in performance, as a simple strategy of betting with the "hot" pitcher yields positive results.

8.5   CONCLUSIONS AND DISCUSSION

"Hot hand" effects, for both teams and pitchers (the "hot arm"), were examined for the betting market of Major League Baseball. Using a sample of 2,430 games during the 2012 season, team and pitcher streaks were calculated and a variety of tests were performed to ascertain the impact of the "hot hand" on prices and quantities in the market itself and returns for simple betting strategies.

The first set of results dealt with quantities and prices in the betting market based upon detailed statistics from www.sportsinsights.com. Their data includes betting volume, percentage bet on each side of the wagering proposition, and the odds themselves. It was found that the betting volume responds to both team and pitcher streaks. Teams or pitchers on streaks make betting on the game more attractive to bettors, leading to an increase in betting volume. Adding this result to volume being affected by team quality, pitcher quality, days with fewer games, and substitution out of the baseball betting market late in the season (due to the start of football season) makes a strong case for the baseball betting market being driven by consumption purposes for a large percentage of the overall betting participants.

The analysis of the betting percentages showed that the percentage bet on the favorite responded to the same factors previously shown in the literature (Paul et al., 2011). Team streaks were shown not to impact the betting percentages, but there was some evidence that the percentage bet on the favorite did respond to various levels of streaks. The odds on the game were also examined, with odds on the favorite being shown to be responsive to a few different levels of team and pitcher streaks, in addition to team quality and home pitcher quality. These tests on the detailed betting market statistics clearly illustrated that streaks impact bettor volume, with lesser impact on the betting percentages and odds in the market.

The data on the baseball betting market was also examined through the calculation of win–loss percentages and returns on simple strategies on a $1 bet based upon various levels of team and pitcher streaks. In relation to the team streaks, the market appears to believe in a mythical "hot hand", as simple strategies of betting against the team on longer streaks (4+ and 6+ games) yielded positive and significant returns. It appears that the odds on the team on the streak are set too high, resulting in positive returns to contrarian bettors.

In relation to the pitcher, however, it appears that pitchers may actually see an impact of a "hot arm", as wagering on pitchers on streaks outperformed betting against them. Betting on the "hot" (or against the "cold") pitcher yielded positive returns for bettors, as the market does not appear to fully incorporate this actual change in performance into the market. Whether this outcome of a real "hot arm" is due to a change in pitcher mechanics or simply due to psychological factors (confidence or lack thereof) is much more difficult to ascertain, but this sample of data suggests that change in pitcher performance during streaks may be real as opposed to simply bettor/fan belief.

Future research may wish to expand upon these results by measuring pitcher quality in different ways to more fully capture both bettor beliefs in change in quality and actual change in pitcher quality. There are also ways to branch this research out beyond baseball into other sports where the performance of a single player, such as a goaltender in hockey or soccer, may have individual impact on the "hot hand" apart from, or in conjunction with, their team's performance.

REFERENCES

Brown, W.O. and Sauer, R.D. (1993). Does the Basketball Market Believe in the "Hot Hand"? *American Economic Review*, **83**(5), 1377–1386.

Camerer, C. (1989). Does the Basketball Market Believe in the "Hot Hand"? *American Economic Review*, **79**(5), 1257–1261.

DeBondt, W.F.M. and Thaler, R. (1985). Does the Stock Market Overreact? *Journal of Finance*, **40**(3), 793–805.

Evan, W.E. and Noble, N.R. (1992). Testing Efficiency in Gambling Markets. *Applied Economics*, **24**, 85–88.

La Porta, R., Lopez-de-Silanes, F., Shleifer, A. and Vishny, R. (1997). Legal Determinants of External Finance. *Journal of Finance*, **52**(3), 1131–1150.

Levitt, S. (2004). Why Are Gambling Markets Organized So Differently From Financial Markets? *The Economic Journal*, **114**, 223–46.

McFall, T.A., Knoeber, T.R. and Thurman, W.N. (2009). Contests, Grand Prizes, and the "Hot Hand". *Journal of Sports Economics*, **10**(3), 236–255.

Paul, R., Humphreys, B. and Weinbach, A. (2013). The Lure of the Pitcher: How the Baseball Betting Market is Influenced by Elite Starting Pitchers. *Oxford University Handbook of Sports Gambling Markets*, Oxford University Press, Leighton Vaughn Williams, editor.

Paul, R., Humphreys, B. and Weinbach, A. (2014). Bettor Belief in the "Hot Hand": Evidence from Detailed Betting Data on the NFL. *Journal of Sports Economics*, **15**(6), 636–649.

Paul, R. and Weinbach, A. (2008). Price Setting in the NBA Gambling Market: Tests of the Levitt Model of Sportsbook Behavior. *International Journal of Sports Finance*, **3**(3), 2–18.

Paul, R. and Weinbach, A. (2008). Does Sportsbook.com Set Pointspreads to Maximize Profits? Tests of the Levitt Model of Sportsbook Behavior. *Journal of Prediction Markets*, **1**(3), 209–218.

Paul, R. and Weinbach, A. (2009). Sportsbook Behavior in the NCAA Football Betting Market: Tests of the Traditional and Levitt Models of Sportsbook Behavior. *Journal of Prediction Markets*, **3**(2) 21–37.

Paul, R. and Weinbach, A. (2010). The Determinants of Betting Volume for Sports in North America. *International Journal of Sport Finance*, **5**(2), 128–140.

Paul, R. and Weinbach, A. (2012). Wagering Preferences of NFL Bettors: Determinants of Betting Volume. *Journal of Prediction Market*, **6**(1), 42–55.

Paul, R. and Weinbach, A (2013). Baseball: A Poor Substitute for Football – More Evidence of Sports Gambling as Consumption. *Journal of Sports Economics*, **14**(2), 115–132.

Paul, R., Weinbach, A. and Humphreys, B. (2011). Revisiting the "Hot Hand" Hypothesis in the NBA Betting Market Using Actual Betting Percentages. *Journal of Gambling Business and Economics*, **5**(2), 42–56.

Sapra, S.G. (2008). Evidence of Betting Market Intraseason Efficiency and Interseason Overreaction to Unexpected NFL Team Performance 1988–2006. *Journal of Sports Economics*, **9**(5), 488–503

Woodland, B. and Woodland, L. (2000). Testing Contrarian Strategies in the National Football League. *Journal of Sports Economics*, **1**(2), 187–193.

9. Investigating the "hot hand" hypothesis: an application to European football

Robert Simmons and Rhys Wheeler

9.1 INTRODUCTION

There is a belief among sports fans that players occasionally exhibit "streak shooting". For example, in basketball, players are often said to have a "hot hand" after scoring several baskets in succession. The "hot hand" hypothesis is precisely this. A rudimentary definition explains that "a player's chance of hitting a shot are greater following a hit than following a miss on the previous shot" (Gilovich et al., 1985, p. 295). Sun (2004) outlines a more contemporary definition that summarizes the concept as a Markov process where players' performance changes with a given probability between hot and cold states, where the former has a higher shooting accuracy than the latter.

We continue to research the topic by investigating whether such patterns occur in European football, adding to many other papers that have extended the hot hand theory to other applications such as baseball (Albright, 1993). Similar to Arkes (2010), team fixed effects models are used to analyse data spanning two decades and 22 European football leagues. We directly investigate if there is a "hot hand" phenomenon in a team context and whether or not this is correctly incorporated into prices offered by betting firms.

9.2 LITERATURE REVIEW

Gilovich et al. (1985) initiated research into the "hot hand" in their seminal paper consisting of three studies. The first identifies a popular belief in the hot hand among basketball fans while the remaining two attempt to find statistical evidence of the hot hand phenomenon using field goal and free throw data.

A survey conducted of 100 basketball fans from Cornell and Stanford University found that "91% of the fans believed that a player has a better chance of making a shot after having just made his last two or three shots than he does after having just missed his last two or three shots" (p. 297). Despite this finding, the following two studies failed to show any significant evidence that the chance of making a shot increased after having made the previous few. Gilovich et al. (1985) concluded that "the frequency of streaks in players' records did not exceed the frequency predicted by a binomial model that assumes a constant hit rate" (p. 309).

In a study of wagers placed on final score outcomes of professional basketball games, point-spread bets, Camerer (1989) revealed overbetting on teams that are on winning streaks. The market systematically overestimates 'hot' teams' performance – although this does not mean that the teams lost, just that they did not exceed the difference in points predicted. Camerer argues that such an overvaluation is a manifestation of a mistaken belief in the hot hand. This chapter later met criticism from Brown and Sauer (1993) who observe that "this conclusion rests on a strong prior that belief in the hot hand is belief in a myth" (p. 1377), which is true insofar as there is no direct testing in Camerer's models for real "hot hand" effects, and assume throughout that it is a myth.

A second study of point-spread betting by Brown and Sauer (1993) relaxes the assumption that the hot hand is a myth. They model hot hand effects in U.S. basketball markets, however unlike the model used in Camerer (1989), Brown and Sauer (1993) are also able to "detect the presence of real hot hand effects in the data" (p. 1377). Their results confirm that the market is affected by a belief in the hot hand such that teams currently on a streak are expected, ceteris paribus, to win by a larger margin than those that are not. Consistency with Camerer ends here, however, as the investigation identifies that the hot hand cannot be ruled out as a myth as their reported findings would be "compatible with real hot hand effects in the score differences" (Brown and Sauer, 1993, p. 1384).

With the exception of Brown and Sauer (1993), the conclusions of Gilovich et al. (1985) and subsequent papers (see Albright (1993); Frohlich (1994) and more recently Clark (2005)) on the topic outline a widespread belief in the hot hand, but that it is nothing more than a belief in a fallacy. Likewise, this had become conventional wisdom in economic popular press with books like *Naked Economics* remarking "there is no evidence that a player's chances of making a shot are greater after making a previous shot" (Wheelan, 2002). However, this does not give a true representation of all the research carried out in this field. There has been much criticism of the methods used in previous studies, in particular questioning the lack of power of previous models. Models in previous research have lacked the ability to reject a null hypothesis of no hot hand effects (a type II error). Considering this, a number of more recent studies have found evidence that it may exist after all (Arkes, 2010).

One criticism of past studies is that the binomial model, which in previous papers had been used as the basis for comparison of the frequency and length of winning streaks, is unlikely to accurately simulate athlete performance; "unlike a fairly flipped coin, athletes compete under varying game conditions and have aches, pains and other human frailties" (Dorsey-Palmateer and Smith, 2004, p. 38). Furthermore, comparison against a binomial model does not account for players mixing difficult and easy shots or how closely a player is being defended. If a player has made several shots in a row, it is likely he will be defended more closely and so the chance of him making the next shot is affected (Arkes, 2010). In other words, the binomial model fails to consider "real world" conditions or exogenous forces that may affect a streak.

Arkes (2013) also addresses the issues surrounding the lack of power of previous tests mentioned above. He argues that since previous studies analyse just one player at a time, previous tests have suffered from a very limited sample size. In fact, in his earlier paper Arkes (2010) uses a player-fixed-effects model and finds that players were 3 per cent more likely to make the second of two free throws had they made the first.

Arkes also uses a suggestion from Stone (2012) to explain that ex-post recording of shots measure the probabilities with an error; thus recording a 1 or 0 to indicate a hit or a miss fails to capture the probability of making a shot effectively. This casts doubt upon the results of previous studies that were mostly concerned with analysis of the autocorrelation between shots. This is verified by Stone (2012) who proves that with shots measuring probabilities plus error, the correlations between shots will be understated compared to correlations between the probabilities themselves. This is something that may have led to false rejection of the "hot hand" in past studies.

Arkes (2013) also suggests that "the frequency of hot hand events is low", causing the effects to be drowned out by observations made when a player is in the normal state. Using randomly generated data, Arkes demonstrates that previous tests fail to detect up to 20 per cent increases in hit probability and concludes that despite much of the previous research on the subject rejecting the hot hand, it could well exist and may have a substantial effect on player and team performance.

Bringing together past research in the field of the hot hand hypothesis and applying it to European football poses an issue to overcome. This is, how well does a "hot hand" translate from player to team analysis? In doing so, this chapter concerns the idea of team momentum, which is the concept of the hot hand applied to a team setting. In his paper examining team momentum in baseball, Vergin (2000) explains how "winning streaks, the hot hand in basketball shooting, and batting slumps in baseball are part of the lexicon of sports and are examples of perceived momentum" (p. 181). Vergin's conclusions reinforce the results of Gilovich et al. (1985). Although there is no evidence of its existence, there is widespread belief that a result in the last event – whether it is a shot in basketball or a victory in the previous game – affects the result of the next.

9.3   DATA

An extensive dataset has been obtained from www.football-data.co.uk and includes the results of most major European football league games from the 1993/94 season up to the start of the 2012/13 season. The dataset also contains pre-match odds from GamesBookers.com – a fixed odds market – for games in the seasons from 2000/01 to the beginning of 2012/13. GamesBookers.com was chosen as it provides the most consistent odds of the available bookmakers. To perform the analysis the data has been stacked, yielding two observations per game: one observation for the home team and one for the away team. This results in a dataset of 272,946 observations, of which 179,252 observations have the bookmaker's pregame odds available.

The "full sample" analysis reported below includes 22 leagues from 11 countries. These are: Belgium (1 league), England (5 leagues), France (2 leagues), Germany (2 leagues), Greece (1 league), Italy (2 leagues), the Netherlands (1 league), Portugal (1 league), Scotland (4 leagues), Spain (2 leagues) and Turkey (1 league).

For a clear exposition, the league-by-league analysis for each model presented in this chapter will be restricted to a set of 15 leagues, which are representative of all the available leagues. The reduced sample includes a mixture of "top" divisions where betting market efficiency is expected to be high, as well as smaller leagues where it may be more likely to see betting market inefficiencies. It also includes leagues of other particular interest such as the top two Italian leagues, which have a history of match fixing and other corrupt activities (Hamil et al. 2010) where the efficiency of the market is uncertain. Leagues where team ability varies widely are also included such as in the Scottish leagues, where long winning streaks may be more common among the stronger teams.

The leagues that are presented individually in the representative sample are as follows: the Belgian First Division, all five available English leagues – the Premiership to the Conference Division, the German Bundesliga 1 and Bundesliga 2, the Italian Serie A and Serie B, the top four Scottish leagues – the Scottish Premiership to the Scottish Football League Third Division and the Turkish Süper Lig.

9.4 NOTATION

This section explains the several variable transformations that were necessary to conduct the analysis presented in the remainder of this chapter. Since the dataset is panel data, each variable has two subscripts where i is the team index which is the cross section of the data, and t denotes the game index which acts as the time series aspect of the dataset and enables the analysis of previous (lagged) games to be implemented.

Home dummy, $HOME_{i,t}$ – This dummy variable indicates whether team i is playing at home for game t:

$$HOME_{i,t} = \begin{cases} 1, & \textit{if team i is playing at home} \\ 0, & \textit{otherwise} \end{cases} \tag{9.1}$$

Win dummy, $W_{i,t}$ – This is a dummy variable indicating whether team i won game t:

$$W_{i,t} = \begin{cases} 1, & \textit{if team i won} \\ 0, & \textit{otherwise} \end{cases} \tag{9.2}$$

Ex-ante probability, $x_{i,t}$ – the probability inferred from the bookmaker's posted odds that team i will win game t. The bookmaker's odds are posted in European decimal format (the total amount returned if the bettor wins), hence, to infer the bookmaker's estimated probability it is necessary to take the reciprocal and divide by the "over-round" or "vigorish" which differs for each game similar to Franck et al. (2010, p. 449). This is done as follows:

$$x_{i,t} = \frac{1/R_{i,t}}{O_t} \tag{9.3}$$

where:

$$O_t = \frac{1}{H_t} + \frac{1}{A_t} + \frac{1}{D_t} \tag{9.4}$$

where $R_{i,t}$ is the odds posted by the bookmaker for team i to win game t and O_t is the "over-round". The over-round is the sum of the reciprocal of the odds posted for the three possible outcomes of game t, where H_t, A_t and D_t are the odds posted for a home win, an away win and a draw respectively. Obviously, $R_{i,t}$ will be equal to either H_t or A_t in each observation.

Streak, $STRK_{i,t}$ – This variable is the number of consecutive games team i has won prior to game t.

Streak Dummy, $ST_{i,t}^n$ – This is a dummy variable used in sections 9.7.3 and section 9.8 to allow for analysis of particular streak lengths. This variable takes the value of 1 if team i's win streak is equal to n (similar to Brown and Sauer (1993)) prior to game t and zero otherwise, where n is a chosen value for the model and stated explicitly. Hence:

$$ST_{i,t}^n = \begin{cases} 1, & \textit{if current streak} = n \\ 0, & \textit{otherwise} \end{cases} \tag{9.5}$$

which of the variables used to analyse the impact of streaks is stated clearly for each of the models in the analysis.

Surprise, $S_{i,t}^n$ – "Surprise" is calculated as the win dummy multiplied by the negative of the natural logarithm of the ex-ante probability that team i would have won each of the previous n games. This provides a method of incorporating into the analysis wins that were perhaps unexpected, thus can be used to identify teams that are performing above average. This method is useful since small probabilities are transformed into relatively high "surprise" and has the potential to provide a more insightful perspective on hot teams and streaks. Formally $S_{i,t}$ is calculated as:

$$S_{i,t}^n = \sum_{t=-1}^{-n} W_{i,t}(-\log x_{i,t}) \tag{9.6}$$

where i denotes the team in question, t is the game reference with $t = -1$ denoting the previous game and $-n$ is the game played n games before. $x_{i,t}$ is the bookmaker's inferred probability of team i winning the game t.

9.5   BOOKMAKER EFFICIENCY

Market efficiency in the context of fixed odds betting can take two forms; "strong form efficiency" posits that all bets should have equal expected value, and "weak form efficiency" asserts that no bets should have a positive expected value (Cain et al., 2000, p. 25). Knowledge of whether the bookmaker is efficient is necessary for analysis of "surprising" winning streaks in section 9.8. Since true probabilities are unobservable ex-ante, we use bookmaker odds to infer them and the reliability of the analysis requires an efficient market as bias may induce inaccurate coefficient estimates. The following simple linear probability model is used to analyse whether bookmakers are efficient in predicting win probabilities:

$$W_{i,t} = \alpha + \beta x_{i,t} \tag{9.7}$$

where variables $W_{i,t}$ and $x_{i,t}$ are the win dummy and ex-ante inferred probabilities as explained earlier.

This section presents an F-test to investigate whether the ex-ante probability coefficient in this equation is statistically different from one. A null hypothesis that this coefficient is equal to one would indicate that the probabilities inferred from the bookmaker's posted odds are efficient estimators of the true probability of a given team, *i*, winning game *t*.

Appendix Table 9A.1 presents the results of the estimated model and an F-test, testing the null hypothesis that $\beta = 1$, for the full sample and each league from the representative sample. An F-statistic of 257.4746 means it is safe to reject the null hypothesis that the coefficient on the bookmaker's ex-ante probabilities is equal to one. The calculated coefficient of 1.128 suggests that the bookmaker is under-pricing favourites. An increase in the inferred probability (which increases as returns from a stake decrease) underestimates the fitted "true" probability. This fits with literature on bookmaker bias in UK fixed odds markets that traditionally exhibit "favourite–longshot bias" which is defined in Cain et al. (2000) as a phenomenon where "favourites win more often than the subjective market probabilities imply, and longshots less often" (p.25) and this violates, at least, strong form efficiency.

Performing this analysis for each league reveals that at the 10 per cent significance level, 11 of the 15 leagues are estimated to have coefficients different to one and that eight leagues have a statistically significant difference at the 1 per cent level. Interestingly, there seems to be no obvious link between the leagues that have coefficients that cannot be said to be statistically different from one. As hypothesised earlier, the leagues expected to have coefficients of one were the "top" divisions in football. However, there is only one top division that fits this theory – the German Bundesliga 1. The English Premier League, Italian Serie A and Scottish Premiership all have coefficients calculated as greater than one. It seems that the problem of favourite–longshot bias may be common across European football fixed odds markets.

9.6   DOES THE MARKET BELIEVE IN THE HOT HAND?

Camerer (1989) and Brown and Sauer (1993) pioneered work on bookmaker belief in the hot hand hypothesis, where they used a pari-mutuel spread betting market to infer market belief in the hot hand. While it is not possible to replicate the models put forward by Brown and Sauer (1993), since our dataset is concerned with a fixed-odds market, it is possible to

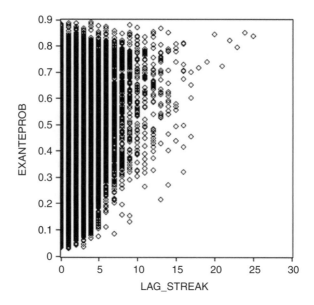

Figure 9.1   Scatterplot of bookmaker probability against streak length

draw some inspiration from their work and provide some insight into the effects of winning streaks on the probabilities advertised by the bookmaker.

Figure 9.1 offers some insight into how a team's winning streak prior to a game affects the inferred probabilities of a win from the bookmaker. It is possible to see that the spread of ex-ante probabilities becomes smaller and the mean skews upwards as streak length prior to a game increases. The trend becomes particularly prominent as streak length becomes long enough to be considered "unusual" as it passes four to five consecutive wins.

Of course, this may be a survivorship bias in the sense that the teams achieving long streak lengths are simply better and would have had higher probabilities at the start of their streak. Formal investigation of the impact of streak length on bookmakers' estimated probability of a win is conducted via a simple OLS regression with team fixed effects:

$$x_{i,t} = \beta_0 + \beta_1 HOME_{i,t} + \beta_2 STRK_{i,t} \qquad (9.8)$$

where all variables are as defined in section 9.4 and the variable of interest, $STRK_{i,t}$, is winning-streak length.

If β_2 is calculated to be positive, it would indicate a belief held by the bookmaker in the hot hand. That is, the bookmaker believes a winning streak increases the chance of winning the next game. A negative β_2 would suggest the opposite – the bookmaker believes winning streaks are abnormal patterns and will reverse in the next game.

Appendix Table 9A.2 shows the estimates of the β_2 coefficient for the full sample and the individual leagues. For the full sample, the β_2 coefficient is indeed statistically greater than zero with a t-statistic of 119.062 and a coefficient of 0.028. This suggests that each consecutive win prior to a game increases the bookmaker's expectation that team i will win by 2.8 per cent. Of course, since this is an estimate for the full sample it may be the case that the bookmaker may consider streaks differently across leagues, particularly where team ability varies greatly.

From the coefficients presented for individual leagues it is possible to infer a large variation in the increase in probability of winning a game from each consecutive win beforehand. The increases range from 1.8 per cent in the English first and third division, and the Italian Serie A, to 3.9 per cent in the English Premier League. It appears that the increase in bookmaker probability from increasing streak length is greatest in leagues where team ability varies the least. This would confirm that the bookmaker does indeed believe in recent "form" and that "hot" teams are more likely to win, particularly when streaks are unlikely because of closely matched team abilities in some leagues. The effect is less profound in leagues where there is great disparity in team ability and long streaks are commonplace for stronger teams.

Bookmakers believe in a continuation of streaks but the extent of their belief differs across leagues as demonstrated by the coefficients estimated by the model. It does not, however, confirm that the hot hand is a real phenomenon, since the bookmaker may be incentivized to increase the inferred probabilities (by reducing returns paid out on bets if the team wins) above their "true" values for their own reasons; for example, balancing wagers to guarantee a profit regardless of the result (Sinkey and Logan, 2012) or to exploit other sources of bias, such as sentiment (Forrest and Simmons, 2008).

9.7 TESTING FOR THE HOT HAND: PART ONE

The sample for the following models is restricted to exclude seasons 2010/11, 2011/12 and the beginning of the season 2012/13 as a hold-out sample to allow forecasting to be performed without influence of the forecast sample on the estimated coefficients.

9.7.1 All Streak Lengths

The existence of a momentum effect in a team context would predict that teams on a winning streak should be more likely to win the next game. The following linear probability model with team fixed effects is estimated using OLS:

$$W_{i,t} = \beta_0 + \beta_1 HOME_{i,t} + \beta_2 STRK_{i,t} \tag{9.9}$$

where the variables included are as described in section 9.4 and $STRK_{i,t}$ is again the streak length variable. If team momentum effects are present it is expected that the probability will increase as streak length prior to a game increases; that is, $\beta_2 > 0$. Extensive research on team performance and home advantage (Pollard, 1986) motivates the inclusion of the home variable and the β_1 coefficient is expected to be positive.

Appendix Table 9A.3 reports the estimation of this model. For the full sample, the estimates show that the hypotheses regarding β_1 and β_2 in this model were correct and the β_2 coefficient is calculated as 0.0104. The coefficient for β_2 suggests that for each consecutive win prior to a given game, team i is a little over 1 per cent more likely to win on average. Although this appears quite small, a streak of five consecutive games would result in an estimated increase in probability of 5 per cent compared to a team that had not won its last game – an indication that momentum may have a real effect on team performance.

Applying the model to individual leagues to investigate the effects across countries and skill levels yields diverse results. When looking at the estimate for the streak length coefficient when the model is run league by league, it becomes apparent that it may have no effect at all in some leagues. In fact, the β_2 coefficient is only significantly greater than zero at the 10 per cent level in eight of the 15 leagues – this diminishes to just three leagues at the 1 per cent level. Furthermore, of the eight leagues in which the coefficient is greater than zero at the 10 per cent level, only four leagues have a coefficient suggesting an increase of more than 1 per cent in probability of winning a game for each consecutive win prior to a match. This finding indicates that the probability inferred by the bookmaker of a team winning a game is affected far more than the true probability by a winning streak before a game. This may leave the bookmaker exposed to bettors who go against the streak and this is investigated in section 9.9.

Insignificant coefficients in this model may be caused by the streak length variable which contains all consecutive wins prior to a game, be that one win or the 25 consecutive wins achieved by Celtic in the 2003/04 season. In the following model we control for this by only examining streaks that are long enough to be considered "unusual", rather than allowing these streaks to be drowned out by more "common" consecutive wins of one or two.

9.7.2 Defining "Hot"

Determining what classifies as a hot streak is not a definite procedure and is very much subject to writers' own judgement. In the seminal paper on the topic, Gilovich et al. (1985) consider streaks of one, two and three hits in a row in both field goal and free-throw data, whereas Brown and Sauer (1993) only consider streaks of two and four games. Arkes (2010) examines the effect of the number of free throws made in the last two to five attempts, but only finds the number of successes in the last two shots had any significant effect on the probability of making the next shot. This is one aspect in which the translation from an individual's hot hand to team momentum raises issues. As such, considering what describes a hot streak will be inferred from the dataset rather than previous literature.

By examining Figure 9.2, some inference can be made as to what constitutes an "unusual" streak. The exponential decay in the frequency of streak lengths is a useful feature in determining which lengths to focus on in the remainder of this chapter. Streaks that are of four consecutive wins or more account for just 5.8 per cent of all runs in the dataset. As such, this should provide an indication of teams that could be considered hot.

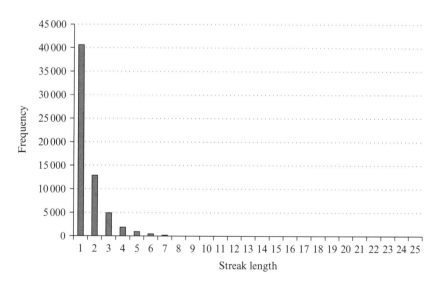

Figure 9.2   Frequency graph of streak lengths

The analysis herein considers a much wider range of consecutive successes than most previous research by analysing streaks between two and seven wins in length.

9.7.3 "Hot" Dummy

The following model is used to investigate specific streak lengths and the impact they have on the probability of winning a game:

$$W_{i,t} = \beta_0 + \beta_1 HOME_{i,t} + \beta_2 ST^n_{i,t} \tag{9.10}$$

where the streak length variable is replaced by a streak dummy variable, with $ST^n_{i,t}$ as outlined in section 9.4. This model is again estimated using OLS with team fixed effects and n ranges from two to seven. Appendix Table 9A.4 presents the β_2 coefficients calculated for the full sample and each league in the representative sample and at each streak length for which the model was estimated.

Looking first at the full sample column, as the number of games in the current streak increases, the coefficient on the streak dummy variable, generally, increases too. The coefficients indicate an increase in probability of winning the game from 1.4 per cent with two consecutive wins prior to a game to a 6.2 per cent increase with six consecutive games. Additionally, all these coefficients were calculated to be statistically different to zero.

Considering the league-by-league analysis however, it appears there is little evidence that winning streaks contribute anything to the probability of winning the next game. The vast majority of coefficients calculated are insignificantly different from zero and a considerable proportion of them are even negative; suggesting that in some leagues, certain streak lengths have a negative impact on a team's likelihood of winning the next game. Of the 13 coefficients statistically different from zero at the 10 per cent level, only one is significant at the 1 per cent level – the German Bundesliga 2 with a pre-game streak of four wins. It is also noticeable that the coefficients found to be statistically significant tend to be rather large, by comparison to the full sample coefficients, the greatest of which suggests a 33 per cent increase in probability if a team in the Scottish Football League 1 has a winning streak of seven wins prior to a match. A possible reason for this may be a very small sample of teams reaching these individual streak lengths, particularly more than five consecutive wins, causing small statistical significance.

9.8 THE ELEMENT OF SURPRISE – TESTING FOR THE HOT HAND: PART TWO

Section 9.7 outlined a model that is limited insofar as it treats streaks of the same length as equally likely and averages the effect accordingly. This section builds upon this model by asking a simple question: what defines a "hot" team? If a team currently at the top of the league wins four or five games in a row, is this a "hot" streak, or just that they have better ability in general? It is much more rational to suggest a team is "hot" if they are winning games against teams that are of an equal or higher ability.

This final model attempts to control for this by considering "surprising" winning streaks. The surprise variable, $S_{i,t}^n$, as defined in section 9.4, provides a measure of how unlikely the winning streak is using the inferred ex-ante probabilities of the team winning each of the games in their streak. In the following model it is worth noting that in section 9.5 it was found that bookmaker's inferred probabilities exhibit favourite–longshot bias, which may exaggerate the surprise variable for unusual wins, since it is the "underdog" wins that will be of most interest.

Estimating the following linear probability model is done using OLS with team fixed effects:

$$W_{i,t} = \beta_0 + \beta_1 HOME_{i,t} + \beta_2 x_{i,t} + \beta_3 ST_{i,t}^n + \beta_4 S_{i,t}^n + \beta_5 ST_{i,t}^n * S_{i,t}^n \quad (9.11)$$

where all variables are as defined in section 9.4. The final term will be the key variable of interest, since this captures the total surprise of teams that have n consecutive wins prior to a game.

Appendix Table 9A.5 reports the calculated β_5 coefficients for this model for the full sample and each league in the representative sample for each streak length considered.

Examination of the coefficients for the full sample show no evidence at any streak length that increasingly surprising winning streaks have any effect on the probability of winning the next game, with none of the calculated coefficients being different from zero. When the model is applied to individual leagues, this pattern remains. Only seven coefficients were calculated to be statistically different from zero, four of which were when the streak prior to a game was equal to three. Additionally, three of the statistically significant coefficients were negative – suggesting a reduced likelihood of winning a game after having a "surprising" win streak. On the whole, however, there is no evidence from this model that having a surprising winning streak has any effect on the likelihood of winning the next game.

9.9   BETTING RULES – CAN THE BOOKMAKER BE BEATEN?

Having determined evidence that there may well be market inefficiencies within the football betting market (section 9.6), we now investigate whether these are exploitable for profits. To do this, data for seasons 2010/11, 2011/12 and the beginning of 2012/13 are used, which were excluded from previous analysis to allow for forecasting here. Appendix Table 9A.6 presents a summary of the betting strategies considered, the total value of stakes placed had a bettor followed the strategy for the period analysed, the total returns (including stakes of winning bets) and the profit/loss for each strategy. Included are strategies in which bets for and against the streak are considered. We compare these to the returns of two simple strategies; betting on all home teams and betting on all away teams. All strategies in this analysis use unit bets for each game that applies to each heuristic strategy.

Examination of the profit/loss columns reveals results that are consistent with the majority of previous research on the hot hand and sports betting markets (Bar-Eli et al., 2006). Only two strategies yield positive returns for the seasons considered. Betting against all teams with streaks equal to seven before a game yielded a 0.49 per cent return. The reliability of this return is questionable given the relatively small number of bets placed for this rule. Betting on all games where the forecast probability of winning was greater than 90 per cent yielded a 2.94 per cent return. Betting against teams on a streak – more specifically, betting that they will lose – typically performs far worse than betting on the streak continuing. Generally, betting the streak will continue outperformed betting on all away teams, but this strategy is no better than betting on all home teams.

Using fitted probabilities from the forecast of Model 3 with a streak of five proved to be one of the best betting methods. However, with the exception of the aforementioned strategy of betting on all probabilities greater than 90 per cent, these too yielded negative returns.

Such wide-ranging returns on these strategies suggest that the market may violate strong-form efficiency. That is, the bets made in these strategies do not yield the same expected value ex-ante. Betting on all games where the probability of winning is greater than 90 per cent yields a 2.94 per cent return and could be interpreted as being indicative of a violation of weak-form efficiency.

9.10 CONCLUSIONS

We have presented results that outline some key features of the European football betting market. In testing for bookmaker efficiency, the results suggest that favourite–longshot bias is present which conforms to prior studies on the efficiency of this fixed odds market. Consistent with much of the research on belief in the hot hand, section 9.6 suggests there is evidence that bookmakers believe in momentum effects from one game to the next. The model presented, however, does not determine the source of this correlation. Findings by Sinkey and Logan (2012) suggest that this may be reflecting bettor belief, rather than the bookmaker belief, as they suggest the bookmaker simply adjusts odds in order to combat behavioural strategies of the bettor to ensure they are not exposed to losses from each game.

In testing for actual momentum effects our model reveals a small, positive effect when applied to all leagues. This suggests an increase in probability of just over 1 per cent for each consecutive win prior to a match. At the individual league level the effect is much less pronounced and is absent in most leagues. This indicates that the bookmaker's probabilities are affected by winning streaks more than the true probabilities. If it is the case that the bookmaker's probabilities are driven by bettor beliefs, this would be consistent with a belief in momentum effects but that such effects are a myth.

When bookmaker probabilities and surprising winning streaks are captured in the model, momentum effects disappear altogether. It seems that European football, with its fixed-odds market and team-based sports setting, conforms to previous research on the hot hand phenomenon and other momentum effects; that belief in such effects exists, but that evidence of them, contrary to work by Arkes (2010) among others, is elusive and they may not exist after all.

Given the lack of evidence of momentum effects, it is unsurprising to find that betting on, or against, teams with winning streaks does not leave the bookmaker open to exploitation for profits on average. However, the results of applying these strategies call into question the efficiency of the markets and further research may uncover other ways in which the market may be exploited. In particular, investigating whether or not the favourite–longshot bias exhibited throughout the European football markets gives bettors the opportunity to profit.

REFERENCES

Albright, S.C. (1993). A Statistical Analysis of Hitting Streaks in Baseball. *Journal of the American Statistical Association,* **88** (424), 1175–1183.

Arkes, J. (2010). Revisiting the Hot Hand Theory with Free Throw Data in a Multivariate Framework. *Journal of Quantitative Analysis in Sports,* **6** (1).

Arkes, J. (2013). Misses on "Hot Hand" Research. *Journal of Sports Economics,* **14** (4), 401–410.

Bar-Eli, M., Avugos, S. and Raab, M. (2006). Twenty Years of "Hot Hand" Research: Review and Critique. *Psychology of Sport and Exercise,* **7**, 525–553.

Brown, W.O. and Sauer, R.D. (1993). Does the Basketball Market Believe in the Hot Hand? Comment. *The American Economic Review,* **83** (5), 1377–1386.

Cain, M., Law, D. and Peel, D. (2000). The Favourite–Longshot Bias and Market Efficiency in UK Football Betting. *Scottish Journal of Political Economy,* **47** (1), 25–36.

Camerer, C.F. (1989). Does the Basketball Market Believe in the "Hot Hand". *The American Economic Review,* **79** (5), 1257–1261.

Clark, R.D. (2005). Examination of Hole-to-hole Streakiness on the PGA Tour. *Perceptual and Motor Skills,* **100** (3), 806–814.

Dorsey-Palmateer, R. and Smith, G. (2004). Bowlers' Hot Hands. *The American Statistician,* **58** (1), 38–45.

Forrest, D. and Simmons, R. (2008). Sentiment in the Betting Market on Spanish Football. *Applied Economics,* **40**, 119–126.

Franck, E., Verbeek, E. and Nuesch, S. (2010). Prediction Accuracy of Different Market Structures – Bookmakers Versus a Betting Exchange. *International Journal of Forecasting,* **26**, 448–459.

Frohlich, C. (1994). Baseball: Pitching No-hitters. *Chance,* **7**, 24–30.

Gilovich, T., Vallone, R. and Tversky, A. (1985). The Hot Hand in Basketball: On the Misperception of Random Sequences. *Cognitive Psychology,* **17**, 295–314.

Hamil, S., Morrow, S., Idle, C., Rossi, G. and Faccendini, S. (2010). The Governance and Regulation of Italian Football. *Soccer & Society,* **11** (4), 373–413.

Pollard, R. (1986). Home Advantage in Soccer: A Retrospective Analysis. *Journal of Sports Sciences,* **4** (3), 237–248.

Sinkey, M. and Logan, T. (2012). Does the Hot Hand Drive the Market? Evidence from Betting Markets. Working Paper.

Stone, D.F. (2012). Measurement Error and the Hot Hand. *The American Statistician,* **66** (1), 61–66.

Sun, Y. (2004). Detecting the Hot Hand: An Alternative Model. In K. Forbus, D. Gentre and T. Regier (eds), *Proceedings of the 26th Annual Conference of the Cognitive Science Society,* Mahwah, NJ: Lawrence Erlbaum Associates Inc., pp. 1279–1284.

Vergin, R.C. (2000). Winning Streaks in Sports and the Misperception of Momentum. *Journal of Sport Behaviour,* **23** (2), 181–197.

Wheelan, C. (2002). *Naked Economics* (2nd edn), New York: W. Norton & Company.

APPENDIX

Table 9A.1 Regression results for market efficiency model

League	Full Sample	Belgian 1st Division	English Premier League	English League 1	English League 2	English League 3	English Conference	German Bundesliga 1
Constant Coefficient	-0.045905	-0.062673	-0.046550	-0.019064	-0.036175	-0.001154	-0.034963	-0.008892
(standard error)	(0.002851)	(0.012214)	(0.010205)	(0.014404)	(0.013311)	(0.015037)	(0.017177)	(0.013457)
Ex-ante Probability Coefficient	1.128524	1.177370	1.125365	1.047666	1.092626	0.995498	1.090724	1.044135
(standard error)	(0.008010)	(0.034757)	(0.028856)	(0.040574)	(0.037407)	(0.041818)	(0.048587)	(0.037832)
F-statistic	257.4746	26.04156	18.87469	1.380099	6.131477	0.011589	3.486583	1.360987
F-test Probability	0.0000	0.0000	0.0000	0.2401	0.0133	0.9143	0.0619	0.2434

League	German Bundesliga 2	Italian Serie A	Italian Serie B	Scottish Premiership	Scottish Football League 1	Scottish Football League 2	Scottish Football League 3	Turkish Super Lig
Constant Coefficient	-0.049554	-0.072007	-0.067492	-0.037862	-0.066012	-0.025090	-0.043952	-0.039623
(standard error)	(0.015824)	(0.009831)	(0.011280)	(0.011698)	(0.024379)	(0.027340)	(0.020277)	(0.012812)
Ex-ante Probability Coefficient	1.138945	1.191956	1.183564	1.119470	1.130557	1.088146	1.158017	1.111654
(standard error)	(0.044746)	(0.028803)	(0.034138)	(0.031756)	(0.066937)	(0.073508)	(0.054825)	(0.036041)
F-statistic	9.642304	44.415750	28.912680	14.153810	3.804270	1.437922	8.307152	9.597425
F-test Probability	0.0019	0.0000	0.0000	0.0002	0.0512	0.2305	0.0040	0.0020

Table 9A.2   *Regression results of streak coefficients with bookmaker win probability as dependent variable*

	Full Sample	Belgium 1st Division	German Bundesliga 1	German Bundesliga 2	English Premier League	English League 1	English League 2	English League 3
Streak Coefficient	0.028368	0.03209	0.027941	0.020095	0.03918	0.018056	0.020382	0.018068
t-statistic	119.0616	24.1786	21.95573	17.7357	31.84227	24.94287	27.97103	25.57552

	English Conference	Italian Serie A	Italian Serie B	Scottish Premiership	Scottish Football League 1	Scottish Football League 2	Scottish Football League 3	Turkish Super Lig
Streak Coefficient	0.022472	0.034136	0.018951	0.034335	0.025188	0.022559	0.030829	0.033775
t-statistic	21.306	26.56184	18.52641	28.98214	16.87711	17.38373	20.02465	25.68371

Table 9A.3 Regression results for team win model

League	Full Sample	Belgian 1st Division	English Premier League	English League 1	English League 2	English League 3	English Conference	German Bundesliga 1
Constant	0.256685	0.270954	0.260512	0.258886	0.269537	0.271444	0.296221	0.258438
Prob.	0.0000	0.0000	0.0000	0.0000	0.0000	0.0000	0.0000	0.0000
Home	0.201467	0.204625	0.199022	0.192022	0.180282	0.168770	0.140500	0.211502
Prob.	0.0000	0.0000	0.0000	0.0000	0.0000	0.0000	0.0000	0.0000
Streak	0.010428	0.008236	0.009208	0.009400	0.005330	0.008649	0.008932	0.006605
Prob.	0.0000	0.0436	0.0097	0.0063	0.1251	0.0151	0.1365	0.1259
Observations	234,840	8,887	13,225	18,744	18,743	18,379	5,145	10,385

League	German Bundesliga 2	Italian Serie A	Italian Serie B	Scottish Premiership	Scottish Football League 1	Scottish Football League 2	Scottish Football League 3	Turkish Super Lig
Constant	0.244208	0.231320	0.207866	0.311236	0.311717	0.325705	0.344897	0.268758
Prob.	0.0000	0.0000	0.0000	0.0000	0.0000	0.0000	0.0000	0.0000
Home	0.231004	0.243262	0.249421	0.127403	0.093891	0.085870	0.063013	0.211954
Prob.	0.0000	0.0000	0.0000	0.0000	0.0000	0.0000	0.0000	0.0000
Streak	0.002743	0.003180	0.007870	0.003666	0.012895	0.010385	0.022330	0.007365
Prob.	0.5743	0.4281	0.1069	0.3359	0.0221	0.0842	0.0001	0.0594
Observations	10,495	11,265	11,166	6,710	5,745	4,672	4,667	9,676

Table 9A.4 Regression results of streak dummy variable coefficients with team win as dependent variable

Streak Length		Full Sample	Belgian 1st Division	English Premier League	English League 1	English League 2	English League 3	English Conference	German Bundesliga 1
2	Coefficient	0.013543	-0.002599	0.037356	0.012087	0.016724	-0.003403	-0.004687	0.016192
	Prob.	0.0002	0.8838	0.0117	0.3350	0.1847	0.7901	0.8426	0.3409
3	Coefficient	0.028438	0.017340	0.000715	0.020738	0.008346	0.041934	0.032387	0.043598
	Prob.	0.0000	0.5167	0.9741	0.2996	0.6735	0.0451	0.3722	0.0862
4	Coefficient	0.057088	0.076710	0.052238	0.042184	0.037951	0.002077	0.018065	0.013498
	Prob.	0.0000	0.0507	0.1149	0.1787	0.2288	0.9494	0.7341	0.7191
5	Coefficient	0.037053	0.015059	-0.033008	0.011754	0.005228	0.131012	-0.012809	-0.070012
	Prob.	0.0022	0.7728	0.4682	0.8084	0.9145	0.0117	0.8731	0.2061
6	Coefficient	0.056998	-0.014463	0.129874	0.094690	0.130446	0.044497	0.229368	0.086443
	Prob.	0.0009	0.8381	0.0519	0.2077	0.0800	0.5518	0.0702	0.3618
7	Coefficient	0.062357	0.003091	0.017506	-0.028664	-0.030048	0.096048	0.209781	0.009848
	Prob.	0.0074	0.9739	0.8300	0.7795	0.7756	0.3886	0.1600	0.9368

Streak Length		German Bundesliga 2	Italian Serie A	Italian Serie B	Scottish Premiership	Scottish Football League 1	Scottish Football League 2	Scottish Football League 3	Turkish Super Lig
2	Coefficient	0.024791	-0.022320	-0.013243	-0.017612	0.006644	0.011777	0.006208	0.027892
	Prob.	0.1480	0.1704	0.4349	0.3934	0.7692	0.6376	0.2592	0.1081
3	Coefficient	-0.016626	0.016113	0.043585	0.002525	0.052926	0.026699	0.019998	0.030590
	Prob.	0.5316	0.5295	0.1265	0.9352	0.1312	0.4830	0.5779	0.2222
4	Coefficient	0.144849	-0.027102	0.084077	0.069672	0.055750	0.076292	0.127675	0.071374
	Prob.	0.0011	0.4793	0.0633	0.1125	0.2724	0.1779	0.0153	0.0446
5	Coefficient	-0.074070	0.022006	0.079561	-0.034351	0.094647	0.125490	-0.009324	-0.049814
	Prob.	0.2252	0.7028	0.2559	0.5324	0.1904	0.1087	0.8948	0.2848
6	Coefficient	-0.090411	0.098416	0.073765	0.026930	0.042261	0.003857	0.126025	0.038129
	Prob.	0.3834	0.1976	0.5025	0.7075	0.6754	0.9707	0.2196	0.5709
7	Coefficient	-0.299405	0.087701	0.197814	0.080543	0.330552	-0.050714	0.127072	0.040979
	Prob.	0.1139	0.3728	0.2853	0.3490	0.0268	0.7386	0.3413	0.6377

Table 9A.5   Regression results for streak length-surprise interaction coefficients with team win as dependent variable

		Full Sample	Belgian 1st Division	English Premier League	English League 1	English League 2	English League 3	English Conference	German Bundesliga 1
Streak = 3	Coefficient	0.004295	-0.010361	0.039422	-0.077652	0.006427	-0.011106	0.158675	-0.074369
	Prob.	0.6361	0.8020	0.2207	0.0961	0.8799	0.8236	0.0087	0.0741
Streak = 4	Coefficient	0.005255	-0.077685	0.024124	-0.022538	0.041025	0.006648	0.005754	-0.018885
	Prob.	0.6234	0.1515	0.4934	0.7395	0.4684	0.9180	0.9360	0.7367
Streak = 5	Coefficient	0.006481	0.008853	-0.015673	0.085202	0.082399	0.054211	-0.042025	0.169785
	Prob.	0.6183	0.8993	0.7424	0.3483	0.2799	0.4967	0.6302	0.0223
Streak = 6	Coefficient	0.008391	-0.028045	-0.035971	-0.068027	0.009879	-0.087989	0.073727	-0.106205
	Prob.	0.6033	0.7657	0.5990	0.5440	0.9193	0.4570	0.5645	0.2544
Streak = 7	Coefficient	-0.013759	0.067753	-0.023367	0.035144	-0.112015	0.017033	-0.029539	-0.113623
	Prob.	0.5176	0.5681	0.8934	0.8208	0.3930	0.9039	0.8184	0.5120

		German Bundesliga 2	Italian Serie A	Italian Serie B	Scottish Premiership	Scottish Football League 1	Scottish Football League 2	Scottish Football League 3	Turkish Super Lig
Streak = 3	Coefficient	0.054927	-0.049997	0.168533	0.000018	-0.006557	0.113254	-0.045888	0.006704
	Prob.	0.3631	0.1887	0.0005	0.9996	0.9319	0.1166	0.4823	0.8594
Streak = 4	Coefficient	0.027048	-0.050083	-0.009906	0.001642	-0.058322	0.137447	0.057706	0.019772
	Prob.	0.7426	0.3339	0.8729	0.9693	0.5434	0.0699	0.4716	0.6491
Streak = 5	Coefficient	0.105553	0.000635	-0.048977	-0.082368	-0.087648	-0.057980	-0.014127	0.038560
	Prob.	0.2538	0.9936	0.5410	0.0910	0.5827	0.4705	0.8776	0.5324
Streak = 6	Coefficient	-0.015645	-0.117331	-0.088519	-0.017840	0.030721	-0.021027	-0.040627	-0.093257
	Prob.	0.9070	0.2718	0.3830	0.8990	0.9134	0.8585	0.7158	0.2507
Streak = 7	Coefficient	0.367641	0.043264	-0.042899	0.216482	-0.459984	0.123184	-0.052890	-0.098184
	Prob.	0.2879	0.7957	0.7241	0.1173	0.5993	0.6363	0.6296	0.6273

Table 9A.6   Betting strategy results

Category	Strategy	Total Value of Stakes Placed	Amount Returned	Profit/Loss	Profit/Loss Percentage
Home/Away	Bet on All Home	£18,723.00	£17,225.29	−£1,497.71	−7.999
	Bet on All Away	£18,723.00	£16,389.32	−£2,333.68	−12.464
Streak = n	Bet on all with streak = 3	£1,191.00	£1,115.61	−£75.39	−6.330
	Bet on all with streak = 4	£519.00	£457.50	−£61.50	−11.850
	Bet on all with streak = 5	£244.00	£235.36	−£8.64	−3.541
	Bet on all with streak = 6	£129.00	£116.35	−£12.65	−9.806
	Bet on all with streak = 7	£67.00	£56.56	−£10.44	−15.582
	Bet against all with streak = 3	£1,191.00	£1,034.62	−£156.38	−13.130
	Bet against all with streak = 4	£519.00	£372.45	−£146.55	−28.237
	Bet against all with streak = 5	£244.00	£190.48	−£53.52	−21.934
	Bet against all with streak = 6	£129.00	£122.26	−£6.74	−5.225
	Bet against all with streak = 7	£67.00	£67.33	£0.33	0.493
Streak > n	Bet on all with streak > 3	£2,268.00	£2,093.13	−£174.87	−7.710
	Bet on all with streak > 4	£1,077.00	£978.75	−£98.25	−9.123
	Bet on all with streak > 5	£558.00	£532.65	−£25.35	−4.543
	Bet on all with streak > 6	£314.00	£288.29	−£25.71	−8.188
	Bet on all with streak > 7	£185.00	£171.94	−£13.06	−7.059
	Bet against all with streak > 3	£2,268.00	£1,860.19	−£407.81	−17.981
	Bet against all with streak > 4	£1,077.00	£825.57	−£251.43	−23.345
	Bet against all with streak > 5	£558.00	£457.12	−£100.88	−18.079
	Bet against all with streak > 6	£314.00	£266.64	−£47.36	−15.083
	Bet against all with streak > 7	£185.00	£144.38	−£40.62	−21.957

Table 9A.6   (continued)

Category	Strategy	Total Value of Stakes Placed	Amount Returned	Profit/Loss	Profit/Loss Percentage
Fitted Values (Model 3) > x	Bet on all with estimated probability > 0.4	£14,757.00	£13,790.92	−£966.08	−6.547
	Bet on all with estimated probability > 0.5	£7,516.00	£7,108.68	−£407.32	−5.419
	Bet on all with estimated probability > 0.6	£3,294.00	£3,196.27	−£97.73	−2.967
	Bet on all with estimated probability > 0.7	£1,391.00	£1,364.13	−£26.87	−1.932
	Bet on all with estimated probability > 0.8	£515.00	£504.59	−£10.41	−2.021
	Bet on all with estimated probability > 0.9	£95.00	£97.79	£2.79	2.937
	Bet on all when estimated probability > Bookmaker's ex-ante probability	£20,725.00	£18,919.44	−£1,805.56	−8.712

10. Sports corruption and developments in betting markets

David Forrest

10.1 INTRODUCTION

The illicit manipulation of individual sporting contests has been documented since the time of the Olympics of Ancient Greece (Weeber, 1991). And the corruption of organized team sports is as old as the sports themselves, as is evident from the known high incidence of fixing in eighteenth and nineteenth century cricket (Gardiner and Naidoo, 2007).

The motives for known historic manipulation have varied from case to case. Often deliberate underperformance by one competitor has been intended to facilitate making a profit in betting markets operating parallel to the sports contest: athletes may trade directly in such markets, wagering that their opponent will win, or they may accept bribes from third parties who plan to make betting gains from such transactions.

In other cases, the primary motivation for a fix has been the achievement of some sporting goal: one competitor "buys" a result by inducing an opponent to underperform to a sufficient degree to bring about the desired outcome. Commonly, such corruption occurs when there is asymmetry between the payoffs from a win to the different competitors. For example, one football club needs to win a match to avoid relegation whereas for its opponent the result has no strong significance. Hill (2009) presented evidence from intercepted telephone calls to document how routine it had become in the Russian football league for clubs needing points to "buy" outcomes of late season matches: this was just part of the "corrupt business environment".

But, even where one, or the primary, motivation may be "sporting" rather than betting gain, the fix is nevertheless often associated with abnormal activity in the betting market. For example, this was the case in the fixing of a football match between Manchester United and Liverpool on Good Friday, 1915. Several players agreed, apparently among themselves, to ensure a United win that would save it from relegation. Evidence of a fix came to light because of heavy betting on a United win: players had sought to gain financially from the agreement. This is illustrative of a more general tendency for the betting market to reflect corrupt actions planned to take place on the field. Participants in a fix, or those to whom information about the planned fix leaks, take the opportunity of pecuniary gain. Indeed, the instigator of bribes to bring about a result for "sporting" reasons may plan actually to finance the transactions by placing and winning bets.

The existence of betting markets on sports events is therefore both a direct source of corruption on the field and a facilitator of fixes for which there are other primary motives. Any change in the availability or organization of betting may thus have potential to change the incidence and nature of corruption within sporting events.

This chapter investigates links between recent developments in the organization and scale of betting markets and the apparent epidemic of match fixing in contemporary sport. It does so with a view to answering the question of how public policy, and sports themselves, should respond to the increase in corruption. For example, should regulators attempt to restrict the terms on which bets can be placed in order to address threats to the integrity of sport?

It is taken as already well established that, in the recent past, integrity has indeed been compromised to a historically unprecedented degree across a range of sports. Public consciousness of the issue was raised by trials in Bochum, Germany, in which a criminal gang was found guilty of fixing 320 football matches in 13 countries. Details are presented in a Report by IRIS (2012) that documented a large number of other football cases that had come to light in just a few years. Since 2012, there has been no let-up in the torrent of revelations, which have led to large numbers of football players and administrators being arrested in countries such as China, Greece, Hungary, Italy, Turkey and Zimbabwe. Indeed, no fewer than 70 countries were reported to have faced football match fixing cases between June 2012 and May 2013 (Abbott and Sheehan, 2013, p. 264). The proven cases have involved betting-related fixes at all levels of the professional and even (as in England and Australia) the semi-professional and amateur games. And problems have extended far beyond football, also implicating sports such as handball, volleyball, motor boat racing, snooker, sumo wrestling and, perhaps especially, cricket and tennis. Further, from the general literature on corruption, it might be speculated that these proven cases are but the tip of the iceberg. For example, Bannenberg and Schaupensteiner (2004) estimated that, at most, 5 per cent of general corruption in Germany comes to light.

It would not be unreasonable to regard the scale of even the proven match fixing as posing an existentialist threat to some sports. Loss of faith in the authenticity of competition following betting scandals led to the collapse of football and volleyball leagues in Asia where fans and sponsors alike shunned the now discredited competitions (IRIS, 2012). Buraimo et al. (2015) provide evidence of substantial and sustained drops in attendance at Italian football clubs implicated in the *Calciopoli* scandal. These examples illustrate that there is a commercial as well as a moral imperative to properly address the threat to integrity. Understanding the reasons for the growth of corruption is a necessary starting-point and central to this must be an understanding of developments in betting markets.

10.2   DEVELOPMENTS IN BETTING MARKETS

As in many other service sectors, the landscape of the betting market has been transformed by technology since around the time of the Millennium. This section of the chapter identifies three major sets of changes: growth in liquidity; proliferation of the subjects on which bets can be placed; and routine extension of the betting period to include the duration of the match itself. Each set of developments is evaluated in terms of whether and to what extent it has raised integrity risk for sports.

10.2.1   The Growth in Liquidity

It is clear that the size of the global betting industry has grown phenomenally since the Millennium. Exactly how fast is hard to assess because a high proportion of stakes are placed illegally or in grey markets. But commercial consultancies, with analysts experienced in the betting industry, attempt to produce "best estimates". Gross Gambling Yield (GGY) is the amount lost by bettors to bookmakers (i.e. stakes minus winnings) and is therefore interpretable as consumer spending, a measure of the popularity of sports betting.

Estimates by CK Consulting in SportAccord (2011) point to a more than tripling of the GGY from sports betting between 2000 and 2010, to €19b per year. But the amount staked, i.e. betting volume, will have grown at a much faster rate than this. The reason is that bookmaker margins were put under intense pressure from new online competition in the many jurisdictions where they had previously enjoyed a measure of monopoly power. Thus a lower proportion of stakes than before was retained (as bettor loss) instead of being paid back as winnings.

An illustration of how much value-for-money improved as competition intensified is that the expected return on football betting with British bookmakers improved from about −11 per cent in 2000 to about −6 per cent in

2010 and the bettor could by then obtain even better value for money by using comparison websites to establish which provider was offering the most generous odds on the particular wager he wished to place (Forrest, 2012). In some other European countries, betting on sport had been either prohibited or available only on very bad terms – as late as the 1980s, returns in Italy had been capped such that only 50 per cent of stakes were returned to bettors (Sorbonne-ICSS, 2014). In these countries, access to a global internet market will have released latent demand for sports betting.

No doubt, greater availability and the improvements in bettor returns associated with the emergence of competitive online markets were each factors, in Europe in particular, in the remarkable growth in the total size of the sports betting market. In Asia, demand was no doubt boosted by the rapid growth of personal incomes in China and in some of the other countries where betting has the strongest cultural grip. And, in all regions, technological change enabling the broadcast and streaming of multiple sports events will have helped the betting market to grow faster because watching and betting on sport are complementary activities: the one makes the other more exciting (for example. betting makes the gambler a stake-holder in the outcome of a game and so even those who are neutral can then find the event more thrilling to view).

Apart from this explosion in the total amount of betting activity (to annual stakes of €200–500b according to Sorbonne-ICSS, 2014, which also quotes even higher Interpol estimates), another significant change was that online trading led to the globalization of the market. For the first time, Europeans could (and do) access Asian bookmakers and Asian operators could (and do) manage risk by laying off bets into Europe. The development of a globalized betting market is illustrated by Grant et al. (2013), who find that significant odds movements in Asia are reflected rapidly in the odds offered by a European bookmaker. As in other financial markets, integration is marked by trading which works in the direction of consistency of prices (odds) across continents. In this particular market, Asia, where betting volumes are higher (and seemingly inclusive of well-informed money), is the leader and Europe the follower.

So, within 10 to 15 years, a global betting market has emerged in which trading volumes are several times larger than in earlier periods. The consequent increase in liquidity in markets on individual sports events is a key factor in understanding why corruption has increased.

Among the defining features of "liquidity" in any financial market is that traders wishing to transact significant volumes over a period can do so at a level not very far from the current price (Black, 1971). In a high-volume financial market, this criterion is likely to be met and informed traders then effectively benefit from "the camouflage of noise traders" (Kyle, 1985), enabling them to make elevated profits. In the particular financial market with which we are concerned, betting, there have been increasing numbers of noise traders (recreational bettors) and this provides an environment in which informed traders (those who know about a fix) can make higher returns because they can place larger stakes without driving prices (odds) against themselves (and without drawing undue attention). Consequently, the money to be made from fixing has been increasing. In the market for fixes, (derived) demand will have shifted to the right, raising the equilibrium quantity of fixes.

An illustration of just how liquid sports betting markets have become is provided by IRIS (2012). IRIS asked experienced betting personnel how much could be placed on the result of a Belgian second division football match through agents in Asia. The consensus was that €200,000–300,000 could safely be staked, as long as the amount was split across a few principal operators. This reflects just how much betting volume there is at even a modest level of competition in a popular sport such as football. The returns that could be made from such stakes are certainly high, relative to athletes' salaries at these levels of sport and it is therefore likely that some of those athletes could be induced to supply a fix for a price that would still leave the fixer with an impressive profit.

That criminals will indeed take advantage of the new opportunities presented by the emergence of highly liquid betting markets is supported by evidence from criminal trials. In the Bochum case, the Prosecution produced evidence that, in a single year, the criminal gang had paid bribes amounting to €12m to make a net profit after bribes and other costs of €7.5m (IRIS, 2012). The list of bets placed included a €36,000 wager on the outcome of a fourth division fixture in Turkey, a further demonstration that relatively high liquidity can extend to low levels of sport.

A second feature conducive to, and perhaps a necessary condition for, extensive fixing is that adequate liquidity should reside in sub-sectors of the market where transactions can take place without effective regulatory supervision. In fact, most betting, even on events held in Europe, takes place in Asia and here fixers can place money without any risk that suspicious transactions may subsequently be traced back to their source. The situation whereby fixers have such free rein has evolved because of the near universal prohibition of sports betting in Asia including the largest countries, China and India. Illegality has shaped the way the industry has developed. The bulk of bets are taken by strictly illegal local bookmakers who manage the risk by selling them on to higher-level operators who then aggregate bets to pool risks. Eventually, further up a hierarchical structure of sports books, much of the money becomes legal when it ends up with one of the four giant operators, the world's biggest bookmakers, which are licensed in Cagayan in the Philippines. These firms routinely deal in aggregated parcels of bets such that betting becomes anonymous. Even where the clients bet directly on computer terminals in illegal betting parlours whose owners are almost in the role of franchisees, the Philippines operators do not have personal records of who places bets and the licensing authority does not require them to "Know their Customer" as financial institutions in Europe, including bookmakers, must. Of course, if "ordinary" bettors are acting illegally at the point where the bet is placed, it is inevitable that the market will come to be organized in such a way as to protect their identity. But this creates a safe environment for fixers and, further, it removes incentives for bets from suspected fixers to be refused: a betting agent who suspects that his client may be a fixer actually has an incentive to cultivate his custom because the agent can add his own money to the parcels of bets to be placed upwards in the hierarchy and thus he too benefits from the fix.

The combination of now highly liquid betting markets and the opportunity to transact with anonymity has created an environment in which fixing offers high financial rewards and little risk of detection. It is therefore unsurprising that criminal groups have been increasingly drawn to the market for fixes. Of course, "petty" crime (players fixing so that they themselves, or their families, can win money from betting, usually on a limited scale) has not gone away. But what is new is the large scale organization of fixing across sport by international organized crime. All the recent criminal trials where multiple sports events have been manipulated have involved international criminal groups such as the Mafia or similar syndicates in Albania, Eastern Europe or Asia. For these groups, fixing sport is now just one more in a portfolio of illicit activities. It has been added to their activities because it has become potentially more lucrative and it also has the attraction that, even where successfully identified and prosecuted, courts tend to impose sentences which are very short relative to those associated with comparably profitable activities such as drug smuggling.

It may be concluded that rising levels of liquidity have greatly increased threats to sports integrity. Betting on sports events is an increasingly popular recreational activity and this provides an environment where criminals can place increasingly large bets and consequently earn increasingly large returns from match fixing.

Sports and competitions where liquidity in betting markets has become high and player wages have remained low are those which have been most endangered by the rapid growth in sports betting. Here the demand for fixes will be relatively strong (because of the potential size of winnings to be made in the betting market) and the willingness to supply fixes may also be relatively high (because players are poorly off and have little to lose if detected and suspended). Mismatch between the volume of betting activity in a competition and the level of player wages is strikingly prevalent in second-level football across much of Europe, where "second-level" refers to second divisions in major countries such as Italy and first divisions in small countries like Finland. Although criminal trials have revealed corruption at all levels of competition, they have featured a disproportionate number of such second-level matches.

So, based on a priori reasoning and a consideration of evidence from criminal trials, it is concluded that the growth of liquidity in betting markets has been the key driver of the substantially raised integrity risk faced by contemporary sport.

10.2.2   Proliferation of Subjects for Betting

As volume in any market grows, consumers are likely to be offered greater choice of product and one form this has taken in the sports betting market is the increasing availability of bets on subjects other than the final winner of the contest. Such bets may appeal to niche groups of consumers either because they offer more fun or interest than traditional bets or because they cater to different risk preferences. For example, with respect to the latter, betting on the winner of a football match seldom offers an opportunity to bet at long odds because leagues are organized hierarchically to limit disparity in ability between teams. Thus a bettor who prefers skewness in returns is not catered for, as he is in a typical horse race where some runners are quoted at long odds. But when the bookmaker offers a bet on which player will be the first scorer in a football match, an array of odds becomes available, allowing more bettors to be drawn in because they can choose a wager according to their risk preference (in this case for betting at long odds). Diversifying the product thus boosts the size of the market and product diversification has been a very visible feature in the development of the sports betting industry in the last decade.

Among the new products, a loose distinction may be drawn between "derivative bets" (relating to a component of the final score, for example, the winner of the first half of a match) and "side bets" (relating to other data in a match such as how many yellow cards are issued). In all sports, bookmakers' websites now routinely offer a large number of both types of proposition on every match on which wagering is possible. Examples of bets available on four popular sports include:

10.2.2.1   Football
What will be the exact final score? What will the half-time 1-X-2 result be? What combination of 1-X-2 half-time and full-time results will occur?

Which team will score first? Will there be a goal in the match? Which player will score first? In live betting, which team will score next? Will the number of goals in a match be above or below a specified figure (most commonly 2.5)? Will the number of goals be an odd or even number? How many corner kicks will there be in the match? Which team will win the first corner kick? How many substitutions will there be in the match? Will there be a penalty in the match? After how many minutes will the first disciplinary card be issued? Will there be a red card in the match? Will the number of disciplinary points be over or under a specified number (with a red card counting two points and a yellow one counting one point)? What will the total of the shirt numbers of players be who score in the match?

10.2.2.2   Tennis

What will the final score be in terms of sets won (2–1 or 2–0 or 1–2 or 0–2)? In live betting, who will win the current set? Who will win the next set? How many points will there be in the match? How many points will a named player win? How many aces will a named player serve? How many aces will there be in the whole match? How many points will there be in the whole match?

10.2.2.3   Cricket

Which batsman will score the most runs for the named team? Which bowler will take the most wickets for the named team? Which of the two batsmen currently at the wicket will get out first? How will the next wicket fall (bowled, lbw, caught, run out, stumped)? How many runs will the named team score in overs 1–10/11–20/etc.? How many runs will be scored before the lunch break? Will a named player score a fifty/a century? What will the difference in total runs be between the teams? Which of two named players will score more runs/take more wickets? How many fours or sixes will a named batsman/bowler score/concede?

10.2.2.4   Darts

What will the exact final score be in the match? Who will win the next set? What will the highest check out be by the named player? How many 180s will a player make in the match? What will the total number of 180s be in the match? How many leg winning doubles will be missed in the match?

These are just some examples. In fact, on major matches, several dozen betting formulae will invariably be displayed by any bookmaker website. This proliferation has been regarded as dangerous by many contributors to the debate on integrity. For example, Rebeggiani and Rebeggiani (2013) note the "inherent cheating potential", of side bets in particular. Such bets may be easy to execute, even by a single player, and sportsmen may be more ready to take part in a fixing activity if it is unlikely to have a decisive impact on the final winner of the event. Employing the framework for determinants of the supply of fixes from Forrest and Simmons (2003), they judge that fixing will be more prevalent where betting is possible on many minor aspects of an event as opposed to only on its winner.

But, while it is plausible that willingness to supply a fix will be greater where a player is required to do something less extreme than delivering a defeat for himself or his team, this will have no practical effect unless there is corresponding demand for the fix. Demand for a fix will be dictated by how much money can be made from a bet on the subject of a fix and this in turn will depend on the depth of the relevant betting market. In general, liquidity is highest in the market on the final result – in the case of football on whether the outcome is a home win, draw or away win (the most popular formula in Europe) or whether a named team does or does not win after application of a handicap (Asian Handicap betting). There is also an active market focused on the total goals in the match. Similarly in basketball, liquid markets relate to which team will win and how many points will be scored in aggregate while in cricket by far the highest volumes are on the winner of the game and how many runs will be scored in a sub-section of the match (for example, overs 21–40). For other derivative and side bets markets in these sports, in practice there is little liquidity, maximum bets will be low, and the potential to make money too limited for them plausibly to be of interest to organized criminals.

Van Rompuy (2015) illustrates that side bets do in fact account for a very limited proportion of football betting volume. Examination of Betfair data on 2,611 matches showed that the results markets accounted for more than 90 per cent of turnover and the main derivatives bets for another 8.5 per cent. All the many side bets available together captured less than one-half of one per cent of turnover. By far the most popular of these side bets was on the identity of the first goal scorer. Even here, and even considering only matches in the highest profile competition, the English Premier League, total transactions per match amounted to less than £42,000. Substantial wagers would scarcely be possible in such a thin market.

A priori reasoning appears to suggest, then, that the development of markets on multiple aspects of a match may not offer significantly increased scope for profitable manipulation of sport by criminal interests. This is supported by the evidence uncovered by prosecutors in criminal trials involving football. In all cases where documentary evidence was gathered, criminals had placed bets (almost invariably through Asia) on final results – the winner, the margin of victory or the total number of goals. None were recorded as having been placed in markets on incidental features of a game. Similarly, in the highest profile American fixing scandal in recent times, where a National Basketball Association referee had been compromised by a criminal gang, the manipulation he carried out was to increase the rate of scoring, to support bets placed in the total points market (Forrest et al., 2008).

A source of more general evidence, exploited by Van Rompuy (2015), is provided by Sportradar, a betting monitoring company. Its "Fraud Detection System" uses algorithms to detect anomalies in movements of odds on hundreds of bookmaker websites across the world. Where anomalies have no apparent innocent explanation, the match is reported to the relevant football authority as suspicious. Van Rompuy looked further at 1,468 matches regarded by Sportradar as "highly suspicious". In the large majority of cases, unexplained and sharp odds movements had been observed in both results and total goals markets, indicating that significant volumes of fixers' money were being placed. But in only 6 of the 1,468 matches was anything detected in side betting markets. Again this is consistent with the notion that criminals are unlikely often to use these markets to profit from a fix.

To be sure, there have been accusations in some fixing cases that derivative and side betting markets have been used by players and their families for personal gain. For example, in a case involving French handball, players were accused of placing bets that their team would trail at half time; in a soccer case, allegations related to a bet that a player would receive a red card. In these cases, amounts of money placed were small but were readily identified as suspicious because the bets were concentrated in small geographical areas. The players and their families had been insufficiently sophisticated to bet outside closely regulated national betting markets.

It cannot be ruled out that such "petty" crime has been facilitated by diversification in the bookmaker product. But a priori reasoning and empirical evidence alike suggest that organized crime, which is implicated as the driving force behind the increase in sports corruption, will not use minor betting markets because trading volumes are too small to support the earning of a significant return.

So the final conclusion of this section is that, based on a priori reasoning and a consideration of evidence from criminal trials, the proliferation of subjects on which bookmakers accept wagers has not been a significant factor in the elevated integrity risk faced by contemporary sport.

10.2.3 The Emergence of In-play ("Live") Betting

While newly available derivative and side betting markets have not captured significant volume relative to the size of the total market, the same cannot be said concerning in-play betting. Other than in the case of competitions spread over many days (for example, golf tournaments or cricket test matches), its provision had been very limited prior to the Millennium: it required heavy input of scarce odds-setting talent (to vary the odds as events unfolded on the field) and there was not much demand because few clients had the physical means of placing new bets quickly as they saw a sporting contest evolve. But Internet and mobile telephone technology gave many the means (and bookmakers learned to programme computers to adjust odds automatically in response both to events, such as the scoring of a goal, and to betting patterns and volumes). Technology thus underpinned the emergence of widely available in-play betting. But the new facility found a receptive audience. It is estimated that 70 per cent of stakes in sports betting are now placed in-play (Sorbonne-ICSS, 2014, p. 27). It is evident that this style of betting has substantial appeal to the public; for example, following a match on television and betting at the same time make both the sport and the betting more exciting. Betting may be perceived as a more challenging and therefore more interesting activity since quick decisions have to be taken given that odds can change very rapidly as play proceeds.

By volume, then, in-play now accounts for an actual majority of sports betting. This relatively new situation raises some questions as to the fairness of betting to the extent that some participants may receive new information faster than others (for example, on fast broadband rather than a television feed with a time delay) and so have an advantage in the market. But does it also compromise the fairness of sport itself? Does it raise integrity risk?

A priori reasoning suggests causes for concern. Use of in-play betting appears to present a number of advantages for criminal interests seeking to exploit betting markets for fraudulent gain. First, it means that the sports authorities are unable to react proactively to the fraud – if suspicious odds movements occur before a match, it can be subject to stronger scrutiny and the players can be warned that they are being observed closely, deterring them from proceeding with the fix. Second, it makes it technically easier to place large stakes because they can be dripped into the market over a more extended period. This allows more profit to be made. Third, the criminals have the opportunity to organize the fix to optimize the odds at which they bet – for example, they may plan that the defence will concede deliberate goals only in the final quarter – as time goes on without goals, odds against the team losing or total goals exceeding a certain number will lengthen, so betting late in the in-play market will enable more profit to be generated.

All these considerations will tend to increase the demand for fixes. As a result, one might expect an increase in total fixing activity.

The live betting market also allows profits to be made from arranging for just one component of an event to be fixed. Willingness to supply may then be greater to the extent that players perceive lower costs to attach to fixing anything short of the final result. Thus a tennis player might be willing to agree to lose the first set but not to undertake to lose the whole match.

How can arranging such a fix be employed in the in-play market to enable profits to be made even though the market on, say, the result of the first set of a tennis match is too illiquid to accommodate large flows of illicit money? Forrest et al. (2008) provide an illustrative example. By "arranging" the outcome of the first set, criminals are acquiring the inside information that prices (odds) will change in a predictable way (lengthening against the corrupted player) as events unfold on the court. This knowledge can be exploited in the same way as it can in any financial market where an insider has advance knowledge of news that will move prices. The fraudsters will bet against the player before the match and will make an offsetting bet that he will win the match after he loses the first set. Because the transactions will be at different prices (odds), by choosing the amounts bet judiciously, it is possible to lock into a certain profit irrespective of the final result (Forrest et al. provide the maths). The manoeuvre achieves a profit for the gang that could be high, given sufficient liquidity in the market on the final result. For both sides of the fix, there is the advantage that the favourite losing a set is likely to attract less suspicion than if he loses the match itself.

Fixing just one element in a contest is commonly termed "spot fixing". It is implausible that this is widespread where the actions are inconsequential. Three Pakistani cricketers were sent to prison in England after agreeing to bowl no balls at specified points in an international match. But it would not be possible to make other than trivial profit from knowledge of what they were going to do. Large bets on such highly specific actions are not possible: there is very little liquidity in the relevant side betting market. Nor could profit be generated in the in-play result market because the actions have almost no implication for which team will go on to win the game: there would be no odds movements from which to profit. This case of the Pakistani cricketers was in fact a newspaper "sting" where no betting activity was actually taking place. The scenario it created was an implausible representation of real-life conspiracies. It would not be profitable for anyone to pay such large sums as were offered to these cricketers for actions of little consequence. On the other hand, "spot fixing" could be profitable where the player's action would be expected to radically shift odds on the final result, for example, if a football player were induced to take a red card at a given point in the match. In the side betting market on red cards, maximum stakes would be too low to gain a substantial pay-off and large bets would certainly attract attention. But the availability of a liquid in-play market would permit significant gains from a combination of bets as in the tennis example. Where there is spot fixing, it is therefore likely to be enabled by the development of in-play rather than by the development of markets on sundry features of a match.

A priori reasoning suggests, then, that the shift to in-play betting introduced new threats to the integrity of sport. But what of the empirical evidence? Records from criminal trials show that fixers readily use both the pre-match and in-play markets. This is consistent with Van Rompuy's (2015) analysis of 1,468 football matches detected as suspicious by Sportradar. In two-thirds of these, betting irregularities were evident in both the pre-match and in-play markets (in another 17 per cent, anomalies were found only in odds movements during the match). Certainly these data are suggestive of a willingness by fixers to take advantage of the possibilities to exploit the in-play market, although it appears typical to make pre-match bets as well. This is not surprising since profit is likely to be increased by exploiting a variety of opportunities, given that too much money put into a market at any one time will raise the risk of detection and perhaps, given limited liquidity, move the odds too much against the interests of the fixers.

From this review, the conclusion is that the shift towards betting taking place in-play is likely to have been a factor behind the raised integrity risk in contemporary sport.

10.3　PUBLIC POLICY TOWARDS BETTING MARKETS

The extent of fixing activity that has come to light in recent years has triggered debates on how it may be combatted. In Europe there have been substantial reports (IRIS, 2012, Sorbonne-ICSS, 2014) that have made recommendations, some of which were embodied, at least in general terms, in the Council of Europe Convention on the Manipulation of Sports Competitions, agreed in September 2014. These recommendations are wide-ranging and targeted at the need for action by a variety of parties such as governments, law enforcement and sports federations. They cover matters as diverse as the need for specific national legislation defining match fixing, the necessity for cooperation between international law enforcement agencies, and the desirability of introducing player education programmes and organized channels for whistleblowing by sports insiders.

This chapter has a narrower focus, on betting markets, and therefore discusses policy specifically regarding the organization and regulation of betting markets. The detailed discussion will be informed by the analysis in the preceding section. But, first, a number of general points should be made.

First, the Asian market accounts for a higher betting volume than the European market and most of the betting related to recent criminal cases has taken place in Asia. This imposes severe limitations on what can be achieved through the regulation of domestic betting operators within Europe.

Second, there is a risk that debate on what measures should be introduced in European regulation in order to address threats to integrity will be distorted by the lobbying of special interest groups. For example, betting in several countries has traditionally been available only from a state-owned or -sanctioned monopoly operator. Governments and monopolists may advocate restrictions on supply that are supposed to reduce integrity risk but they also preserve economic rents and the potential to turn these into government revenue. Similarly, sports federations may seek to gain control of rights to use fixture lists for betting purposes on the grounds that this would enable them to control integrity risks, but a system of licensing by sports organizers might also allow them to generate new revenue streams from selling those rights.

Third, if policy-formation is to be based on the traditional approach suggested by welfare economics, evaluation should include consideration of the interests of consumers of gambling services. Sports betting is a popular leisure activity, indeed increasingly so, and the majority of participants bet without any evidence of problem levels or styles of play (see, for example, Wardle et al., 2010). Given this, considerable consumer surplus attaches to sports betting (Australian Productivity Commission, 2010) and policies based on restricting the supply of betting services may lead to a significant loss of consumer surplus.

Of course, the dominant form of regulation of sports betting across the world is simple prohibition. For example, this is the current regime in the United States (outside Nevada) and in China. But, despite prohibition, China appears to have the largest betting volume in the world (Sorbonne-ICSS, 2014); and the United States, which has long had a large street bookmaker sector (Strumpf, 2003), is now also served by several off-shore online bookmakers located in the Caribbean and specializing in the American market. They survive despite active measures against them such as the blocking of financial transactions with American residents. These examples underline that prohibition of gambling tends to be ineffective. It also runs the risk of aggravating integrity risk because illegal betting is inevitably non-regulated and non-transparent. Hill (2010) notes that evidence from the memoirs of players and administrators suggests there was a high level of corruption in English football in the 1950s whereas no such evidence has emerged for the decades that followed. He links the cleansing of the sport to the legalization of sports betting in the United Kingdom in 1961. With legalization, the underground bookmaker industry disappeared as leisure bettors took the opportunity to bet within the law at new high street retailers. Fixers could not readily follow them because there was effective monitoring of the legal market. There was still liquidity but it now resided in a well-regulated environment.

The Council of Europe Convention does not go so far as to advocate prohibition. But Article 9 does invite signatory states to consider "the limitation of the supply of sports betting, following consultation with the national sports betting operators".

What form could limitation on sports betting take? France permitted online sports betting in 2010 (Loi, 2010: 476); but licensed operators were restricted to offering bets only on sports events and competitions approved by the regulator (ARJEL) and only betting formulae approved by the regulator. The list of approved competitions is wide ranging in all the popular sports but includes only the top two divisions in domestic football and excludes football and basketball matches where at least one of the teams has nothing at stake in terms of League standings. An inspection of the list of authorized formulae presented on the ARJEL website reveals that a similar range of derivatives is offered in France as by international bookmakers; but that no side bets are included. The same restriction against side betting applies in Germany.

In-play betting has also been frowned upon by some national legislators. In Australia it was made illegal for licensed bookmakers to offer the product as early as 2001 (the Interactive Gambling Act). In Germany, it is restricted to bets on the final result. Other European countries do not appear to have made any explicit rules to prevent in-play betting (Van Rompuy, 2015).

French legislation also limits the price of betting services by setting a cap of 85 per cent on the pay-back ratio in sports betting. This is said to limit the profitability of fixing as well as securing other goals such as anti-money laundering and deterrence of problem gambling.

In light of our previous discussion, is there any evidence base to support a restriction on the supply of betting services as a means of mitigating integrity risk?

A restriction against side bets appears likely to have little relevance because side betting markets offer little liquidity and appear not to be of interest to the criminal gangs responsible for extensive manipulation of European sport. On the other hand, there is likely little social cost to prohibition given that few consumers in fact make side bets in markets where they are freely available.

Restrictions against in-play betting have some rationale to the extent that the product was evaluated above as having raised integrity risk. If in-play betting were curbed worldwide, integrity risk might, then, be lowered (although at the cost of a considerable loss of consumer surplus given the strength of bettors' revealed preference for this style of play). But of course, such international regulation is unlikely to be implemented and prohibition of in-play betting just at the level of the nation state, or even at the European level, is unlikely to comprise an effective policy. Wherever they are based, criminals appear overwhelmingly to use Asian markets because they offer higher returns, allow larger bets and permit essentially anonymous betting. If anything, depriving European bettors of the opportunity to bet live with local operators will shift some of the demand to international unregulated markets, enhancing liquidity in the sector where criminals operate.

Similarly, holding bettor returns below the world level is likely to hurt unsophisticated bettors who do not know how to circumvent restrictions on accessing foreign operators, while diverting the demand of more sophisticated players from well-regulated European markets to unregulated and non-transparent offshore and Asian markets. The advantage in terms of mitigating integrity risk is unclear given that significant crime does not take place in the domestic market anyway. It is not even clear that the policy is consistent with protecting vulnerable problem gamblers whose losses would be aggravated if their demand were inelastic (Forrest, 2008; Rowell and Gyrd-Hansen, 2015).

An emphasis on restricting the choices of European bettors appears not to have much to commend it as a means of addressing the serious threats faced by European sport. This is not to say of course that regulation of European markets should be other than rigorous. The Council of Europe Convention sets out many potentially useful provisions, such as reporting requirements where a fraud is detected, which are already in place in countries such as France, Italy and the United Kingdom but not yet in many of the countries which agreed to the Convention. Such requirements are effective in terms of detecting and therefore deterring small-scale local fixes. But European sport is far more threatened by the existence of highly liquid and barely regulated betting markets outside its borders and, while these continue to operate, greater protection is likely to be secured by focusing on other areas of policy than local regulation of gambling.

10.4   CONCLUDING REMARKS

One obvious thought is that sport can have little influence on the demand for fixes, which is high because liquidity is so high in the global betting market. But it can influence the supply of fixes because that comes from sports personnel, be they players, referees, owners or officials. So what can sport do for itself?

Clearly it needs to persuade its sports players not to supply criminals with fixes. One economic approach is to rebalance the structure of prizes to make winning more rewarding. For example, in tennis it was identified that first round matches of important tournaments attracted the attention of fixers because the prize money for advancing to the second round (where many players would expect to be beaten) was usually derisory. According to Rodenberg and Feustel (2014), some tournament organizers appear to have responded by changing the structure of prizes in a way that indicates they understand the problem. Another classic approach from economics (Forrest and Maennig, 2015) would be to offer deferred payment for sportsmen such that part of their remuneration would be payable only at the end of a guilt-free career. This would perhaps especially deter wrongdoing by veteran players who may currently perceive themselves as having nothing to lose from taking bribes given that they will shortly retire.

Some sports, among them football and snooker, have emphasized education, particularly through detailed programmes for early career sportsmen, as a means towards reducing the willingness to supply fixes. In the United Kingdom, three betting operators fund education for youngsters in a range of sports. And indeed Article 6 of the Council of Europe Convention explicitly states the need for such activities. No doubt they have value. It may be necessary to explain to naïve young players that they might be groomed by older players and sophisticated criminals to become future participants in fixing. Certainly they are unlikely to be fully aware of the dangers associated with entrapment, which may turn into long-running relationships with criminal gangs. Educating them can therefore only be good in terms of deterring the supply of fixes. On the other hand, too much should not be expected of education. It is hard to think of many areas of society where education alone has been found to have strong deterrent effects in terms of an activity that is anti-social but rewarding or profitable for the individual. In any case, the evidence from criminal trials is that more veteran than youth players have been implicated in the organization and execution of fixes which have come to light.

Education is of course a relatively easy option for sports to take forward. It is likely to be much more uncomfortable for sports to recognize that their own poor governance has allowed them to fall victim to match fixing and that reform of governance has to be an important part of any agenda to combat the problem. Aspects of governance in football that have allowed fixing to spread include the following. First, the sport has allowed infiltration by criminal interests. Several waves of arrests have included league officials as well as players. Cases in Belgium and Finland have featured the purchase of clubs by criminals, to be used subsequently for regular rigging of matches. Fit and proper person tests have plainly been inadequate. Second, poor financial discipline is evident throughout the professional game, resulting in owners resorting to fixing to pay bills, and failing to pay player wages. Reneging on contractual obligations to players is notoriously common in Eastern and Southern Europe and it is unsurprising that evidence from FifPro (2012) clearly shows that players from those regions who have been cheated of their wages are disproportionately likely to be targeted by fixers. Third, malpractice among owners and leaders of national federations and of FIFA itself is regularly revealed. Players and other employees are more likely to commit offences such as fixing if they perceive that those who employ them also engage in a corrupt and lucrative exploitation of the sport (the notion of negative reciprocity).

Sport may blame betting markets for the increasing threat to its integrity (though it may also seek to profit from betting interest, for example, all clubs in the English Premier League have a commercial relationship with a betting firm and several have a bookmaker as shirt sponsor). Sport has a point. The level of fixing activity has indeed increased as a direct result of the growth of liquidity in betting markets. But sport would more effectively withstand the threat, and would certainly more easily take the moral high ground, if it were better governed. That some sports might require government encouragement towards better governance is hinted at in Article 7 of the Council of Europe Convention which commits signatories to inducing "compliance by sports organizations and their affiliated members with all their contractual or other obligations". This will presumably include paying their players.

REFERENCES

Abbott, J. and Sheehan, D. (2013). 'The INTERPOL approach to tackling match fixing in football', in Haberfeld, M.R. and Sheehan, D. (eds), *Match-Fixing in International Sport. Existing Processes, Law Enforcement and Prevention Strategies*, Cham, Switzerland: Springer, pp. 263–287.

Australian Productivity Commission (2010). 'Gambling', Report no. 50, Productivity Commission, Canberra.

Bannenberg, B. and Schaupensteiner, W. (2004). *Korruption in Deutschland. Portrait einer Wachstumsbranche*, Munich: Verlag C.H. Beck.

Black, F. (1971). 'Towards a fully automated exchange, Part I', *Financial Analysts Journal*, **27**: 29–34.

Buraimo, B., Migali, G. and Simmons, R. (2015). 'An analysis of consumer response to corruption: Italy's *Calciopoli* scandal', *Oxford Bulletin of Economics and Statistics*, **78**: 22–41.

FIFPro (2012). *Black Book*, available from www.fifpro.org.

Forrest, D. (2008). 'Gambling policy in the European Union: Too many losers?', *FinanzArchiv/Public Finance Analysis*, **64**: 540–569.

Forrest, D. (2012). 'Online gambling: an economics perspective', in Williams, R., Wood, R. and Parke, J. (eds), *Routledge International Handbook of Internet Gambling*, Abingdon, UK: Routledge, pp. 29–45.

Forrest, D. and Maennig, W. (2015). 'The threat to sports and sports governance from betting-related corruption: causes and solutions', in Heywood, P.M. (ed.), *Routledge Handbook of Political Corruption*, Abingdon, UK: Routledge, pp. 328–346.

Forrest, D., McHale, I. and McAuley, K. (2008). *Risks to the Integrity of Sport from Betting Corruption*, London: Central Council for Physical Recreation.

Forrest, D. and Simmons, R. (2003). 'Sport and gambling', *Oxford Review of Economic Policy*, **19**: 598–611.

Gardiner, S. and Naidoo, U. (2007). 'On the front foot against corruption', *Sport and the Law Journal*, **15**: 6–27.

Grant, A., Johnson, J.E.V. and Oikonimidis, T. (2013). 'Bettors vs. bookmakers: 1–0! Examining the origin of information in football betting markets', Working Paper, University of Sydney.

Hill, D. (2009). 'To fix or not to fix? How corruptors decide to fix football matches', *Global Crime*, **10**: 157–177.

Hill, D. (2010). 'A critical mass of corruption: why some football leagues have more match-fixing than others', *International Journal of Sports Marketing and Sponsorship*, **11**: 221–235.

IRIS (2012). *Paris sportifs et corruption: Comment préserver l'intégrité du sport*, Paris: IRIS éditions, Institut de Rélations Internationales et Stratégiques.

Kyle, A.S. (1985). 'Continuous auctions and insider trading', *Econometrica*, **53**: 1315–1336.

Rebegggiani, L. and Rebeggiani, F. (2013). 'Which factors favour betting related cheating in sports? Some insights from political economy', in Haberfeld, M.R. and Sheehan, D. (eds), *Match-Fixing in International Sport. Existing Processes, Law Enforcement and Prevention Strategies*, Cham, Switzerland: Springer, pp. 157–176.

Rodenberg, R.M. and Feustel, E.D. (2014). 'Forensic sport analytics: detecting and predicting match-fixing in tennis', *Journal of Prediction Markets*, **8**: 77–95.

Rowell, D. and Gyrd-Hansen, D. (2015). 'Could a Pigouvian subsidy mitigate poker machine externalities, in Australia?', *Economic Papers*, **33**: 327–338.

Sorbonne-ICSS (2014). 'Protecting the integrity of sport competition: the last bet for modern sport (Executive Summary)', University Paris 1 Panthéon-Sorbonne, Paris and the International Centre for Sport Security, Doha.

Sport Accord (2011). *Integrity in Sport: Understanding and Predicting Match Fixing*, Moudon, Switzerland: Sport Accord.

Strumpf, K. (2003). 'Illegal sports bookmakers', Working Paper, University of North Carolina at Chapel Hill.

Van Rompuy, B. (2015). 'The odds of match fixing: facts and figures on the integrity risks of certain sports bets', T.M.C. Asser Instituut, the Hague, Netherlands.

Wardle, H., Moody, A., Spence, S., Orford, J., Volberg, R., Jotangia, D., Griffiths,

M., Hussey, D. and Dobbie, F. (2011). *British Gambling Prevalence Survey 2010*, London: The Stationery Office.

Weeber, K.-W. (1991). *Die unheiligen Spiele. Das antike Olympia zwischen Legende und Wirklichkeit*, Zurich and Munich: Artemis & Winkler Verlag.

Index

absolute value of the odds (ABS Odds)
  betting percentages 126
  betting volume 121, 122, 123
access, to sports betting 5, 6, 7, 8, 16–17, 18
accuracy, probability of forecasts 72, 105
actual "hot hand" 120
advertised probabilities 146–7
advertising 29
AIDS model 5, 6, 13, 14, 15, 18
Albania 167
Alberta 8
Ali, M.M. 54, 97, 101
amateur sports leagues 8
American Civil War 22, 23
American Revolution 21, 22
anomaly (Tote–SP) 92, 93, 99, 102
anonymous betting 167, 177
anti-gambling lobbying group 7
ARJEL 176
Arkes, J. 139, 141, 149, 153
"arranging" first set tennis outcomes 173
arrests, in football 178–9
Arsenal vs. Tottenham (2010) 57, 58
Article 6 (Council of Europe Convention) 178
Article 7 (Council of Europe Convention) 179
Article 9 (Council of Europe Convention) 176
Asch, P. 54
Ashley, T. 30
Asia 164, 165, 166, 167
Asian markets 175, 177
Asimakopoulos, I. 114
asset prices 52, 53
Aston Villa, Everton vs. (2011) 57–60
asymmetric information 80, 107

Atlantic Canada 8
Atlantic City 24, 27
attendance, at spectator sports
  consumer spending study
    AIDS model estimates 15
    estimated income and price elasticities 16
    SHS data 9, 10
    use of CPI 13
  non-regulation 6
  and spending on betting as complements 1, 6, 17
Australia 40, 107, 163, 176, 179
Austria 43
average betting odds 74, 76, 77, 108, 114
away wins
  in fixed odds betting 38
  forecasting match results (study) 73, 88
    odds descriptive statistics 74, 75, 76, 77, 78
    performance analysis 86
    take-out rates 79, 80, 81–2, 83
  handball betting study 109, 110, 111, 112, 113, 114
  probability evaluation, in-play betting (study) 57, 61, 62

balanced book hypothesis 119, 120, 125, 127
Ball, R. 54
Banks, J. 14
Bannenberg, B. 163
baseball 3, 8, 25, 55, 118, 119, 121, 122, 124, 125, 131, 133, 135, 136, 137, 139, 142
  team momentum in 142
  see also Major League Baseball (MLB); National League (baseball)

basketball
  fixing scandal 170–71
  "hot hand" studies 118
  liquid markets 170
  point spread betting 38, 140
  see also National Basketball
    Association (NBA)
behaviour (bettor) 41, 71, 97, 153; *see*
  also prospect theory
behavioural bias 120
behavioural hypotheses 55
Belgium 166, 179
benchmarks, price changes 52
best estimates 164
Bet & Win (BW)
  forecasting match results (study) 71
    odds descriptive statistics 74, 76,
      77, 78
    performance analysis 85, 86, 87
    take out rates 80, 83
  see also Bwin
Bet365 (B365) 40, 43, 44
  forecasting match results (study) 71
    odds descriptive statistics 74, 76,
      77, 78
    performance analysis 85, 86, 87
    take-out rates 80, 83
  over-round charges 45
Betfair 50
  betting data 170
  in-play betting, probability
    evaluation study 52–68
  influence on over-round charges 39,
    42, 43, 44, 46, 48, 49–50, 51
  revenue growth 47
betting, *see* sports betting
betting coupons 8, 73
betting exchanges 43, 51; *see also*
  Betfair; World Bet Exchange
betting markets
  analysis of favourite–longshot bias
    107
  compared to asset markets 92
  corruption
    developments in 164–74
    and public policy 174–7
    see also fixing
  efficient, *see* efficient markets
  market imperfections and profit
    generation 1

see also football betting markets;
  handball betting markets
betting odds
  forecasting results (study) 74–8
  goals-based 55, 60, 61, 62
  "hot hand" effects 128–31, 137
  information efficiency studies 54, 106
  longshots 107
  suspicious movements 172
  team quality 118, 128, 131
  Tote vs. bookmaker 93, 94, 96, 97,
    98, 99, 100, 102
  underdogs 3
  see also average betting odds;
    decimal odds; fixed odds;
    fractional odds; unfair odds
betting percentages, hot hand in
  120–21, 125–8, 136–7
betting rules 54, 106, 114, 152
betting shops 40, 43, 44, 50, 51
betting strategies 106, 120, 131, 133,
  136, 137, 152
betting volume
  Asian markets 175
  China 175
  competition and 166
  high profile matches and 8
  "hot hand" effects 121–5, 136
  mismatch, level of player wages and
    168
  offer of favourable odds for
    attracting 54
  online betting and 40
  side bets, football 170
  United States 175
betting windows, racetracks 25
bettor belief 153
bettors
  behaviour 41, 71, 97, 153
    see also prospect theory
  biased 42, 54
  casual 107
  insider 107
  reaction to streaks 118–38
  recreational 101, 122, 166
  risk-loving 107
  unbiased 42
  unsophisticated 177
  valuing of probability events 72, 80
  see also football pools bettors

bias(es), *see* behavioural bias;
    favourite–longshot bias; optimistic
    bias; sentiment bias; survivorship
    bias; systematic biases
biased bettors 42, 54
Bill C-290 (Canada) 7
binomial model, winning streaks 140,
    141
Birmingham, Sunderland vs. (2010) 57,
    59
Black Sox scandal (1919) 26
Blalock, G. 30, 36
Bochum case 163, 166
bookmaker margins 54, 57, 97, 98, 100,
    102, 103, 164
bookmakers
    belief in "hot hand" 145–7
    efficiency
        win probabilities 144–5, 153
        see also market efficiency
    facilities at football stadia 1
    informational efficiency studies 54
    odds offered by
        on longshots 107
        Tote odds vs. 93, 94, 96, 97, 98, 99,
            100, 102
    and profit, *see* profit making; profit
        maximizing
    as shirt sponsors 179
    see also experts; illegal bookmakers;
        market traders; online
        bookmakers
Boulier, B. 90
bribes/bribery 22, 162, 163, 166, 178
Brier, G.W. 84
Brier scores 72, 84, 85, 86, 87, 88
Brinner, R.E. 36
British Columbia 8
British odds, *see* fractional odds
Brown, P. 54
Brown, S.J. 54
Brown, W.O. 54, 118, 119, 120, 140,
    145, 149
Bruce, A.C. 93, 102
budget, consumer spending study 11,
    13, 14
Buraimo, B. 164
Busche, K. 107
Bwin 40, 43, 44, 45; *see also* Bet & Win
    (BW)

Cain, M. 54, 95, 145
Calciopoli scandal 164
California 27
*California v. Cabazon Bank of Mission
    Indians* (1987) 24
Camelot 23, 28, 31
Camerer, C. 118, 119, 120, 140, 145
Cameron, A.C. 90
Canada
    consumer spending study 5–19
        conclusions 17–19
        data description 9–13
        empirical methods 13–14
        results and discussion 14–17
    decimal odds 40
    sports betting 5, 7, 8, 9, 16–17
Canton Bulldogs–Massillon Tigers
    betting scandal 26
card sharps 23
Caribbean 175
casinos (US) 8, 23–5, 26, 27
casual bettors 107
Central City 23, 24
cheating potential, side bets 169–70
Chicago White Sox 26
China 163, 165, 166, 175
Choi, D. 55
CK Consulting in SportAccord 164
Clark, R.D. 140
Class I, II and II gaming (Indian) 24
Clotfelter, C.T. 30, 36
collusion 42
Colorado 23, 24
commercial consultancies 164
commercially operated casinos 24
commission, in point spread betting
    39
compensated price elasticity estimates
    14, 16, 17
competition
    absence in point spread betting, US
        50
    and betting volume 166
    decline in over-round charge 39, 40
    loss of faith in authenticity of 164
    and price changes 42, 43, 44, 50, 51
competitive balance, Spanish League
    74–5
complements, betting and viewing/
    attendance as 1, 6, 7, 8, 17

Consumer Price Index (CPI) 13
consumer spending 164
    on sports betting
        and attendance as complements 1,
            6, 17
        and spending on exercise and as
            substitutes 6, 17
    see also expenditure
consumer spending study 5–19
    analytical models 5–6
    conclusions 17–19
    data description 9–13
    empirical methods 13–14
    gambling, exercise, and attendance
        6–9
    results and discussion 14–17
consumer surplus 175, 177
consumption-based motives 124, 136
continental odds, *see* decimal odds
contracts, preventing privatization of
    lottery profits 29
contractual obligations, reneging on
    179
contrarian strategies 120, 133, 137
Cook, P.J. 30, 36
corners-based bets 55
Corrado, C.J. 54
correlation analysis, forecasting (study)
    72, 77, 78, 88
corruption 7, 142
    betting markets
        developments/changes in, and
            164–74
        public policy 174–7
    historical aspect 162
    public consciousness 163
    sports implicated, *see* individual
        sports
    US sports leagues 25, 26
Council of Europe Convention on the
    Manipulation of Sports
    Competitions 174, 176, 177, 178,
    179
cricket
    bets available 169
    corruption 162, 163, 170, 173
Criminal Code (Canada) 5, 7
criminal interests
    in-play betting and advantages for
        172

infiltration, football 178–9
    see also fraud; organized crime
Cripple Creek 23, 24
cross-price elasticities, consumer
    goods and services 5–6, 15, 16, 17
Croxson, K. 55
Cumulative Prospect Theory (CPT)
    97–8, 101, 102, 103

darts 169
days of the week
    betting odds 128, 129, 130
    betting percentages 125, 126, 127
    betting volume 121, 123, 124
Deadwood 23, 24
Deaton, A. 13, 14
DeBoer, L. 30
decimal odds 40, 41, 57, 71, 105, 108,
    114
deferred payments, player
    remuneration 178
Delaware 8, 22, 26, 27
Delaware Lottery 26, 27
demand
    for fixing 167–8, 170, 172, 177–8
    for sports betting 7, 165
Denmark, market efficiency, handball
    league (study) 109, 110, 111, 112,
    113, 114
deregulation 1
derivative bets 168, 170, 171, 176
Direr, A. 105
dismissals, and adjustment of betting
    odds 60
District of Columbia 21, 22
Dobson, S. 52
Dowie, J. 54
draws
    in fixed odds betting 38
    forecasting match results (study) 73,
        88
        odds descriptive statistics 74, 75,
            76, 77, 78
        performance analysis 85, 86
        take-out rates 79, 80, 81, 82, 83
    handball betting study 109–10, 112,
        113, 114
    probability evaluation, in-play
        betting (study) 57, 60, 61, 62
duopolies 42, 44

Eastern Europe 167, 179
economic models, market structure and
    price setting 42, 44, 50
economic-based test of market
    efficiency 106, 114
education, to reduce fixing 178
efficiency, state-owned operations 28
efficient markets 3, 119
efficient markets hypothesis (EMH)
    betting markets and analysis of 105
    semi-strong form 52, 53, 54, 55, 63,
        68
    strong form 53
    weak-form 53, 54
    see also market efficiency
El Quinigol 72
elasticity 14, 16, 17, 19
elite starting pitchers 118
employment status, SHS data 11, 13
endogeneity problems, regression
    analysis, over-round charges 51
English football
    corruption 163, 175
    forecasting match results 71
    informational efficiency studies 54
English Football League 56, 110
English Premier League (EPL) 89, 145
    belief in the "hot hand" 147
    commercial relationships with
        betting firms 179
    in-play betting market, probability
        evaluation study 52–68
    over-round in 39–40
        conclusions 50–51
        empirical analysis 44–50
    side bets 170
entertainment 6, 13
Europe
    analysis of favourite–longshot bias
        107
    corruption, second level football
        168
    reneging on contractual obligations
        179
    reports on extent of fixing 174
    sport betting operations 1
    see also individual countries
European football
    "hot hand" hypothesis 139–53
        betting rules 152

bookmaker efficiency 144–5
conclusions 153
data 142–3
literature review 139–42
market belief in 145–7
notation 143–4
testing 147–51
shirt sponsorship 1
see also individual leagues
European odds, *see* decimal odds
Evans, L.B. 43
event studies 52, 53–4
Everton vs. Aston Villa (2011) 57–60
ex-ante probabilities 143, 144, 145, 146,
    151
excess returns 120
exercise 5, 6, 15, 16, 17, 18
expectation-based errors 120
expected news, under-reaction to 55
expected return, on football betting
    with British bookmakers 164–5
expenditure
Canada
    government-sponsored lotteries
        8
    SHS data 9, 10–12
    single-event sports betting 7
United States
    horse racing 25
    sports betting 26
see also consumer spending
experts, forecasting performance 71,
    72, 84, 85, 88

fair values, spread bets 55
fairness 172
Fama, E.F. 53, 54, 105
Fantasy NASCAR 27
Fantasy NFL 27
favourable odds 54
favourite(s) 76, 106, 125; *see also* home
    favourites; road favourites
favourite–longshot bias 68, 72
    1996 British horse races
        ranked by SP 94
        ranked by Tote odds 94
    bookmaker efficiency 153
    fixed odds betting markets 54
    insiders and bookmaker odds 100,
        102

and market efficiency (study) 105–14
  conclusions 114
  empirical analysis 110–13
  empirical strategy and data
    108–10
  literature review 106–8
  risk-seeking behaviour 97
  Spanish football market 80–81, 82,
    88
  in US Tote 97
  see also reverse favourite–longshot
    bias
FC Barcelona 74, 76
Feustel, E.D. 178
FIFA 179
FifPro 179
financial discipline 179
financial transactions 6, 163, 166, 170,
  173, 175
Finland 168, 179
first round matches (tennis) 178
Fitt, A.D. 55
fixed odds 41, 42, 92, 100, 102
fixed odds betting
  lottery-based, Canada 8–9
  market efficiency 144
fixed odds betting markets 38–51
  bookmaker profits 38
  favourite–long shot bias 54
  informational efficiency studies 54
  literature review 41–2
  market structure and price setting
    42–4
  over-round
    in EPL betting 39–40
      conclusions 50–51
      empirical analysis 44–50
      understanding and calculating 38,
        40–41
fixing
  in basketball 170–71
  betting markets as a source and
    facilitator 163
  in cricket 162, 163, 173
  demand for 167–8, 170, 172, 177–8
  factors conducive to 166–7
  in football, *see* football, match fixing
  legal sports betting and easier
    detection of 18
  motivation for 162

profitability in 166
reports on extent of 174
side bets and prevalence 170
single-event sports betting and
  likelihood of 7
flexible demand models 5–6, 14
Florida 24
football
  forecasting match results (study)
    71–90
    concluding remarks 88
    descriptive odds statistics 72,
      74–8
    performance analysis 84–8
    statistical models 71
    take-out rates 79–83
  "hot hand" studies 118
  leagues, *see* individual leagues
  match fixing
    arrests 178–9
    aspects of governance allowing
      spread of 178–9
    England 162–3, 175
    Italy 80, 142, 163, 164, 168
    loss of faith in authenticity of
      competition 164
    public consciousness 163
    reducing 178
    at second level 168
    spot fixing 173–4
  see also European football
football betting
  bets available 168–9
  expected return, Britain 164–5
  point spread 38
  reverse favourite–longshot bias 107
  side bets and betting volume 170
  stadia facilities 1
football betting markets
  Spain 72–83
  see also fixed odds betting markets;
    in-play betting market
football clubs
  corruption and decline in attendance
    164
  criminal infiltration 179
football pools
  Spanish, *see* La Quiniela
  United Kingdom 38
football pools bettors 71, 72, 84, 88

forecasting football match results
  (study) 71–90
  concluding remarks 88
  descriptive odds statistics 72, 74–8
  performance analysis 84–8
  statistical models 71
  take-out rates 79–83
Forrest, D. 7, 8, 18, 54, 71, 73, 84, 90,
  170, 173
Fracsoft 57
fractional odds 40
France
  handball
    corruption 171
    market efficiency (study) 109, 110,
      111, 112, 113, 114
  public policy, betting markets 176,
    177
Franck, E. 42, 54
Franklin, B. 21
fraud
  in-play betting and 172, 173
  privately run lotteries 22
  reporting requirements 177
Fraud Detection System 171
free markets 28
Frees, E.W. 30, 36
Friedman, M. 101
Frohlich, C. 140

Gabriel, P.E. 92, 93, 98, 99
gambling, *see* sports betting
Gamebookers (GB)
  forecasting match results (study) 71
    odds descriptive statistics 74, 76,
      77, 78
    performance analysis 85, 86, 87
    take-out rates 80, 83
GamesBookers.com 142
Gandar, J.M. 54, 107
García, J. 8, 73
Garen, J. 30
German Bundesliga 145, 150
Germany
  Bochum case 163, 166
  favourite–longshot bias analysis 107
  market efficiency, handball league
    (study) 109, 110, 111, 112, 113,
    114
  public policy, betting markets 176

Gibraltar 43
Gilovich, T. 139, 140, 142, 149
globalization 7, 165
goals-based bets 55
goals-based betting odds 55, 60, 61,
  62
Goddard, J. 52, 114
Golec, J. 54, 101
governance, spread of football fixing
  178–9
government intervention 28
government-sanctioned lotteries, *see*
  lotteries
Grant, A. 165
Gray, P.K. 107
Gray, S.F. 107
Great Depression 25
Greece 163
Gross Gambling Yield (GGY) 164
GTECH 23

Hall, C.D. 107
Hancock, J. 21
handball, match fixing 163, 171
handball betting markets
  market efficiency and favourite–
    longshot bias (study) 105–14
    conclusions 114
    empirical analysis 110–13
    empirical strategy and data
      108–10
    literature review 106–8
hazard functions, in-play betting
  probability model 53, 56
health 6, 17, 18
high probability events, undervaluing
  72, 80
high-profile football matches 8
highly liquid betting markets 166, 167,
  170
Hill, D. 162, 175
hockey
  "hot hand" effects 137
  see also National Hockey League
    (NHL)
home favourites, betting odds 111, 128,
  129, 130
home pitcher loss streaks
  betting odds 129, 130, 131
  betting percentages 126

betting returns 134
betting volume 123
home pitcher win streaks
  betting odds 129
  betting percentages 125, 126, 127,
    128
  betting returns 134, 135
  betting volume 121, 123
home team loss streaks
  betting odds 129
  betting percentages 126
  betting returns 132
  betting volume 123
home team quality, betting percentages
  127
home team win streaks
  betting odds 128, 129
  betting percentages 125, 126
  betting returns 132, 133
  betting volume 121, 123
home wins
  in fixed odds betting 38
  forecasting match results (study) 73,
    88
    odds descriptive statistics 74, 75,
      76, 77, 78
    performance analysis 85, 86
    take-out rates 79, 80, 81, 82, 83
  handball betting study 109, 110, 111,
    112, 113, 114
  probability evaluation, in-play
    betting (study) 57, 60, 61, 62
Hong Kong 107
horse racing
  favourite–longshot bias 81
  reverse favourite–longshot bias 107
  United Kingdom
    average pari-mutuel returns 92
    Tote–SP relationship 94, 95, 96
  United States 25
    explanatory power of CPT for
      pari-mutuel data 101
  see also racetrack betting
"hot hand" and "hot arm"
  Major League Baseball (MLB) 118,
    119
    betting odds 128–31
    betting percentages 125–8
    betting returns 131–6
    betting volume 121–5

conclusions and discussion 136–7
literature review 119–21
testing 119
"hot hand" hypothesis 118
  European football 139–53
    betting rules 152
    bookmaker efficiency 144–5
    conclusions 153
    data 142–3
    literature review 139–42
    market belief 145–7
    notation 143–4
    testing 147–51
  studies 118
hot streaks 149–50
household spending, see consumer
  spending
household type, SHS data 11, 12–13
housing tenure, SHS data 11, 12
Hui, S.K. 55
Humphreys, B.R. 107
Hungary 163

illegal bookmakers 7, 166
illegal sports betting 6, 18, 175
Illinois Lottery 23, 27, 28
  privatization study 29–36
implicit probabilities 75, 105, 108, 110,
  111, 112, 114
implied probabilities
  forecasting (study) 79, 81, 82, 84,
    86
  in-play betting (study) 56, 57, 58, 59,
    60, 63, 64, 66, 68
in-play betting
  corruption 171–4
  public policies 176, 177
in-play betting market, probability
  evaluation 52–68
  computation of match outcomes
    56
  conclusion 68
  in-play betting odds data 57–68
  literature review 53–5
income
  consumer spending study 11, 12, 15,
    16
  and demand for betting 165
  and lottery sales 30
  and lottery transfers 32, 33, 34

India 166
Indian Gaming Regulatory Act (1988)
    24
Indiana lottery 23, 27, 35
industrial organization, and price
    setting 42–4
inferred probabilities 143, 144, 145,
    146, 147, 148, 149, 151
information asymmetry 80, 107
information availability
    and asset prices 52
    betting markets 92
    determination of optimal fixed odds
        42
    forecasting (study) 76
    and market efficiency 105
informational efficiency
    in sports betting 41, 53, 54, 106
    tests of 52
    see also market efficiency
informational inefficiency, and betting
    odds 60, 68
informational uncertainty
    in event studies 52
    fixed odds betting 42
informed traders 165, 166
inside information 92, 173
insider bettors 107
insider traders 52, 97, 98, 100, 102
integration (betting market) 165
integrity risk 164, 168, 171, 172, 174,
    175, 176, 177
inter-market arbitrage opportunities 54
international organized crime 167
Internet 8, 29, 172; *see also* online
    betting; online bookmakers
Interwetten (IW) 40, 43
    forecasting match results (study) 71
        odds descriptive statistics 74, 76,
            77, 78
        performance analysis 85, 86, 87
        take-out rates 80, 83
    over-round charges 45
IRIS 163, 166
Italian Serie A 145, 147
Italy
    corruption in football 80, 142, 163,
        164, 168
    private operation of public lottery 23
    reporting requirements, fraud 177

James I 21
Jamestown 21
Japan 107
Johnson, J.E.V. 93, 102
Johnson, R.S. 108
joint-hypothesis problem 52
Jullien, B. 97, 101

Kahneman, D. 97, 103
Kentucky 22, 25
Koning, R.H. 43, 108, 111, 114
Kothari, S.P. 54
Kuypers, T. 39, 41, 42

La Quiniela 71, 72, 73
    aggregate statistics 73
    complementarity, watching sport
        and betting 8
    determinants of demand for 73
    entry fee 73
    forecasting football match results
        (study)
        odds correlation matrix 78
        odds descriptive statistics 75–6
        performance analysis 84–8
    high profile matches and betting
        volume 8
    minor prizes 73
    pari-mutuel betting 38
    take-out rate 73
laboratory experiments, favourite–long
    shot bias 108
Labour Force Survey (LFS) sampling
    frame 10
Ladbrokes (LB) 43, 44
    competition from online
        bookmakers 43
    forecasting match results (study) 71
        odds descriptive statistics 74, 76,
            77, 78
        performance analysis 85, 86, 87
        take-out rates 80, 83
    over-round charges 39, 40, 45, 46–7,
        48, 49–50, 51
Las Vegas 8, 39
Law, D. 101
league sports
    informational efficiency studies 54,
        55
    see also individual sports

learning process 88
legal sports betting
    easier detection of match fixing
        18
    North America
        access to 7, 8, 16–17, 18
        challenge to, and concerns about
            8, 18, 27
        expansion 5, 6
        relationship between sports
            leagues and 8
        regulation and availability analysis
            6–7
    Spain 72
    unintended consequences of access
        to 6, 18
legalization
    casino gambling, United States 24
    sports betting
        Canada 5, 7, 16–17
        United Kingdom 176
        United States 5, 7–8, 26, 27
leisure-related spending 5, 6, 17, 18
Levitt, S.D. 39, 50
Lindsey, G.R. 55
liquidity, in betting markets 164–8
live attendance, *see* attendance
Liverpool, Manchester United vs.
    (2015) 162–3
lobby groups, and regulation of
    gambling 6–7
Logan, T. 153
logit models 90
    forecasting results (study) 72, 86, 87,
        88
    handball betting markets (study)
        111, 112, 113, 114
Long Island 25
long-odds bets 63, 68
long-odds high-prize betting 71, 73
longshots 93, 101, 107; *see also*
        favourite–longshot bias; reverse
        favourite–longshot bias
losing streaks
    betting odds 129, 130, 131
    betting percentages 125, 126,
        128
    betting returns 132, 134
    betting volume 122, 123, 125
    "mythical" hot hand 120

lotteries
    government-sanctioned, Canada 8
        consumer spending study
            AIDS model estimates 15
            estimated income and price
                elasticities 16
            SHS expenditure data 10, 11
            profit making 9
    private operation of public 23
    United States 21–3, 26, 27
    see also state lotteries
lottery tickets
    Canada 8, 9
        consumer spending study 13,
            18–19
    United States
        banning of interstate
            transportation of 22
        illegal sale of 22
        parlay-style 26, 27
        sales 29, 30
lottery transfers 29, 30–31, 32, 33, 35
Lottomatica 23
Louisiana State Lottery Company 22
Louisville Grays 26
low probability events, overvaluing 72,
    80
luxury goods, expenditure on 14

MacKinlay, A.C. 54
Mafia 167
Major League Baseball (MLB) 25
    challenge to legalization of sports
        betting 8
    "hot hand" and "hot arm" 118–37
        betting odds 128–31
        betting percentages 125–8
        betting returns 131–6
        betting volume 121–5
        conclusions and discussion 136–7
        literature review 119–21
        testing 119
    probability evaluation, match
        outcomes 55
    reverse favourite–longshot bias 107
    starting pitchers 118–19
major league sports, informational
    efficiency studies 54, 55
Makropoulou, V. 42
malpractice, national federations 179

Manchester United
  vs. Liverpool (2015) 162–3
  vs. Manchester City (2011) 41
  vs. Newcastle (2010) 57, 58
manipulation of sport 162, 167, 170,
    171, 174, 176
Manitoba 8
Markellos, R.N. 42
market efficiency
  European football 142
  and the favourite–longshot bias
      (study) 105–14
    conclusions 114
    empirical analysis 110–13
    empirical strategy and data
        108–10
    literature review 106–8
  fixed odds betting 144
  information availability 105
  privatization and 1
  probability model 144–5
  strong-form 144, 152
  Tote–SP relationship 100
  weak-form 105, 112, 144, 152
  see also efficient markets
market entry, and price changes 39, 42,
    43, 44, 50
market failures 28
market imperfections, and profit
    generation 1
market inefficiency 92, 93, 102, 142,
    152
market size 168
market structures
  and price setting 42–4
  wagering 92
market traders
  reaction to news 55
  see also bookmakers
Markov process, hot hand as 139
Markowitz, H.M. 101
Marsden, J.R. 92, 93, 98, 99
Maryland 25
Massachusetts 22
Metrick, A. 107
Mikesell, J.L. 30
Miller, T.W. 30, 36
mining towns, casinos in US 23, 24
minutes elapsed, match results
    probabilities (study) 63–8

minutes of play, match results
    probabilities (study) 57, 58, 59,
    60
mispricing 57, 60, 63
Mississippi River 23, 24
Missouri 22
mobile telephone technology 172
momentum effect 141–2, 148, 149,
    153
monopolies 6, 22, 24, 28, 42, 164, 175
Montana 8, 26
Montana Lottery 27
months of the season
  betting odds 128, 129, 131
  betting percentages 125, 126, 127
  betting volume 121, 123, 124
moral objections 22, 23
Muellbauer, J. 13, 14
mythical "hot hand" 119, 120, 125,
    133, 136, 137, 140

Naked Economics (Wheelan) 140
National Basketball Association
    (NBA) 7, 8, 26, 107, 108, 119, 120,
    122, 171
National Collegiate Athletic
    Association (NCAA) 7, 8, 17, 26,
    27, 107
national federations, malpractice 179
National Football League (NFL) 7, 8,
    26, 27, 107, 108, 120, 122
National Hockey League (NHL) 7, 8,
    107, 122
National League (baseball) 25–6
Native American casinos 24–5
natural monopolies 28
neoclassical approach, Tote–SP
    relationship 97
Nevada 8, 23, 24, 26, 27
new firms, *see* market entry
New Hampshire 21, 22
New Jersey 7–8, 23, 24, 27, 36
New Orleans 23
New York 22, 25, 30
New Zealand 107
Newcastle, Manchester United vs.
    (2010) 57, 58
NFL parlay lottery tickets 27
noise traders 165, 166
non-expected utility models 101

non-parametric regressions, market
 efficiency, handball betting leagues
 110, 111, 112, 114
North America, *see* Canada; United
 States
Northstar Corporation 23, 35
Northstar NJ 23
Nyberg, H. 108, 109, 114

objective probability 97, 98, 100,
 102
odds, *see* betting odds
offshore bookmakers 7, 121, 175
Ohio 35
Ohio League 26
Oller, P. 25
online betting
 exchanges 43
 France 176
 growth of sports betting 1
 in-play 54–5
 over-round charges 40
 Spain 73
online bookmakers 7, 39–40, 43, 55;
 see also individual bookmakers
Ontario 8
optimal fixed odds 42
optimistic bias 54
ordered logit model, forecasting (study)
 72, 86, 87, 88, 90
Oregon 8, 26
Oregon Lottery 26, 27
organized crime 167
outsiders 97
over betting, winning streaks 140
over-estimation
 "hot" teams' performance 140
 winning probability of longshots
 107
over-reaction, surprise news 55
over-round 38, 39
 Canadian sports betting 9
 in EPL betting 39–40
 conclusions 50–51
 empirical analysis 44–50
 and favourite–longshot bias 79–83
 understanding and calculating 38,
 40–41
overvaluing, low probability events 72,
 80

Page, L. 54
Pakistani cricketers' case 173
Pankoff, L.D. 54
Pari Sportif 8
pari-mutuel betting 25, 38, 71, 73, 89,
 92, 101
parlay-style betting 7, 9, 26, 27
participation, in physical activity 5, 6,
 17, 18
Paul, R. 120
Pawlukiewicz, J.E. 108
pay-back ratio, 85 per cent cap, France
 176
Peel, D.A. 41, 54, 101
Pennsylvania 22, 23, 27, 35
Pérez, L. 8, 73
perfect competition, and price change
 43
petty crime 167, 171
Philadelphia 21
Philippines 167
physical activity 1, 5, 6, 9, 13, 17, 18
pitcher quality 137
 and betting odds 128, 131
 betting percentages 127
 betting volume 121, 122
pitcher streaks
 betting odds 128, 129, 130, 131
 betting percentages 125, 126, 127,
 128
 betting returns 133, 134, 135, 136,
 137
 betting volume 121, 122, 124–5
 "mythical" hot hand 119
pitchers, in MLB 118–19
player wages/remuneration 168, 178
player-fixed-effects model 141
point spread betting 38
 absence of competitive effects, US
 50
 Canada 8
 commission charged in 39
 in-play 55
 "mythical" hot hand 120
 over-betting on winning streaks 140
Poisson processes 55
Poland, market efficiency, handball
 league (study) 109, 110, 111, 112,
 113, 114
pool cards 26

Pope, P.F. 41, 54
population
  and lottery sales 30
  and lottery transfers 32, 33, 34
pre-match fixing 174
price changes
  competition and 42, 43, 44, 50, 51
  consumer spending study 14, 16
  event studies 52, 53–4
  in-play betting markets 55
price elasticities, consumer spending
  study 5–6, 14, 15, 16, 17, 19
price scaling 14
price setting 42–4; *see also* over-round
private operation, public lotteries 23
privately operated casinos, legalization,
  US 24
privately run lotteries 21, 22
privatization
  state betting operations 1
  state lotteries 23, 27, 28–9
    revenue generation (study)
      conclusions and future research
        35–6
      model and methodology 29–32
      results 32–5
prize money, tennis tournaments 178
pro-gambling consumers 6–7
Pro-Line 8
probabilistic model, forecasting
  performance analysis (study) 84,
  86, 87, 88
probabilities, winning streaks and
  advertised 146–7
probability distortion 101
probability evaluation, in-play betting
  (study) 52–68
probability model, market efficiency
  144–5
product diversification 168, 171
product innovation 1
productivity 18, 28
Professional and Amateur Sports
  Protection Act 1993 (PASPA) 8,
  26, 27
professional gamblers 23
professional sports leagues 6
  lottery-based games, Canada 8
  opposition to legalization of sports
    betting 8, 18, 27

relationship between legal sports
  betting and 8
profit making
  corruption 162
  fixed odd betting 38
  Illinois lottery (2012) 35
  in-play market 172, 173
  informed traders, financial markets
    165–6
  lottery corporations, Canada 9
  market imperfections and 1
  pari-mutuel betting 38
  see also over-round; returns
profit-maximizing 54
profit-maximizing models 41, 42
prohibition
  lotteries, US 22
  sports betting 7, 26–7, 165, 166, 175,
    176
prospect theory 30; *see also* Cumulative
  Prospect Theory (CPT)
public choice model, regulation and
  availability of legal gambling 6–7
public perception, legal sports betting
  and concerns about 8, 18
public policy contexts
  betting markets 174–7
  privation of lotteries 28–9
  sports betting 7

Quandt, R.E. 97, 101
Quebec 8

racetrack betting 54, 107; *see also*
  horse racing
Ray, R. 14
Reade, J.J. 55
Real Madrid CF 74, 76
Rebeggiani, F. 169
Rebeggiani, L. 169
recreational bettors 101, 122, 166
recreational facilities, consumer
  spending study 10, 13, 18
recreational gambling 23
red cards, spot fixing 173–4
reference person, SHS data 11, 12
regression models
  forecasting 106
  "hot hand" effects 121–31
  market efficiency 106

handball betting markets (study)
110–13, 114
over-round changes, EPL 44–51
privatization of lotteries (study)
29–32
Tote–SP relationship 96–100
regression-based test of market
efficiency 106, 114
regulation
fixing due to lack of 166
gambling 6–7
lotteries, US 21–2
sports betting 175
see also prohibition
remuneration (player) 168, 178
reporting requirements, fraud 177
resource allocation (optimal) 28
returns
for betting on favourites, *see*
favourite–longshot bias
to betting strategies involving streaks
131–6
to winning bets 92
see also excess returns; expected
returns; Tote–SP relationship
revenue generation
gambling as 6
sports betting 7
state lotteries
effects of privatization (study)
conclusions and future research
35–6
model and methodology 29–32
results 32–5
privatization as public policy
question 28–9
US casinos 24, 25
reverse favourite–longshot bias 107–8
risk-averse 101
risk-loving bettors 30, 107
risk-seeking 97, 101
risky choice 101, 102, 103
riverboat gambling 23, 24
road favourites
betting odds 128, 129, 130, 131
betting percentages 125, 126, 127
betting volume 121, 122, 123
road pitcher loss streaks
betting odds 129, 130
betting percentages 126, 128

betting returns 134
betting volume 123
road pitcher quality, betting
percentages 127
road pitcher win streaks
betting odds 128, 129, 130, 131
betting percentages 126, 127
betting returns 134, 135
betting volume 121, 123
road team loss streaks
betting odds 129, 130
betting percentages 126
betting returns 132, 134
betting volume 123
road team quality, betting percentages
127
road team win streaks
betting odds 128, 129, 130
betting percentages 126
betting returns 132, 133
betting volume 121, 123
Rodenberg, R.M. 178
Rodríguez, P. 8, 73
Rossi, M. 80, 81, 89, 90, 108
Russian football league 162

Salanié, B. 97, 101
San Francisco 23
Saskatchewan 8
Sauer, R.D. 6, 54, 55, 89, 92, 107, 108,
118, 119, 120, 140, 145, 149
Savage, L.J. 101
Schaupensteiner, W. 163
Schnytzer, A. 107
Scientific Games 23
Scott, F. 30
Scottish football 54
Scottish football leagues 142, 143, 150
Scottish Premiership 143, 145
second-level football, corruption in
168
sedentary lifestyle 1, 17
selection, consumer spending study 10
semi-strong form efficient markets
hypothesis (EMH) 52, 53, 54, 55,
63, 68
Seminole Tribe 24
Seminole Tribe v. Butterworth (1981) 24
sentiment bias 54, 107–8, 147
Shin, H.S. 54, 97, 98

shirt sponsorship 1, 179
short-odds bets 63, 68
side bets 168, 169–70, 171, 173, 176
Siegfried, J.J. 43
Simmons, R. 6, 7, 18, 54, 71, 90, 170
simulations
    in-play match outcome probabilities
        56, 57–68
    returns to betting strategies
        involving streaks 131–6
simulcast betting 25
single-event sports betting 7–8
Sinkey, M. 153
Slutsky decomposition 14
snooker 163, 178
Snowberg, E. 97, 107
soccer, "hot hand" effects 137
soccer leagues, analysis of favourite–
    longshot bias 107
socialization of losses (lottery) 29
Sociedad Estatal Loterías y Apuestas
    del Estado (SELAE) 73, 75
South Dakota 23
Southern Europe 179
Spain
    football betting market 72
        favourable odds in 54
        see also La Quiniela
    market efficiency, handball league
        (study) 109, 110, 111, 112, 113,
        114
Spanish National Lottery Agency
    (SELAE) 73, 75
spectator viewing
    and sports betting as complements
        1, 6, 7, 8, 17
    see also attendance, at spectator
        sports
sport, relationship, sports betting and 7
Sportingbet (SB) 40, 43
    forecasting match results (study) 72
        odds descriptive statistics 74, 76,
            77, 78
        performance analysis 85, 86, 87
        take-out rates 80, 83
    over-round charges 45
Sportradar 171
Sports Action 8
sports betting
    access to 5, 6, 7, 8, 16–17, 18

betting against the streak 120, 131,
    132, 133, 134, 135, 137, 152, 153
betting with the streak 120, 131, 132,
    133, 134, 135, 137, 152
consumer spending, *see* consumer
    spending study
demand for 7, 165
economic and public policy contexts
    7
Europe, *see* Europe
expansion of opportunities 5, 7
"hot hand" hypothesis 119–20
learning process 88
and legality, *see* illegal sports betting;
    legal sports betting; legalization
negative aspects 7
North America, *see* Canada; United
    States
popularity and growth 1, 7
proliferation of subjects for 168–71
regulation 175
relationship, sport and 7
scandals, *see* corruption
and spending on exercise as
    substitutes 6, 17, 18
state-owned operations 1
and viewing/attendance as
    complements 1, 6, 7, 8, 17
see also betting markets; fixed odds
    betting; in-play betting; online
    betting; pari-mutuel betting;
    parlay-style betting; point
    spread betting
sports books 26, 27, 39, 166
    reaction to streaks 118–37
Sports Select 8
sports teams
    concerns about legal sports betting
        18
    legal sports betting and revenue
        generation 6
spot fixing 173–4
spread bets, *see* point spread betting
Stan James (SJ)
    forecasting match results (study) 72
        odds descriptive statistics 74, 76,
            77, 78
        performance analysis 85, 86, 87
        take-out rates 80, 83
Stardust 26

Starmer, C. 103
starting pitchers 118–19
starting price (SP), and Tote, *see* Tote–
  SP relationship
state lotteries
  privatization 23, 27, 28–9
    revenue generation (study)
      conclusions and future research
        35–6
      model and methodology 29–32
      results 32–5
    state-owned 23
    state-sanctioned 22
state-owned enterprises 1, 23, 28, 175
state-sponsored monopolies 6
statistical models, forecasting 71, 106
Statistics Canada 9, 10
Stekler, H. 90
Stone, D.F. 141
streak length 122, 133, 146, 147, 148–9,
  150
streak shooting 139
streaks
  bettor and sports book reaction to
    118–37
  see also unusual streaks; winning
    streaks
strong-form efficient markets
  hypothesis (EMH) 53
strong-form market efficiency 144, 152
Strumpf, K. 6
subjective probability 54, 80, 98, 102,
  145
subjects for betting 168–71
substitutes
  betting and spending on exercise as
    6, 17, 18
  bookmaker-based betting 44
Sun, Y. 139
Sunderland vs. Birmingham (2010) 57,
  59
surprise news, over-reaction 55
surprising winning streaks 144, 151,
  153
Survey of Household Spending (SHS)
  5, 9–13
survivorship bias 146
suspicious bets 173
suspicious matches 171, 173, 174
suspicious odds movements 172

Sweden, market efficiency, handball
  league (study) 109, 110, 111, 112,
  113, 114
systematic biases 41, 80

t-tests, forecasting (study) 76–7
take-out rates, forecasting (study) 72,
  73, 75, 79–83
Tamarkin, M. 54, 101
tax law change, sports gambling 26
team fixed effects models 139, 148
team quality
  betting odds 118, 128, 131
  betting percentages 127
  betting volume 121
team streaks
  betting odds 128, 129, 130, 137
  betting percentages 125, 126, 127,
    137
  betting returns 132, 133, 135, 136,
    137
  betting volume 121, 122–4, 125
  "mythical" hot hand 119
technological change 165, 172
tennis
  analysis of favourite–longshot bias
    107
  bets available 169
  match fixing 163, 173, 178
Thaler, R.H. 92, 105, 106, 107
tickets, *see* lottery tickets
Tote–SP relationship 92–103
  conclusions 102
  discussion 100–101
  empirical (regression) results 98–100
  literature studies 93–6
  theoretical exposition 96–8
Tottenham, Arsenal vs. (2010) 57, 58
traditional bookmakers 43, 44, 46, 51
Trivedi, P.K. 90
true probabilities 68, 144, 145, 148, 153
Turkey 163, 166
Tversky, A. 97, 103

unbiased bettors 42
uncertainty
  Tote odds 93, 95, 101, 102
  see also informational uncertainty
uncompensated price elasticity
  estimates 16, 17

under-betting 3
under-pricing 145
under-reaction, expected news 55
underdogs 3, 41, 119, 120, 151
underground bookmaker industry
        (UK) 176
underperformance 162
undervaluing, high probability events
        72, 80
unemployment
    and lottery sales 30
    and lottery transfers 32, 33, 34, 35
unfair odds 101, 102
United Kingdom
    private operation of public lottery
        23
    race-track betting, favourite–
        longshot bias analysis 107
    reporting requirements, fraud
        177
    sports betting
        expected return, football 164–5
        facilities at football stadia 1
        legalization 176
        stability of over-round in fixed
            odds betting 39
    see also English football; English
        Football League; English
        Premier League (EPL)
United States
    betting volume 175
    casinos 8, 23–5, 26, 27
    fixing scandal 170–71
    league sports, *see* individual sports
        and leagues
    lotteries 21–3, 26, 27
    race-track betting
        favourite–longshot bias analysis
            107
        pari-mutuel 25
    sports betting 1, 25–7
        access to legal 7
        illegal 6, 18
        legalized 5, 7–8
        point spread 50
        prohibition 175
    see also individual states and cities
universities, lottery-funded US 21
unusual streaks 146, 149
urban households, SHS data 11, 12

Van Rompuy, B. 170, 171, 174
VC Bet (VC)
    forecasting match results (study) 72
        odds descriptive statistics 74, 76,
            77, 78
        performance analysis 85, 86, 87
        take-out rates 80, 83
Velzen, B. van 43
Vergin, R.C. 142
video lottery terminals 29
Virginia 21
Virginia City 23
Virginia Company 21
volleyball 163, 164

wagering markets, *see* betting markets
Wardle, H. 175
Warner, J.B. 54
Washington, G. 21
weak-form efficient markets hypothesis
        (EMH) 54
weak-form market efficiency 105, 112,
        144, 152
Weinbach, A. 120
Weinberg, G. 107
Weitzman, M. 97, 101
welfare 7, 28
welfare economics 175
William Hill (WH) 43, 44
    competition from online
        bookmakers 43
    forecasting match results (study) 72
        average take-out rates 80
        odds descriptive statistics 74, 76,
            77, 78
        performance analysis 85, 86, 87
        over-round charges 39, 40, 45–6, 47,
            48–9, 50, 51
win–loss percentages
    betting odds 128, 129
    betting percentages 125, 126
    betting returns 132, 134, 137
    betting volume 121, 122–4
winning bets, returns to 92
winning streaks
    betting odds 128, 129, 130, 131
    betting percentages 125, 126, 127,
        128
    betting returns 120, 132, 133, 134,
        135

betting volume 121, 122, 123, 125
binomial model 141
inferred probabilities 146, 147,
    148
over betting 140
profitability of betting against 120
surprising 144, 151, 153
winnings, Canadian sports betting 9

wisdom-of-crowds hypothesis 71
Wolfers, J. 97, 107
Woodland B.M. 54, 107, 120
Woodland L.M. 54, 107, 120
World Bet Exchange 42

Ziemba, W.T. 92, 105, 107
Zimbabwe 163